States has been on the side of counterrevolution. We have justified such actions on the grounds that they were necessary to contain Soviet communism, but in fact most of the revolutions we opposed were led by noncommunists. This policy is all the more futile in that the revolutions of rising expectation are irrepressible, Lens says, and will doubtless flare anew in the present period of worldwide economic stress.

In great detail, Lens demonstrates that our reliance on the nuclear weapon as our security shield is counterproductive. This most useless weapon in all history brings us neither diplomatic victory nor the hope of military victory. Worse still, it leads us inexorably to the very catastrophe it is supposed to avoid.

Moving from history to policy, Lens offers a program for joining the revolution of rising expectations and initiating the process of world disarmament. Along with the late U.N. Secretary-General, U Thant, he favors establishment of international agencies with sovereign powers to curb nuclear proliferation, fight poverty, eliminate pollution, and control population. This, he says, is the next step toward the "one world" now dictated by history.

The Maginot Line Syndrome is a meticulously documented and incisively argued book.

Sidney Lens, a well-known writer and lecturer, is senior editor of *The Progressive*. He has published numerous articles in such magazines as *Harper's, Harvard Business Review, New Republic,* and *Nation,* and innumerable newspapers; and has lectured and taught at many universities. His books include *The Day Before Doomsday, The Military-Industrial Complex, The Labor Wars,* and *Radicalism in America.*

THE MAGINOT LINE
SYNDROME

THE MAGINOT LINE SYNDROME

America's Hopeless Foreign Policy

SIDNEY LENS

BALLINGER PUBLISHING COMPANY
Cambridge, Massachusetts
A Subsidiary of Harper & Row, Publishers, Inc.

International Standard Book Number: 0-88410-842-2

Library of Congress Catalog Card Number: 82-20652

Printed in the United States of America

Library of Congress Cataloging in Publication Data

Lens, Sidney.
    The Maginot Line Syndrome.

    Includes bibliographical references and index.   1. United States—
Foreign relations—1945-   2. United States—National
security.   I. Title.
E840.L43 1982   327.73   82-20652
    ISBN 0-88410-842-2

CONTENTS

Acknowledgments   vii

Chapter 1
The Maginot Line Syndrome   1

Chapter 2
The Mirage of Containment   9

Chapter 3
The Wrong Weapon   37

Chapter 4
The Wrong Enemy   59

Chapter 5
The Irrepressible Revolution   85

Chapter 6
Will the Soviets Disappear?   119

Chapter 7
Strategy for Survival   149

Notes   169

Index   185

About the Author   195

ACKNOWLEDGMENTS

I am indebted to a number of people, whose wisdom I have tapped, for giving me suggestions and criticisms that I hope have made this book a little stronger: John M. Swomley, Jr., Erwin Knoll, Daniel Ellsberg, Saul Mendlovitz. And of course special thanks again to my helpmate and wife of many, many years, Shirley.

THE MAGINOT LINE SYNDROME   1

The men and women who run the United States are not lunatics or Dr. Strangeloves. They do not want a nuclear war. They do not want the nation destroyed; and if they occasionally argue that such a war is "survivable," they nonetheless know that it would cause casualties beyond anything the human species has ever endured. They have wives, husbands, children, friends whom they cherish; and they are as attached to the United States of America as most of us are. They do not want their families and children to die or their nation to be annihilated, if only because it would also mean—to be crass—their own eclipse as persons of power. If their judgment is wrong, it is not because they are *deliberately* steering the United States toward suicide.

But basing themselves on false assumptions and projections, these people have fashioned a foreign policy that has the opposite effect of what they desire and that, if continued, will lead to unparalleled catastrophe. They believe that we face a mortal enemy—the Soviet Union—that threatens our way of life, our free enterprise system, and our prosperity, and must therefore be forced to change its character decisively or be vanquished by whatever means possible. This policy, meant to contain the influence of the Soviet Union, and where possible to roll it back until it becomes minuscule or disappears entirely, is called "containment." Proponents of this policy believe that the dozens of national and social revolutions that have erupted since World War II and that threaten the world order that the United States hopes to retain are either caused directly by the Soviet Union or sustained by it. And they believe that the primary means of containing and rolling back both the Soviet Union and the revolutions is military power, the centerpiece of which is the nuclear bomb. They have spent trillions of dollars in furtherance of this foreign policy, and though it has met with many setbacks, particularly in recent years, they are convinced it will ultimately bring victory.

In the third of a century since this policy was developed, it has become part of the American mystique, accepted almost without question by both the establishment and a sizable majority of the population. But there is now a considerable mass of evidence to indicate that it has been ill-advised. We have been focusing on the wrong enemy and relying on the wrong weapon. This is not unique, for throughout history nations have relied on strategies that had worked previously, only to find them useless or counterproductive in the war at hand. Sometimes the strategies had become obsolete; sometimes they proved inappropriate because—as in the present instance—the new enemy was of a different nature than the old one. The best known example of this sort in recent years was France's World War II fixation on its famed Maginot Line, but the Maginot Line syndrome has affected other countries at other times.

Many centuries ago, according to H.G. Wells, Carthage was vanquished by Rome in the first Punic War because she mistakenly believed that her previously invincible mercenaries, quinqueremes (boats with five banks of oars), and elephants were still invincible. But the Romans used free citizens as soldiers, added a corvus to their ships which hooked enemy boats and prevented them from ramming, and adopted effective methods for dispersing the elephant brigades.[1] Carthage was destroyed; Rome went on to become the world's most powerful nation.

In the British war against the American colonists from 1775 to 1783, the strategies by which Britain had defeated France in the four wars of the previous century that became known as the Second Hundred Years' War were unavailing against a much weaker adversary in the New World that relied heavily on guerrilla warfare. Despite an advantage of three to one in population, a navy second to none, and immensely greater wealth, Britain was defeated, in part because it was unprepared to wage a new type of warfare. The British general

John Burgoyne wrote in 1777: "Wherever the King's forces point, militia to the amount of three to four thousand assemble in twenty-four hours; they bring with them their subsistence, etc., and the alarm over, they return to their farms."[2] From July 12 to August 27, 1780, there were fifteen major guerrilla skirmishes in Georgia and South Carolina alone. The results reflected, among other miscalculations, the British failure to prepare for this kind of war.

An equally serious error caused the naval defeat of the sixteenth century Spanish empire at the hands of the British. The Spanish had prepared for the wrong war. "With their long swift galleys, rowed by slaves and criminals," writes historian W. N. Weech,[3] "Spanish sailors learned to grapple and board" ships of Moslem corsairs in the Mediterranean. But this method of warfare was of little use against British ships in open sea. "The Spaniard remained an expert hand-to-hand fighter; he never became an efficient navigator. The smaller English vessel, part merchantman, part privateer . . . could easily elude the more cumbersome [Spanish] galleon, sail closer to the wind, and by clever maneuvering, put its shot into the enemy, while the return fire passes harmlessly through its rigging."[4] The outcome was a factor in the ultimate decline of the Spanish empire and steady expansion of the British empire.

In our own times, the best known instance of a nation that prepared for the wrong war with the wrong weapons was France before World War II. The words "Maginot Line" conjure up an image of military futility today, but in the prewar years, the French believed this awe-inspiring structure guaranteed victory in any war with Germany. Nor were they alone in their belief, for the leaders and people of Britain, the United States, and other Western nations agreed. As it turned out, however, the Line was useless—worse than useless, in fact, for the illusions it fostered prevented preparation for a realistic defense.

French strategists believed the lessons they learned in World War I to be applicable to World War II. Their great success at Verdun in 1916 had persuaded them that defense had a far greater chance of success than did offense. They planned for the next war, therefore, from the narrow prism of the previous one. "It is a joke in Britain to say that the War Office is always preparing for the last war," Winston Churchill wrote in his history of World War II. "But this is probably true of other departments and other countries, and it was certainly true of the French Army."[5]

World War I had been a "war of positions." Soldiers in defensive trenches shot at enemy troops in trenches a few hundred yards away, and, when enough of the other side had been killed or disabled, "went over the top" to capture the position. When enough positions had been captured, the enemy presumably would be compelled to sue for peace. There were, of course, tanks, planes, cannon, and other forces involved as well, and many nuances of strategy. But there was a widespread belief that an army on the offensive would need two to three times as many troops as an army defending its positions, and that the offensive army would soon be enervated. As its resources and reserves dried up, it would be forced to surrender.

From this erroneous assessment was born the Maginot Line and the Maginot Line mentality. If a war of position—a defensive war—succeeded in 1914 to 1918, reasoned the French generals, why not cover the whole Franco-German frontier with one long, unbreachable "trench" to guarantee an equally successful outcome.[6] "Choose the best points from which your artillery can fire," advised Marshall Henri Philippe Petain, "then create fortified works to protect your guns, and then link up the fortifications where you can by underground galleries."[7] The result was the Maginot Line, named after War Minister André Maginot.

Begun in 1929, completed in 1934, and constantly improved thereafter, the Line was an impressive piece of work. It spanned from Switzerland in the south to Longwy—the intersection between France, Luxemburg, and Belgium—in the north.[8] The Belgian border was left unfortified because the Ardennes were thought to be an impassable obstacle. Nonetheless, some fortifications were emplaced in that area in 1939 (and along the Swiss frontier to the south as well).[9] To the French and to most people in the West, the "war of position" strategy seemed unassailable.

"No army can break down the Maginot Line," boasted the French newspaper *Le Soir*. "The French believe," said the *Literary Digest* of January 29, 1938, "that the Maginot Line will prevent any possibility of invasion." German planes, it conceded, might wreck French cities behind the Line, but "no hostile force can occupy their territory until the Maginot Line is destroyed. . . . They believe that Line to be inviolable." So did innumerable experts in Britain and America. "Thanks to the fortification with which she has had the wisdom to protect herself," wrote "Gallicus" in the magazine *19th Century*,

"France is in the position to face any attack and to safeguard the integrity of her domain."[10]

The Line was truly striking, a masterpiece of technological achievement. It included thousands of ramparts, forts, garrisons, antitank defenses, machine-gun posts, and fields of barbed wire to a depth of fifteen to eighteen miles. If German troops, tanks, or cavalry were to break through the first set of defenses, they would still have to contend with other traps.

Little of the Line was visible. Where the ground was flat, the fortresses were dug into the earth; where there were hills or ridges, forts were burrowed into the sides. The reinforced concrete was painted an earthen color to camouflage its existence. Thus, an innocent passer-by would see only a peaceful panorama of grass-covered terrain and grazing cattle. Most of the forts were two stories high, forty to sixty feet each, one below ground, one above. A gunner below would not necessarily have to take the elevator to the chamber above; he could spiral his weapon sixty feet upward until it reached the surface turret, and by using an ingenious periscope device, fire in comfort.[11] To make his job even easier, he only had to press a button for automatic delivery of ammunition. Famed columnist Dorothy Thompson reported being in one of the fortifications after the war had started. She took an elevator eleven floors to a chamber ten feet square, which had painted walls and ammunition boxes. She heard the word "fire," but all was so quiet she didn't think anything was happening. The next day she learned that what she had seen "had been real fighting that day in the neighborhood of Weisenburg, and the enemy had been repulsed."[12]

Sheltered electric plants provided power for the elevators, for narrow-gauge railroads, and for ventilation. It was claimed that a million French troops could live in Maginot Line quarters below the surface for three months in relative comfort.[13] The forts were linked by underground tunnels, so the general staff could move forces around almost as if they were above ground. Here and there a lake, interspersed between the forts, was drenched with petroleum, ready to be set afire as the enemy approached. The artillery was placed on turrets capable of a complete circle, just in case an adversary did breach the immediate forts. If, despite all calculations, the Line was overrun, there was a secret chamber far underground, known only to a handful of people, where the pressing of a button would blow up hundreds of miles of fortifications.[14] In the opinion of the *Literary Digest*, it was "inconceivable to the French" that the button would ever be used. Pierre Belperron, biographer of Andre Maginot, estimated the cost of the Line as equal to that of 100 battleships of the Queen Elizabeth class, or $3 to 5 billion—a vast sum at that time.[15]

People spoke of the Line in undiluted superlatives. Belperron, for instance, wrote just a few weeks before France was conquered that "the Maginot Line stands like a great shield across the face of France," making the "greatest single contribution to the assured victory of the allies." Thanks to this rampart of western civilization, France could "devote her energies to prosecuting the war unhampered by fears of blitzkrieg invasion."[16] The entire French populace accepted the conventional wisdom that it was secure behind those millions of square yards of concrete and steel.

As it turned out, of course, the Maginot Line was a catastrophe; worse, it was irrelevant. On May 10, 1940, German forces invaded the Netherlands and Belgium. Two days later, they sped across the French frontier at high speed, and on May 15, General Ewald Von Kleist's troops broke through the defenses into open country. Their momentum took them almost fifty miles westward the next day, and by May 26 the rout was so thorough that Britain was forced to evacuate 198,000 of its own plus 140,000 allied troops in the historic drama at Dunkirk. The next German offensive, begun on June 5, ended nine days later when the Germans entered Paris. Simultaneously, on June 14, the Germans drove into the heart of the Maginot Line at Saarbruecken. In forty-eight hours, records Winston Churchill, "the German penetration to Besancon had cut off retreat. More than four hundred thousand men were surrounded without hope of escape."[17] The "great shield across the face of France" had proved worthless. By June 22, the Republic of France had signed an armistice punctuating the most humiliating defeat in its history. In just six weeks it had managed—despite the Maginot Line—to lose the war.

The French tragedy, clearly, could not be blamed on Nazi superiority. In manpower, the two sides—including British forces in France—were about on a par; if it were true, as many believed, that three times as many troops were needed to mount an offensive as to hold defensive lines, the odds were with France. But there had been a depressing and unexpected failure of strategy. The French were fighting a war of position at a time when positions had become vulnerable to artillery-resistant Panzer tanks and Stuka dive bombers;

the Germans, though they too had hastily built a defensive Siegfried Line, were fighting a war of movement. The French had simply closed their eyes to a technological revolution; the Germans had made full use of it. It was now possible to produce heavy tanks that were almost cannonproof and that moved at almost the speed of an automobile. It was also possible to produce bombers that could swoop down to create a breach in defensive lines. While the French dispersed their tanks in small numbers to infantry divisions, the Germans aligned their tanks in divisional and corps strength. The Stukas, Panzers, and infantry became team partners in a strategy of *movement*, with the planes creating holes in an enemy position, the Panzers speedily driving through to encircle the position, and the troops following to hold it. Even Churchill, who concurred with French defensive strategy at the outset, admits he "did not comprehend the violence of the revolution effected since the last war by the incursion of a mass of fast-moving armor."[18] Over and over again he was dismayed by France's inability "to resist the combination of tanks and dive-bombing." It was out of touch with the new reality; it had allowed its success in World War I to blind it to new conditions.

The Maginot Line syndrome is relevant to post-World War II America—not in the sense that the United States is building useless lines of fortifications to defend itself against a Soviet invasion, but in the broader and more subtle sense that we are focusing on the wrong enemy and relying on weapons and strategies that were made for another kind of war. We have defined the enemy as "Soviet communism," when in fact the challenge has come from far-flung national and social revolution. And we have based our security on nuclear weapons and the strategy of containment, both of which have proven to be counterproductive.

* * * * * * *

American economic and military power remains formidable—a gross national product approaching four trillion dollars and a military arsenal that includes enough nuclear weapons to kill everyone on Earth many times over. No other nation can remotely match that power, not even the Soviet Union, whose GNP is about half that of the United States.

Yet there is a spreading malaise in our country. Aside from the Left, which has always believed that capitalism is on an inevitable slide toward eclipse, many at the Center and even on the Right of the political spectrum now wonder about the future. Among those who predict there will be a nuclear war before the end of this century, for instance, are a former science adviser to President Eisenhower, a former deputy chief of the CIA, and many who once held high posts in the State Department and the Department of Defense, and on the staffs of congressional committees. The "father" of the nuclear submarine, Admiral Hyman G. Rickover, stated on retiring early in 1982, that the nuclear arms race is senseless: "I think we're probably going to destroy ourselves."[19] What Henry Luce once termed "the American century" is now mocked by a steady erosion of the American standard of living—under Republican as well as Democratic presidents—as well as by foreign policy reverses that a great power with the enormous resources of the United States should not have to sustain.

Great imperial nations do not lose wars to such small states as Vietnam, which has a GNP of barely $8 billion—one four-hundredth the American GNP. Nor do they stand by helplessly while their leading client in the critical Persian Gulf, the Shah of Iran, is overthrown by Islamic revolutionaries who, at the outset, have not even a platoon of soldiers under their command. Nor do great imperial nations pay tens of billions per year tribute to such weak nations as Saudi Arabia, Nigeria, Venezuela, or Algeria for oil that is priced 30 to 100 times above the cost of producing it. A generation ago it was possible for the CIA to overthrow the government of Mohammed Mossadegh in Iran because he nationalized the oil industry. It would be impossible for the CIA to topple the governments of the fourteen OPEC nations today.

The postwar institutions, strategies, and weapons that were expected to guarantee American predominance far into the future are beginning to be regarded as exercises in futility. Perhaps it is time to take another look.

THE
MIRAGE
OF
CONTAINMENT

2

The history of the containment policy is relevant to an analysis of it, for it gives us a clue as to its effectiveness and potential. Though the actual term—containment—did not come into vogue until 1947, the policy itself has had two incarnations, the first one spanning from the Russian Revolution in 1917 to World War II, the second, since World War II. It is a history of a strategy that has been tried twice, both times for decades and both times failing.

In 1917, the leaders of the United States, Europe, and Japan made the same kind of assumptions that our policymakers make today: that Soviet communism was determined to spread its revolution worldwide (which was true in 1917), that it was fomenting revolutions that otherwise would not occur (which was not true), and that it had to be contained and rolled back by political and economic pressure if possible, by military force if necessary. Winston Churchill urged the West to strangle "the baby in its crib."[1] "The whole of American policy during the liquidation of the Armistice," wrote Herbert Hoover in 1921, "was to contribute everything it could to prevent Europe from going Bolshevik or being overrun by their armies."[2] Though no one used the word at the time, this was in fact the strategy of containment.

Fourteen foreign armies, including an American contingent of 7,000 soldiers, occupied parts of the Soviet Union from 1918 to 1920, and Britain and France contributed many millions to Czarist officers engaged in a counterrevolution against the Soviet regime.[3] What happened in that period is instructive. The Allied leaders had a choice between seeking a modus vivendi with the Bolsheviks or trying to crush them. In the four months from November 1918 to February 1919 the Soviet foreign office sent seven notes to the Allied powers, written, as correspondent William Henry Chamberlin observed, "in the most conciliatory language." After receiving one, Woodrow Wilson sent William C. Bullitt of the State Department, and Lincoln Steffens, the well-known journalist, to Moscow to negotiate.[4] The two men met with Lenin and concluded an agreement highly favorable to the West: The Bolsheviks agreed that all governments in Russia—White as well as Red—would retain jurisdiction over the areas they then held, and outstanding debts incurred by the Czar would be honored. In return, the West would lift its blockade, withdraw its troops, and reopen communications. Bullitt was elated, but his plan was never even considered. As British Prime Minister David Lloyd George explained to him, he could not "expect us to be sensible about Russia" in the present climate of opinion. President Wilson refused to see Bullitt because, as *New York Times* correspondent Walter Duranty suggested, by this time the White armies were winning (momentarily, it turned out). Wilson evidently believed there was no need to deal with the Soviet regime, thinking it would soon be a limping memory.

There was much self-delusion in that period, as there is today. In a study of news dispatches carried by the *New York Times* in the two years after November 1917, Walter Lippmann and Charles Merz listed ninety-one reports of how "the Soviets were nearing their rope's end, or actually had reached it."[5] It was true, of course, that the Russian economy was falling apart: computed in 1913 prices, total Soviet production fell from seven billion rubles in 1913 to one and a third billion for the year 1920/21. The grain harvest was only 40 percent of prewar levels; industry was operating at 15 percent of normal. The daily bread ration in the big cities in 1918 was one ounce, and even that was often unavailable. By late 1920 and early 1921, the situation was catastrophic. Millions were dying of hunger, typhus, and battlefield injuries. Not less than a million died during Admiral Kolchak's retreat across Siberia alone.[6]

But there was more inner vitality to Soviet communism than the West had anticipated. Trotsky appealed to the patriotism of 30,000 former czarist officers and was able to mold them into the nucleus of a Red Army. Lenin's regime distributed land to the peasants and won their support for a guerrilla war behind White Guard lines. Soviet appeals to tired Western troops to stop fighting were effective with allied soldiers who were sick of war and confused by the realignment of friend and foe. American troops sang "Home toot sweet" and staged a near-mutiny to force their repatriation. A mutiny by the French fleet in Odessa caused France to evacuate its forces. By the end of 1919 the White armies were in retreat, and by early the following year the Bolsheviks had won.[7] In retrospect, Wilson could have secured a better outcome — from the Allied point of view — if he and the other Western leaders had been less bellicose. But the mood in the United States then, as in this generation, was not amenable to calm reflection. Those who counseled moderation were labeled Reds. Senator Robert M. La Follette, Sr. of Wisconsin was called a "Bolshevik spokesman in America" because he proposed that U.S. troops be withdrawn from Archangel. Colonel Raymond Robins was denounced as a Red when he insisted that Lenin and Trotsky were not "German agents." Such organizations as the National Council of Churches and the Foreign Policy Association were tarred with the same brush—Red.[8]

Rhetoric, unfortunately, was no substitute for policy. The reality was that the West, too, was bedeviled by problems that put it on the defensive. The 1917 Russian Revolution, however one may assess it now, inspired emulation. Tens of thousands who had never heard the name Lenin before converted to Leninism overnight. A conference of Socialist party leaders in the United States proclaimed that "since the French Revolution established a new high mark of political liberty in the world, there has been no other advance in democratic progress and social justice comparable to the Russian Revolution."[9]

When the successful uprising in Petrograd was followed by the revolt of German sailors at Kiel and the establishment of Soviet republics in Bavaria and Hungary, the impression was of an incipient tidal wave. Mutinies shook the French army; Italian workers seized the factories in larger cities; general strikes erupted in a number of countries; and English laborers formed a radical shop steward movement. The young Winston Churchill expressed the anxiety of many Western leaders in a letter to David Lloyd George: "We may well be within measurable distance of universal collapse and anarchy throughout Europe and Asia."[10] If any of the three revolutions that racked Germany between 1919 and 1924 had succeeded, his fears might have proved correct.

Under the circumstances, the West was in no position to undertake another military intervention. Instead, with the United States in the forefront, it pursued a policy of economic containment, refusing long-term credits to the Soviets at a time when large sums— $13 billion in the postwar decade—were being granted to other nations in Europe. "We cannot recognize, hold official relations with, or give friendly reception to the agents of a government which is determined and bound to conspire against our institutions," said Secretary of State Bainbridge Colby in August 1920.[11] (A century and a half earlier—after the American Revolution—the Russian czars had taken the same attitude, refusing diplomatic recognition to the United States for thirty-three years.) A few months later, when the Russians asked that trade be resumed, Charles Evans Hughes, Colby's successor, rejected the request on the grounds that the Soviet Union did not recognize the rights of private property, free labor, and the sanctity of contracts.[12] Other governments, beginning with the United Kingdom in 1924, did recognize the Soviet Union, and trade slowly resumed. But long-term investments and long-term loans were negligible, despite generous terms offered by Lenin and his successors. By 1927, only twenty-three foreign firms were engaged in Soviet manufacture, and only seventeen in mining. Both together accounted for less than one half of one percent of Soviet industrial output. The best Moscow could accomplish in this period was a few hundred million dollars of short-term commercial credit.[13]

Nonetheless, Soviet Russia did not collapse. A bitter, three-way dispute broke out among three of Lenin's heirs—Bukharin, Trotsky, and Stalin—over how to form capital for industrial development in the absence of foreign credits. When the most extreme position—Stalin's—prevailed, the Soviet people paid a harsh price for their isolation. Living standards dropped severely and, as popular resistance grew, Stalin resorted to strong police measures to discipline the population. But communism was not rolled back.

Despite the tough talk, so similar to that of today's American leaders, it was soon apparent that Western power—American power in particular—was not limitless. A new intervention against the Soviet Union could not be mounted; it would have been met by guerrilla resistance and by strikes throughout Europe, where conditions were still far from stable. Something of a stand-off prevailed; communism did not expand to other countries, but neither was it liquidated in Soviet Russia.

By the 1930s, the United States and its allies were consumed by the worst economic depression in history and confronted by a vigorous and determined enemy—Nazi Germany—which they considered a greater *immediate* threat than the Soviet Union. Communism may have been the more formidable challenge in the long run, but in the late 1930s the urgent problem was Nazism. The equivocal position of our establishment was reflected in a suggestion by Senator Harry S. Truman, shortly after the Nazi armies invaded the Soviet Union, that "if we see that Germany is winning the war we ought to help Russia, and if Russia is winning we ought to help Germany, and in that way let them kill as many as possible." [14]

The policy of containment and rollback now had to contend not only with Soviet communism but also with instability and fissures in the capitalist world. The United States had no choice but to seek a wartime alliance with the Soviet Union, for while American technology and dollars were indispensable, victory might have been long delayed, and perhaps even rendered unattainable without the Soviet effort. Had Hitler been able to draw on Russia's sizable resources and transfer his Eastern troops to fight on the Western front, World War II would have lasted much longer and, perhaps, culminated in another wave of European revolutions.

As it was, the Left almost limped to power in France and Italy at the end of the war. The communists had played primary roles in the European resistance. Of the five members of the Bureau of the National Council of Resistance (CNR) in France, three were communists, and of the three members of CNR's Committee of Military Action (Comac), two were communists. In Italy, the communists had formed a partisan movement known as Garibaldini, which organized a general strike in Northern Italy in March 1944, described by Hugh Seton–Watson as "the most impressive action of its kind that took place at any time in Europe under Hitler's rule." [15] In both countries resistance fighters seized control of the factories when liberation came, and with their following and their stockpile of armaments, they might have marched full speed to political power. But, at the urging of General Charles de Gaulle, Stalin ordered the French communists to evacuate the factories and disarm the partisans. Stalin issued similar instructions in Italy, and the revolutionary threat waned. Yet in a war that took 52 million lives and destroyed such vast resources, the impulse toward revolution was bound to endure. Communism came to power in Yugoslavia and China despite Stalin's orders that Tito and Mao Tse-tung serve as subordinates in the respective governments of King Peter and Chiang Kai-shek. And communism was imposed on Eastern Europe and North Korea by Soviet military forces.

Thus, the policy of containment and rollback proved futile in its first test. The West certainly enjoyed military superiority over the Soviet Union, but it failed to reverse the Russian Revolution, in part because it was itself enervated by World War I and in part because it was divided and unable to take a common course. The military superiority of the capitalist world was canceled by the conflicts between capitalist nations or blocs as well as by the weakness of their economies. That was the state of affairs leading to failure of containment in its first application; after more than a quarter of a century, not only was the Soviet Union a functioning, if badly damaged, entity, but its sphere of influence had appreciably widened. What heartened the American establishment and encouraged it to try containment again after World War II was the most powerful weapon human ingenuity had ever created, the nuclear bomb.

* * * * * * *

The second attempt to contain and roll back communism in our time has been even less successful than the first. The United States, and the West generally, won its share of victories suppressing revolutionary forces in many places, just as it had done after World War I, and making life difficult for the Soviet bloc through economic pressures. But once again the Soviet Union survived. This time, in fact, it formed a bloc of a dozen nations, supplemented by the support of many other states, such as India and Libya, that are closer to Moscow than to Washington.

Many people ascribe this expansion to successful Soviet export of revolution and our own failure to prevent it, but since 1924 the Soviet leadership has done little to advance world revolution. Once the 1919 to 1924 wave of social upheavals had spent itself, Moscow repudiated the long-held theory that socialism could survive in Russia only if the revolution spread to other countries. It adopted, instead, the doctrine of "socialism in one country," which held that Russian socialism could survive whether revolutions took place elsewhere or not. Only Trotsky's faction adhered to the concept of "permanent revolution," and it was quickly defeated and dispersed. The main branch of communism took a turn toward moderation, opting to work within "class-collaboration" unions such as the AFL (instead of within "dual" unions of their own), supporting reform-oriented labor and farmer-labor parties, and generally toning down revolutionary rhetoric. Stalin rejected the notion of a proletarian revolution in China, instructing the Chinese communists instead to affiliate with Chiang Kai-shek's Kuomintang and work for a "bourgeois" revolution. "For the Russian communists in 1927–28," writes historian D. F. Fleming, "it was a case of here and now or never. The world revolution might be cherished as a far-off ideal, but it definitely had to be put in the background."[16]

There was a return to revolutionary rhetoric for a few years after Trotsky was expelled, when Stalin nursed the fear of a second military intervention by the Western powers, and again from September 1939, when Stalin signed a pact with Hitler, to June 1941, when Hitler invaded Russia. The Soviet Union, isolated and impoverished, held few cards other than the threat of revolution against the West, which it periodically used. But in general it took the other course. After Roosevelt extended diplomatic recognition and France signed a treaty of alliance, Moscow reverted to a nonrevolutionary policy. Local communists joined the Popular Front government in France, praised and endorsed Franklin Roosevelt in the United States, and everywhere muted propaganda for class warfare. The Soviets seemed to be seeking a modus vivendi with the liberal wing of capitalism, if only to stave off an attack by Nazi Germany.

During World War II, the communists made new overtures to the West for long-term collaboration. "We frankly declare," said the American communist leader, Earl Browder, after the Teheran Conference between Roosevelt, Churchill, and Stalin in December 1943, "that we are ready to cooperate in making capitalism work effectively in the post-war period. . . ."[17] Communists pledged to give up the right to strike after the war just as they had during the war. The Communist International, symbol in the West of world revolution, was dissolved.

Leading figures in Roosevelt's entourage, including the president himself, believed the communists would help maintain social stability in the postwar world just as they had during hostilities. They would be transformed into social democrats and live as a left opposition *within* the capitalist system, like the Labour Party in Britain or the socialist movement in France. "We really believed in our hearts," said Harry Hopkins, Roosevelt's closest adviser, "that this was the dawn of a new day we had all been praying for and talking about for so many years. . . . The Russians had proved that they could be reasonable and far-seeing, and there wasn't any doubt in the minds of the President or any of us that we could live with them and get along with them peacefully for as far into the future as any of us could imagine."[18] Clearly, it was not Soviet adherence to revolution that caused the schism with the United States.

During the war, the allies had been united on seeking the military defeat of the Axis, but not on the shape of the future. For Churchill, the major goal was to save the British empire. He—and his successors—sought to restore the old order and the old colonial empires with as little modification as possible. They reimposed monarchies in Greece, Belgium, and Italy, and helped restore French rule in Indochina and Dutch rule in Indonesia (Dutch East Indies). "It seemed," according to Robert Sherwood, "that Britain was backing the most conservative elements . . . as opposed to the liberals or Leftists who had been the most aggressive in resistance to the Germans and Fascists."[19]

If the status quo were to be preserved, it was also necessary to contain the Soviet Union, which Churchill considered an enemy of the Empire. Even during the war, differences about the shape of the future had given rise to disputes over military strategy. In 1942, for instance, the British had opposed a second front across the English Channel, which the Soviets desperately sought so as to relieve German pressure against their forces in the East. Instead, the British favored a south–north second front through Sicily and Italy into Central Europe, the Balkans, and finally, Germany. As Churchill saw it, if American and British armies could be placed flush against or close to Soviet borders, the Russians would be confined to their old domain. On the other hand, an assault from the West, across the Channel, would make it easier for the Red Army to overrun Eastern and Central Europe.

For Stalin, the wartime objective was to weaken the old order and the old balance of power that Churchill so fervidly cherished. He expected to break out of the *cordon sanitaire* that the West had forged around his nation and to establish a buffer zone—Rumania, Bulgaria, Yugoslavia, Albania, Czechoslovakia, Poland, and Hungary—between Russia and the rest of Europe. He was thinking not of revolution but of de facto control over the corridor of small countries through which German troops had marched into Russia twice in the previous quarter-century. The Germans "will recover, and very quickly," Stalin predicted the very month Hitler was defeated, April 1945. "Give them twelve to fifteen years and they'll be on their feet again. And that is why the unity of the Slavs [including the Soviet Union] is important."[20]

For Roosevelt, the American objective was not merely to thwart the ambitions of the Axis powers but also to replace the older British and French imperialism with a softer imperialism in which America would predominate. In Roosevelt's design, the new approach to the underdeveloped countries would be to "give them a share." His bias against the old colonialism was so evident that during an informal dinner at the Atlantic Conference in August 1941, Churchill pointed a stubby finger at the American chief executive and exclaimed: "Mr. President, I believe you are trying to do away with the British empire. Every idea you entertain about the structure of the postwar world demonstrates it."[21]

But while the goal was clear, it is obvious in retrospect that Washington's specific plans for establishing a Pax Americana were far from complete. Little thought had been given to the effects of national and social revolutions. Implicit in every war is the possibility of revolution, but American leaders were caught off guard when independence movements erupted after World War II.

Four months before Pearl Harbor, Churchill and Roosevelt, meeting secretly "somewhere in the Atlantic," proclaimed "the right of all peoples to choose the form of government under which they will live."[22] But no rules or guidelines were established for implementing this right. When the peoples of Madagascar and North Africa attempted, toward the end of the war, to secure independence, France suppressed the movements with military force, and the United States did nothing to help the nationalists. In retrospect, it seems clear that both Roosevelt and Truman had assumed a Pax Americana could be arranged with the modest effort of not much more than monetary measures, international relief, a mechanism for resolving disputes (the United Nations), and judiciously placed loans. At Bretton Woods, New Hampshire, delegates of forty-four nations met in the summer of 1944 to adopt proposals for two bodies that would facilitate trade and development — the International Bank of Reconstruction and Development and the International Monetary

Fund. A short time later, officials of the United States, Britain, the Soviet Union, and China met at Dumbarton Oaks, an estate in Washington, to lay plans for a new world organization to preserve the peace – the United Nations. But none of this sufficed to cope with the explosion of nationalism that erupted beginning in 1944. Churchill's explanation at the Yalta Conference of how national problems would be disposed of indicates how unprepared the West was. Suppose, said Churchill, that China demands the return of Hong Kong, or Egypt requests the return of the Suez Canal. In each case the grieving country would be given the opportunity "to make a broad submission to the opinion of the world" [the United Nations], but Britain would not be obligated "to give Hong Kong back to the Chinese," or the Suez to Egypt, "if we did not feel that was the right thing to do."[23] Stalin asked Churchill what would happen if the Chinese or Egyptians were not satisfied with just *talking* about their problem and wanted something done about it. That question was not answered; it was to become the main source of friction in the postwar era.

* * * * * * *

Coexistence with the Soviet Union demanded adjustments on both sides. The Soviets, for instance, would have to permit a greater degree of democracy in their client states and a loosening of the reins. The United States would have to agree to finance Soviet reconstruction without laying down conditions that would, in effect, eviscerate Russia's planned economy. And there would have to be an understanding about the atom. On September 11, 1945, only a month after nuclear bombs were dropped on Hiroshima and Nagasaki, Secretary of War Henry L. Stimson (with the support of three other members of the cabinet) proposed to Truman an "atomic partnership" with the Soviet Union. The alternative, he said, would be "a secret armament race of a rather desperate character," and the day would come when seemingly weak nations would be able to threaten strong ones.[24] Atomic partnership was essential if the two great nations were to live together in some measure of harmony. There was a need, too, to find a formula for policing the world against "little" and "big" wars – something that was provided for in the United Nations Charter but would not be effectuated without superpower agreement.

Unfortunately, a modus vivendi became impossible under President Truman. It might not have happened under Roosevelt, either, but his less flexible successor was convinced the United States did not have to make any concessions or adjustments. Moscow's wartime losses were staggering — 20 million dead; 15 large cities, 1,710 towns, 70,000 villages, 32,000 factories, 1,135 coal mines, 3,000 oil wells, and 10,000 power stations destroyed.[25] American officials did not think the Soviets would be able to mount much of an economic challenge for a long time, just as they were certain Russia would not acquire the Bomb for many years. Somewhere along the way, then, Truman and his advisers decided the United States could work its will as it saw fit, and that the Soviets would be no obstacle. Both Gar Alperovitz, in *Atomic Diplomacy: Hiroshima and Potsdam*, and Martin J. Sherwin, in *A World Destroyed*, claim the atom bomb was dropped on Hiroshima in August 1945 more as a warning to the Soviet Union than as a final, devastating blow to force a Japanese surrender.[26] The Bomb, combined with a heavy industry that had doubled its capacity, gave the Truman Administration a feeling of invulnerability and steered it in old directions for old objectives — markets, profits, strategic gain — at a time when history was dictating new directions.

The Soviets were again willing to de-emphasize class warfare, as they had in the 1930s, in return for reconstruction aid and political coexistence with the United States. But Washington's attitude stiffened. Eleven days after he took office, Truman castigated Soviet Foreign Minister Molotov in what Admiral William D. Leahy described as "blunt language unadorned by the polite verbiage of diplomacy."[27] Two weeks later, Truman ended lend–lease shipments and offered no substitute loans. In the Soviet economy's weakened state, this was a major disaster, for there was no other source of credit. Truman eventually offered some aid, but only under terms the Soviets felt would make them pawns of the United States. In March 1946, Moscow was advised that the United States might consider a $1 billion credit if the Kremlin would settle its lend–lease account, join the International Monetary Fund and World Bank, and live up to their rules against discrimination in international trade. This, of course, would have forced not only the Soviet Union, but also its buffer states, into the "American system." It would have compelled Eastern Europe (except for Czechoslovakia) to remain a raw-material-producing area. These countries, like the United States itself after the Civil War, required a protectionist policy—high tariffs, quotas, and similar devices—for their nascent industries, not free trade. Soviet specialists who asked to be anonymous, expressed the view to an American in London that the "real object . . . in advocating freer trade was to hold the markets for manufactured goods in the less developed countries and to check their industrialization." The Russian argued that "protection was necessary for the industrialization of Eastern European countries, and their industrialization was necessary to free them from economic domination by the capitalist countries."[28]

The chasm widened and the differences ultimately were concretely defined first by the Truman Doctrine, then by an article in *Foreign Affairs*, "The Sources of Soviet Conduct," by the director of the Policy Planning Staff of the State Department, George F. Kennan. Though there are differences within the American establishment regarding emphasis and implementation, these documents remain the cornerstone of U. S. policy.

* * * * * * *

On March 12, 1947, Truman told a joint session of Congress that "the peoples of a number of countries of the world," including Poland, Rumania, and Bulgaria, "have recently had totalitarian regimes forced upon them against their will."[29] That was true, of course. The 1947 Soviet-sponsored elections in Poland, for instance, were preceded by severe repression against resistance fighters friendly to Britain and the London-based Polish government-in-exile. Sixteen leaders of this resistance, including two socialists, Puzak and Pajdak, were invited for consultation by Soviet military authorities in Poland, under the assurance of safe conduct, only to be bundled off to Moscow in a military plane, tried, and (all but three) sentenced to prison terms. Fifty thousand members of the Home Army were disarmed and sent to Siberia; 300 socialists were arrested prior to the elections, and 149 Peasant Party candidates were jailed (18 of them executed) during the campaign.[30] On the other hand, as historian Walter LaFeber points out, "The Soviets held elections which allowed a non-Communist government to gain power in Hungary, suffered an overwhelming defeat in the Russian-controlled zones of Austria, supervised elections in Bulgaria, which satisfied British if not American officials, and agreed to acquiesce in the coming to power of an independent, non-Communist government in Finland . . . if that government would follow a foreign policy friendly to Russia."[31] There was also the fact, on the other side of the ledger, that Britain, France, Holland, Belgium, and others were guilty of dictatorial measures similar to those the Russians were imposing—in Greece, the Dutch East Indies, Indochina, the Gold Coast, Cyprus, Belgian Congo, among others. The only difference was that repression in those colonial and semicolonial areas had long been accepted as the "normal" condition of an imperial world.

After providing his description of events in Eastern Europe, Truman pointed to an international dichotomy:

> At the present moment in world history nearly every nation must choose between two alternative ways of life. . . . One way of life is based upon the will of the majority and is distinguished by free institutions, representative government, free elections, guarantees of individual liberty, freedom of speech and religion, and freedom from political oppression. The second way of life is based upon the will of the minority forcibly imposed upon the majority. It relies upon terror and oppression, a controlled press and radio, fixed elections, and the suppression of personal freedom.[32]

American policy, Truman said, should be "to support free peoples who are resisting attempted subjugation by armed minorities or by outside pressures." This call to quarantine Soviet communism reflected the influence of Admiral William D. Leahy, chairman of the Joint Chiefs of Staff, a hard-liner on the issue of communism, Truman's principal adviser after Roosevelt's death, and the advisor of the former British prime minister, Winston Churchill. On March 5, 1946, with Truman sitting on the podium, Churchill made his historic "iron curtain" speech at Fulton, Missouri. The Soviet Union, he said, was an expansionist state.

> From Stettin in the Baltic to Trieste in the Adriatic, an iron curtain has descended across the continent. . . . The world is now divided into capitalist and communist blocs. To check the expansion of the communist bloc, the English-speaking peoples—a sort of latter-day 'master-race'—must sooner or later form a union. They should immediately contract a military alliance and coordinate their military establishments. They must lead a 'Christian' civilization in an anti-communist crusade.[33]

Truman's young adviser, Clark M. Clifford, had prepared a 62-page position paper in 1946, "A Summary of American Relations with the Soviet Union," in which he concluded that since the Soviets were "vulnerable to atomic weapons, biological warfare, and long range air power . . . the U.S. must be prepared to wage atomic and biological warfare."[34] This position, Clifford wrote, was concurred in by all the leading members of the cabinet and the intelligence community. The Truman Doctrine carried much of this flavor. The exact tactics for quarantining communism were not specified, but they ranged from economic and military aid for those who opposed communism to direct military measures by the United States itself.

The other document that has had a major impact on American policy was Kennan's *Foreign Affairs* article, published under the pseudonym "X." Deftly written and displaying considerably more sophistication than Truman's speech, the article, originally drafted as a paper for Secretary of the Navy James Forrestal, was softer in tone than Truman's rhetoric, but it carried the same thrust. There existed, wrote Kennan, an "innate antagonism between capitalism and socialism" that must lead, in the Soviet view, to "the eventual fall of capitalism." Fortunately the communists "were in no hurry about it" but "the main thing is that there should always be pressure, increasing constant pressure toward the desired goal." These aggressive tendencies, inherent in communism, Kennan argued, require "long term, patient but firm and vigilant containment" by applying "counterforce at a series of constantly shifting geographical and political points, corresponding to the shifts and maneuvers of Soviet policy." For the next ten or fifteen years, Kennan proposed, the United States should "promote tendencies which must eventually find their outlet in either the break-up or the gradual mellowing of Soviet power."[35] As columnist Walter Lippmann saw it, the "X" article and Truman Doctrine constituted a call for "unending intervention in all countries that are supposed to 'contain' the Soviet Union."[36]

Many years later, in his memoirs, Kennan regretted that he had not made it clear that he was calling for nonmilitary action. "I saw no necessity of a Soviet–American war," he wrote in 1967, "nor anything to be gained by one, then or at any time." Kennan was confident that American support for resistance movements within the Soviet sphere, coupled with the Soviet Union's own internal weakness, would be enough to "moderate Soviet ambitions" within a reasonable time.[37]

Kennan's afterthought notwithstanding, however, the two 1947 documents spurred uncompromising rhetoric and plans for military action. In 1946, Truman threatened to use nuclear weapons against the Soviet Union unless it withdrew its troops from Azerbaijan.[38] When the Chinese communist revolution triumphed, many rightists in the United States charged government officials with "treason." Right-wing theorist James Burnham asserted in his book, *Containment or Liberation*, that revolution was the result of "the activities of a trained and centralized international enterprise with headquarters located in the Soviet Union and agents operating everywhere on earth." Poor social conditions, he implied, had nothing to do with it.[39] More and more one heard the words "liberation" or "roll-back" coupled with "containment"; and James F. Byrnes, one of Truman's closest associates, talked of "measures of last resort"—presumably war—unless the Russians were prepared to "retire in a very decent manner" from their position in Eastern Europe.[40]

Many zealots, confident that U. S. economic and military positions were impregnable, talked of a "preventative war." Major General Orville A. Anderson, commandant of the Air War College, lectured on "the advisability of launching an A-bomb attack on Russia." "Which is the greater immorality," he asked, "preventative war as a means to keep the U.S.S.R. from becoming a nuclear power; or, to allow a totalitarian dictatorial system to develop a means whereby the free world could be intimidated, blackmailed, and possibly destroyed?"[41] Secretary of the Navy Francis Matthews advocated "a war to compel co-operation for peace. . . . We would become the first aggressors for peace." *Christian Science Monitor* columnist Joseph C. Harsch described the "aggressor for peace" scenario: Washington would deliver "a disarmament ultimatum to Moscow and then when that ultimatum had been rejected, as it undoubtedly would be rejected, treat that rejection as a *casus belli* and go to war with all its atomic weapons in a total effort to destroy the military power of the Soviet bloc."[42] However, a "preventative war" was not winnable, and Truman was realistic enough to reject the idea, at least for the time being.

* * * * * * *

There was an apocalyptic aura to the containment policy, noticeable particularly with the political Right, as if there were no limits to the exercise of American power. It could do as it pleased to achieve what it wanted, if only it acted resolutely. Jeane J. Kirkpatrick, President Reagan's ambassador to the United Nations, describes with nostalgia the period from 1945 to 1968 (the year it became clear the

Vietnam War was lost), when that power was triumphant. This, Kirk-patrick says,

> was a relatively happy respite during which free societies were unusually secure. The West was united, self-assured, and strong. The United States and the democratic ethos we espoused were ascendant in the world if not every-where triumphant. . . . We were strong and prosperous. No country or group of countries could compete on equal terms with us economically or could successfully challenge our military power.

This apocalyptic strain remains part of the American mystique even today when it is evident that our power is on the wane. The more fervid advocates of containment, in the conservative and neo-conservative camp, attribute the decline to an erosion of will, a fail-ure to exercise the power we have. Kirkpatrick denigrates the period from 1968 to the election of Ronald Reagan as an "era of detente" in which our leaders acquiesced to "the relentless expansion of Soviet military and political power" and accepted with little chal-lenge "a corresponding contraction of American military and politi-cal power." Within the United States, "an attitude of defeatism, self-doubt, and self-delusion . . . displaced what had been a distinctly American optimism about the world and our prospects as a nation." Detente, in her schema, reflected the fact that we had lost our deter-mination to fight back, and that the Soviets, spurred on, had taken the offensive to "relentlessly" expand.[43]

In the apocalyptic view of our recent history, the advocates of containment—especially its extremist wing—see our foreign policy failures as defeats that happened only because we lacked determi-nation. Thus Norman Podhoretz, editor of *Commentary* and an authentic voice of neoconservatism, berates President Eisenhower for accepting a stalemate by which North and South Korea retained pre-war borders after the Korean war, rather than pushing ahead to *liberate* North Korea from communism. Three years later, in 1956, the Eisenhower Administration was similarly overcautious in Hun-gary; when "the Hungarians rose up against their Soviet masters the United States looked on sympathetically but took no action."[44]

Podhoretz forgets two relevant points concerning Korea: first, that Truman and General Douglas MacArthur did try to "liberate" North Korea in 1950, with the disastrous result that China entered the fray and, within three weeks, drove the American armies hundreds of miles back until they were below the 38th parallel; second, there was a possibility—as many in Washington believed—that the war in Korea was a diversion for a Soviet attack on Western Europe. As for Hungary, critics are understandably vague about how we could have halted the advance of Soviet tanks in Budapest in 1956 without triggering a third world war.

There are Americans who still blame the "do-nothing" policy of the Truman Administration for "giving" China to the communists in 1949, heedless of the fact that we allocated $3 billion in military aid to Chiang Kai-shek's anticommunist forces—a respectable sum at that time and much more than the Russians had given Mao's communists. Whenever a bastion is lost there is a tendency to attribute it to erosion of will if not duplicity. Again to quote Podhoretz, "No sooner had Vietnam fallen than Soviet proxies in the form of Cuban troops appeared in Angola, and again the United States refused to respond. . . . Within the next few years . . . six more countries (Laos, Ethiopia, Mozambique, Afghanistan and Cambodia) were taken over by factions supported by and loyal to the Soviet Union, while the United States looked complacently on."[45]

This is too blatant a misrepresentation of history to go uncorrected. The United States in fact did respond to events in Angola, giving covert support to South African troops that drove hundreds of miles into Angola from the south and to Zaierean troops that advanced dozens of miles toward the capital, Luanda, from the north. What irks the *Commentary* editor, however, is that these U.S.-aided groups having failed, we didn't do more—including, perhaps, sending in American troops. Nor did the American government look "complacently" on as Laos and Cambodia went communist; Kennedy considered using nuclear bombs against Laos in 1961 unless the Pathet Lao agreed to become part of a tripartite government, and the American intervention in Cambodia included not only CIA support for the ouster of Prince Norodom Sihanouk and military aid to Lon Nol, his successor, but also years of secret bombing by U.S. planes of Khmer Rouge positions.[46] American intervention in Ethiopia consisted of training 2,800 of Haile Selassie's officers, giving him hundreds of millions of dollars in military aid, and, when the emperor was deposed by rebels while traveling abroad, returning him to the country in an American plane and ferrying his loyal troops to Addis Ababa to restore him to power. As for Afghanistan, the United States imposed harsh sanctions on the Soviet Union after its troops were sent in, including an embargo on the sale of grain. In Mozambique, our military supplies were a major factor in helping Portugal suppress rebel forces for decades.

In the real world, American presidents, despite their acceptance of the containment policy, have had to adjust their sights and trim their hopes to the dimensions of the possible. Certainly Truman would have preferred to roll back communism in Eastern Europe and China; Eisenhower would have chosen to "save" Hungary from the Russian tanks and North Korea from Kim Il Sung; Kennedy would have opted for Castro's ouster in Cuba. For various reasons, none of this was possible. One factor a president must take into consideration is the effect on his constituencies of a given course of action. Nixon was worried in 1969, for instance, that he might not be able to enact his domestic program if the opposition to his Vietnam policy continued to grow. Another factor that affects policy is the possibility of enlarging a war; Lyndon Johnson worried constantly about that, as Doris Kearns records in her memoir of the president. There are a host of other considerations, such as the attitudes of our allies or the ability of the economy to absorb the cost of a military venture.

The feeling of power that came with the atom bomb and postwar economic dominance, however, has made it difficult for many Americans to reconcile themselves to stalemates or setbacks. Perhaps there is a lingering envy for the ease with which older imperial powers once were able to seize and retain colonies – 50,000 British troops once overpowered India; 20,000 French troops subdued Indochina. In their frustration, conservatives and many moderates press for more effort and determination. Even those who contend that the United States should not have blundered into the Vietnam quagmire also say that once it did become involved, it should have "fought to win"–by which they mean the Pentagon should have used all necessary force, including nuclear bombs on North Vietnam and possibly China, to bring Hanoi to brook. And having designated Iran and its Shah as the fulcrum of American security in the Persian Gulf, the United States should not have permitted the Islamic revolution of Ayatollah Khomeini to succeed; it should either have prodded the Iranian military to execute a coup d'état or, if that was not feasible, sent in American troops. The Nixon Doctrine, which called for passing the major burden of fighting in their own countries to such allies as the Thieu government, is called by Podhoretz a move "towards withdrawal, retrenchment, disengagement" from a policy of "containment to strategic retreat."[47]

As the bulk of such people see it, "strategic retreat" encourages the Soviet Union to build up its military force and increase its influence around the world. Ultimately, if this process continues and the Kremlin gains superiority, it will not have to occupy the territory of our allies or ourselves to impose its will, any more than it now has to occupy Finland to impose its will there. Its mere existence and clear cut military superiority would force the whole world, including the United States, to accept Moscow's dictates.

James Fallows, in his book *National Defense*, describes the Finlandization scenario thus: The Soviet Union acquires a capability to destroy the 1,000 American land-based Minutemen missiles in a surprise first strike, leaving perhaps 10 percent functional. In the same nuclear sweep, the other two legs of the U.S. defense triad are also damaged. Eighteen of the forty-one nuclear-missile submarines are demolished while in port awaiting repairs or "changing crews," and two-thirds of the B-52 bombers at America's disposal are similarly flattened.[48] The United States, Fallows points out, would still have enough warheads left, especially in its nuclear submarines, to "destroy every large and medium-sized city in the Soviet Union." But, in the opinion of the Right, an American president would not strike back because in these circumstances he would not have enough warheads to "kill" the remaining Soviet missiles aimed at American cities. He would, therefore, accept the initial death toll of two to ten million and take no retaliatory steps, fearing that the next round would result in 100 million deaths, not to mention destruction of industrial facilities and infrastructure. The surprise attack, in other words, would immobilize a rational U.S. president. He would swallow his pride and supinely agree to Soviet domination.

It is to avoid that prospect that the United States must act resolutely, willing to fight and die to contain and roll back communism. So-called moderates disagree with the tone and sometimes with the specifics of this thesis—for instance, as to whether the United States should have fought in Vietnam, or fought so long—but they accept most of its conclusions, as evidenced by the near-doubling of military spending during the four "moderate" Carter years and the continued support by a vast majority of liberals in Congress of whatever military projects the Pentagon proposes. As Henry Kissinger defined it, the difference is "between those who regard as inevitable an apocalyptic showdown with the Soviet Union and those who think that managing the competition will remain a permanent feature of our foreign policy—with a gradual erosion of the Soviet system but no clear-cut terminal point."[49] The methods, in other words, differ, but the objective is the same.

* * * * * * *

The containment policy, however, has been a failure, in its second incarnation as in its first. George F. Kennan had been confident that it would succeed because rapid industrialization had exacted so many economic sacrifices from the Russian people, and the war had left them "physically and spiritually tired."[50] It did not seem possible that the Soviet Union could resist additional pressures. But it did.

The Soviets were able to explode their own nuclear device by 1949, just four years after the United States had done it, and they retained a conventional force that everyone, including the U.S. National Security Council, conceded could overrun virtually all of Europe in a few days. Cutting through the knot of economic containment proved more arduous and forced the Soviets to take harsh measures. But though the Russian people paid dearly for the effort, that too was accomplished. The Kennan–Truman assessment that severe pressure on Moscow would force it to become pliable to American purposes was proven wrong.

In the absence of loans or grants from the only available source — the United States — Stalin's regime acquired capital for reconstruction by "squeezing" its own citizens and, even more, the 110 million people in the seven East European buffer states that were now part of the Soviet sphere of influence. Under the Yalta and Potsdam agreements, Moscow was entitled to reparations from former enemy countries—Germany, Hungary, Bulgaria, Rumania—and took them now with a harsh hand. Enormous quantities of machinery were dismantled and shipped to the Soviet Union. By the calculation of an anti-Soviet economist, J. Wszelaki, the value of such seizures was $20 billion—$15 billion from East Germany alone. Two-fifths the Rumanian budget of 1946/47 and one-fourth of the Hungarian one went to satisfy reparations.[51]

Another source of capital was a series of special economic agreements that favored the Kremlin. Poland, for instance, was compelled to deliver 8 million tons of coal to the Soviet Union in 1946 and 12 to 13 million tons in subsequent years at below-world-market prices. The Kremlin reaped a harvest from dozens of joint companies formed with bloc countries to exploit petroleum, quartz mining, bauxite, transportation, and shipping. The joint companies were joint in name only. A Soviet–Yugoslav undertaking for transport on the Danube charged the Soviet Union 38 cents for every ton-kilometer shipped while charging Yugoslavia 80 cents. Milentije Popovic, in his *Economic Relations Amongst Socialist States*, estimated that, in its joint ventures with Bulgaria, Russia received the equivalent of 2.7 man-days of labor for every day of its own.

Such measures cost the Soviet Union a heavy price in world esteem, and the political steps that accompanied them cost even more. As the burdens imposed on the East European people inevitably increased their hostility toward Moscow, Moscow's response was to tighten the reins. In one country after another, noncommunist parties that had been permitted to exist with some degree of independence were dissolved or forced to merge with the communists. The policy reached a climax in February 1949, when the Czech communists managed a bloodless uprising against the government of Eduard Benes. The inevitable step was a purge of nationalist elements within the Communist parties. Many communist leaders, especially those who had fought in the World War II underground, responded to popular sentiments by urging more consumer goods and less coercion. One of the "crimes" listed against Wladyslaw Gomulka of Poland, for instance, was that he had promised the peasants they would not be collectivized. Leaders of this sort were purged and, in some instances, executed. Politbureau member and Minister of Interior Laszlo Rajk of Hungary was tried in September 1949 as an "American and Yugoslav agent" and was executed. Traicho Kostov, a deputy prime minister in Bulgaria, suffered a similar fate. More than half the ninety-seven members of the Czech Central Committee were removed, along with Deputy Prime Minister Rudolf Slansky. Hundreds of thousands—a U.S. estimate put it at 1.75 million—were ousted from the six parties, and in Russia itself followers of Andrei Zhdanov were similarly eliminated.[52]

Stalin's methods were undoubtedly harsher than necessary, and they fueled the flames of anticommunism in the West. But any leadership in the communist world during those years would have had to exact sacrifices that were not required in Western Europe because of U.S. loans and grants. Nonetheless, despite containment, Soviet industry rebounded. Having reached what economists call the takeoff point, the Soviet economy forged ahead from 1947 to 1950 at a growth rate of 20 to 26 percent a year. Steel production, a good barometer of material progress, jumped from 18 million tons in 1940 to 27 million in 1950 and 45 million in 1955. Output of electric power leaped in the same time span from 48 billion kilowatt hours to 91 billion to 170 billion.

Pressure from the United States and its allies propelled the Soviet bloc into emergency improvisations that distorted economic planning into a caricature of what it ought to be. On March 26, 1948, Truman banned the sale of aircraft to Eastern Europe and Russia. In November, more items were added to the proscribed list and special measures were taken to prevent American merchandise sold to Latin America from being resold to the Soviet bloc. The big blow came with the passage of the Export Control Act of 1949, which prohibited the sale of military or strategic goods to the communist states. The words "military" and "strategic" were so broadly construed that in September 1949, the United States shipped only $100,000 worth of cargo to the Soviet Union. In March 1950, 600 types of products were listed as requiring export licenses and, as a corollary to the Marshall Plan, the United States decreed that all recipients of U.S. aid join the embargo or lose their grants and loans. Even technical know-how was ultimately included in the embargo.[53]

The impact of these pressures on the Soviet bloc economy was immense — as Kennan and Truman had foreseen. A leading Czech economist explained the ripple effect on the ban of one item, sulfur. With the foreign supply cut off, the Soviet bloc had no choice but to reactivate certain Czech mines that provided a low-grade ore at a cost two and a half times the world price of sulfur. Thus, all products in which sulfur was used became much more costly and much less competitive than similar products in the capitalist world. The example of sulfur, multiplied by hundreds, gives an idea of the nightmarish problems faced by the communist countries. Yet they survived; none were lured back to capitalism, and where there were revolts — as in East Germany, Hungary, and Czechoslovakia — the rebels were usually "socialists with a human face," not procapitalist. (Some of the leaders of the Polish Solidarity movement in 1980 to 1982 may have been an exception to this rule — may have preferred, that is, reversion to a nonsocialist society. But they too were committed to a worker self-management system like the one in Yugoslavia.)

Cut adrift from the world market by the American-sponsored embargo and by discrimination against its exports, the communist world turned inward. What could have been bought cheaper on the "free world" market had to be reassigned for production to bloc countries at higher cost. Planning programs had to be coordinated to limit duplication, and since there could be no thought of free trade under the circumstances, a new mechanism had to be established for commercial intercourse. In January 1949, the Soviet Union and five Eastern European nations formed the Council for Mutual Economic Assistance (Comecon), later adhered to by East Germany, Outer Mongolia, North Korea, Vietnam, and Cuba. Here, business was conducted on a semibarter basis, with each nation entering into a host of bilateral agreements. It was an unwieldy and insular arrangement, but inevitable under the circumstances. By 1953 more than four-fifths of Soviet commerce was within its own bloc.

Comecon's plan for a self-sufficient "socialist international division of labor" resulted in many maladjustments. Czechoslovakia, to cite one example, had once been one of the most efficient industrial states in the world, noted for high-grade engineering at its Vitkovice iron works and Skoda auto factories and also for its high quality glassware, textiles, shoes, and chinaware. But forced into a market system with a low level of quality, Czech products also deteriorated toward the common denominator. Since it could not buy higher grade machinery in the West, it lost its place as a marvel of efficiency and product excellence.

There is no denying that containment forced the communist world to take many defensive measures, and it certainly kept living standards lower in the Soviet bloc than they would otherwise have been. But it did not cause "either the break-up or the gradual mellowing of Soviet power," as Kennan had predicted. The "Soviet empire" was not rolled back; on the contrary, it expanded a little, now exercising what the Center for Defense Information calls "significant influence," which it did not have before 1947, in Afghanistan, Angola, the Congo, Cuba, Ethiopia, Laos, Libya, Mozambique, Syria, South Yemen, and Vietnam.[54] To be sure, China and Yugoslavia have seceded from the Soviet bloc since the policy of containment was formulated, but no communist country has been "liberated" in the sense of returning to capitalism. If the policy of containment were to eliminate the Soviet Union as an obstacle to America's international ambitions, the policy has failed. There is no sign of terminal enfeeblement in the Soviet system; though it remains authoritarian and controls its East European allies with an iron fist, its GNP is second only to that of the United States, and though it has chronic agricultural problems and its rate of industrial development has slowed, at the moment it is neither in danger of economic or military collapse.

What accounts for communism's ability to hold on? History records few revolutions that have been reversed (we refer to "social" revolutions in which an entirely new set of institutions replaces an old one, not "political" revolutions in which one government or one dictator replaces another). Revolutionary regimes may undergo drastic changes in leadership, but they almost never succumb to counter-revolution. The bifurcated English Revolution from 1642 to 1688 changed leaders many times, for example, but it did not restore the old feudal class to power. It takes desperate people to make a revolution, and they usually cling tenaciously to the social structure they have created. The Concert of Europe, an alliance of reactionary monarchs guided by Prince Klemens von Metternich of Austria, tried feverishly from 1815 to 1846 to undo national revolutions and to prevent others from succeeding. But the revolutionary spark, once ignited, could not be extinguished; such patriots as Giuseppe Mazzini and a host of others, described by historians as Romantic nationalists, led a wave of uprisings that spread in 1848 to Prussia, Austria, Hungary, Italy, and other countries. The bourgeois revolution, once started, did not reverse course.

The Russian Revolution, too, seems to have had that power to endure against great odds and outside pressures. With all its shortcomings, the Soviet system is not likely to be rolled back to capitalism or feudalism any more than the United States is likely to submit once more to the sovereignty of the British monarchy. And so long as the Soviet Union exists, with its vast resources and a GNP approaching $2 trillion annually, it will attract to its side developing nations that seek help against the West. In politics, "the enemy of my enemy is my friend," and revolutionaries who have been fighting an American puppet—in Ethiopia or El Salvador, for example—are not likely to turn to the United States for aid once they have won, but rather to the "enemy of my enemy," the Soviet Union. The thirteen American colonies did exactly the same thing during the Revolutionary War when they turned to France for economic and military assistance. In a world in revolution—six dozen nations have been involved in national upheavals since World War II—Moscow has a large number of potential allies and a strong base from which to resist containment.

Another factor that may explain the durability of revolutions is that they often result from a severe crisis of the old order—when it has been weakened by war, for instance, and lacks the power to fight back effectively. The 1905 revolution in Russia took place soon after the Czar's defeat in the Russo–Japanese war; the spate of revolutions after 1917 took place against a background of world war in which all the powers, and especially the defeated ones, were enervated. And the dozens of revolutions since World War II were helped by the impotence of all imperial powers—except the United States. Britain was forced to grant independence to India because it no longer could police its jewel colony or protect the sea lanes that connected it to the island empire. Britain, France, Holland, and Belgium were all too weak to put down revolutions with the ease to which they had become accustomed over more than a century. Eduard Benes, the noncommunist Czech president, showed keen insight into the historical process when he warned in 1946, after Churchill's "iron curtain" speech, that "there can be no world war today which would not be followed by revolution—greater revolution than has taken place this time. Undoubtedly there are people who would like to see war between the East and the West but the revolution which would follow such a contest would defeat the very ends for which they wished it."[55]

Still another factor in the durability of revolutions is the tendency of a revolutionary people who have tried it once to try it again. Revolution becomes part of a nation's consciousness. The defeat of the 1905 revolution in Russia was followed by victory in 1917; the defeat of half a dozen revolutions in Cuba and Nicaragua in the last century was followed by victorious ones in recent years; the setback for the Chinese revolution in Sun Yat-sen's day was followed by Mao's victory more than a generation later; the defeat of the noncommunist Algerian revolution in 1945 was followed by a victorious guerrilla war that ended, after seven and a half years, in 1962.

A second revolutionary wave in the less-developed countries is today more than a remote possibility. The economies of the less-developed countries, including those in the Western Hemisphere as well as in some oil-producing states, are suffering from a common malady: they are heavily in debt. Having bowed to the U.S. State Department's condition that they must allow free trade if they are to receive economic and military aid from Washington, they find that they have more money going out (in repatriated profits and an un-favorable balance of payments) than coming in. In consequence, their debts have mounted by almost geometric progression; as of the end of 1980, the Third World as a whole owed private banks, gov-ernments, and various international agencies $580 billion. More than a fifth of the export earnings of these countries goes to service their foreign debts; not a few find themselves in technical default: Peru in 1978, Zaire many times, Turkey in 1979, Brazil in 1980.[56] Usually the banks and the International Monetary Fund space out the debt repayment to avoid collapse of their clients, but almost always they demand such concessions as the imposition of an "austerity" pro-gram. The countries are expected to reduce national spending, delay social improvements, cut subsidies for food and other necessities, and generally reduce their living standards. Inevitably, there is resis-tance—riots in Peru, for instance, after it agreed to austerity—and should the situation worsen as the great nations themselves suffer depression, the chances of social turmoil in the less-developed coun-tries grow apace. Though new revolutions are not inevitable, there seems to be a strong impulse for them in circumstances where the first revolution has failed to solve social problems.

All this means that the Kennan–Truman containment policy is a narrowly focused and ultimately futile response. Not only does it fail to recognize the vitality of revolutionary forces, but it provides no clear vision of how the Soviet Union itself can be contained or rolled back. Both Kennan and Truman suggested the Soviet system had to be fundamentally changed—in Truman's view, to a society "based upon the will of the majority" and in Kennan's, to "either the break-up or gradual mellowing of Soviet power." But what does this mean? Certainly no one believes that a semifeudal czarism can be restored in Russia or, for that matter, a "free-enterprise" capital-ism. Where would the capital come from to buy out trillions of dol-lars of plant and infrastructure? Capitalism could be imposed on the Soviet Union only by force of arms—a new military intervention—and that option, too, is unavailable in the nuclear age. On the other hand, it is hardly likely that Kennan or Truman (or any of our pres-ent leaders) considered the "solution" to the Soviet "problem" to be democratic socialism.

One reason for the failure of containment was that its goals were unclear, perhaps because the true objective of containment was not

Soviet communism, as such, but all revolution, communist or non-communist.

The first attempt at containment, from 1917 to World War II, failed for three reasons: First, the Bolsheviks were able to win the Russian people by offering land to the peasants and peace to the public at large. Second, the established world order was preoccupied with its own inner crisis through most of this period, initially by the wave of revolutions from 1917 to 1924, then by the Great Depression. Third, the fissures within the Western world were so deep that it was never able to unite for a military assault on Soviet communism.

The second attempt at containment failed for more fundamental reasons: First, the "enemy" was no longer a single revolution but six dozen revolutions, and while the vast majority of these were non-communist in character, inherent in each was always the possibility it might move toward communism, or at least toward neutralism; in that sense, what was to be contained was no longer containable — it was too massive, too irreversible, too much of an idea whose time had come. Second, the nuclear bomb, in a strange and paradoxical manner, made war largely obsolete as an instrument for resolving international disputes between the superpowers, and hence also outdated old-style diplomacy. The Bomb, far from making the West all-powerful, limited both its vision and its options.

THE
WRONG
WEAPON

3

"This is the greatest thing in history," said President Truman when he was informed that an atom bomb had just destroyed Hiroshima.[1] He and his aides were certain the Bomb would enable the United States to dominate international affairs for a long time to come. At the very least, as James F. Byrnes observed even before the first nuclear device was detonated, it "might well put us in a postion to dictate our own terms at the end of the war,"[2] and "make Russia more manageable in Europe." Elder statesman Bernard Baruch put it more forcefully: "America can get what whe wants if she insists on it. After all, we've got it—the Bomb—and they haven't and won't have it for a long time to come."[3] The expectation was that the Russians could be compelled to retreat on the Balkan, Polish, and Manchurian issues, and perhaps even to retire from Eastern Europe.

As it turned out, however, the Bomb paid few dividends. Dropping it on Hiroshima and Nagasaki in August 1945 may have shortened the war by a few weeks or months—though even that was disputed by some authorities who argued that Japan was already beyond hope of victory and had made overtures for surrender. A group of experts from the United States, sent to Japan in 1946 to assess the effect of the atom bombs on Japan's decision to surrender, concluded that "the Hiroshima and Nagasaki atomic bombs did not defeat Japan, nor by the testimony of the enemy leaders who ended the war did they persuade Japan to accept unconditional surrender." In the survey's opinion, the Japanese government would have surrendered "in all probability prior to 1 November 1945 . . . even if the atomic bombs had not been dropped, even if Russia had not entered the war, and even if no invasion had been planned or contemplated."[4] The Bomb may have been the deciding factor in the Soviet's 1946 decision to relinquish Azerbaijan and Kurdistan, two Iranian provinces that they had occupied during the war by agreement with the United States and Britain. Senator Henry Jackson claims that Truman told him of an ultimatum given Soviet Ambassador Gromyko to evacuate Iran within forty-eight hours or suffer a nuclear attack on the Soviet Union itself.[5] However, it is difficult to think of any other instances when the Bomb enlarged American influence. Eisenhower threatened to use atomic weaponry against North Korea in 1953 to force an armistice in the three-year-old war, and Kennedy weighed the same strategy against the Pathet Lao in Laos in 1961 to force it into a three-sided coalition government. But in neither of these instances did the United States expand its worldwide "assets" in any way: the Korean War ended in a stalemate, and the United States and its clients ultimately lost in Laos.

In 1962, John F. Kennedy won a widely acclaimed "victory" when he mobilized nuclear and conventional forces against Cuba for allowing Soviet missiles on its soil, thereby bringing the world "eyeball to eyeball," as Secretary of State Dean Rusk put it, to a nuclear confrontation. The Russians withdrew their launchers and warheads, but Cuba gained a political victory of sorts when Kennedy secretly agreed, as a quid pro quo, to curb Cuban exile invasions originating on U.S. soil. Again, there was no expansion of American influence—communist Cuba remained communist.

"The nuclear bomb," said George F. Kennan in May 1981, "is the most useless weapon ever invented. It can be employed to no rational purpose."[6] Henry Kissinger made a similar point in a 1976 speech in London: "For centuries," he said, "it was axiomatic that increases in military power could be translated into almost immediate political advantage. It is now clear that in strategic weapons new increments of weapons or destructiveness do not automatically lead to either military or political gains. The destructiveness of strategic [nuclear] weapons has contributed to a nuclear stalemate."[7]

Theoretically, a military instrument so powerful should have endowed its possessor with political omnipotence—when the possessor had a monopoly or near-monopoly. The London *Observer* of June 27, 1948, commented exuberantly, "It is we who hold the overwhelming trump cards. It is our side, not Russia, which holds atomic and post-atomic weapons and could, if sufficiently provoked, wipe Russia's power and threat to the world's peace from the face of the earth."[8]

But American monopoly of the Bomb in the first few years of the nuclear age was not enough to assure victory, and in later years the American arsenal was counterbalanced by a smaller but nonetheless deterring Soviet arsenal. Raymond Aron of *Le Monde*, one of Europe's most authoritative writers, says about the period when the United States had a corner on atom bombs, "United States superiority over the Soviet Union in the nuclear field was offset . . . by Russian superiority in conventional arms and by the Red Army's continued ability to overrun Western Europe in a matter of days, as during the years from 1946 to 1953, or with more difficulty in the years after 1953."[9] The National Security Council, in a secret document, NSC–68, corroborated this estimate. "The Soviet Union and its satellites," it said, had the capability at that time (1950) "(a) To overrun Western Europe, with the possible exception of the Iberian and Scandinavian Peninsulas . . . (b) To launch air attacks against the British Isles and air and sea attacks against lines of communication of the Western Powers in the Atlantic and Pacific. . . . The United States now has an atomic capability . . . to deliver a serious blow against the war-making capacity of the U.S.S.R." But the NSC memorandum went on to doubt "whether such a blow, even if it resulted in the complete destruction of the contemplated target systems, would cause the U.S.S.R. to sue for terms or prevent Soviet forces from occupying Western Europe against such ground resistance as could presently be mobilized." While the Soviet Union was being bombarded with atom bombs, its Red Army would seize all of Western Europe up to the English Channel "in a matter of days."[10]

Assuming that the United States had enough fission bombs to devastate the Soviet Union, it would be a pyrrhic victory if the Red Army concurrently occupied the heartland of the Western alliance — Germany, France, the low countries, Italy. In fact, however, the United States had only enough nuclear weapons at that time to "wound" the Soviet Union, not "kill" it. According to "U.S. sources" quoted by British Nobel laureate P.M.S. Blackett in his *Studies of War*, a Hiroshima-type bomb could inflict approximately the same damage as 2,000 tons of chemical explosives. Extrapolating from this figure, Blackett estimates that to wreak the same damage on Russia as 1.2 million tons of traditional bombs did on Germany in the peak bombing period from January 1943 to the end of World War II would require 600 A-bombs—and we did not have nearly that number in 1945 or 1949.[11]

An atomic attack, it is true, would concentrate the blow in a brief time span, but European Russia alone was eight times larger in area and three times more populous than Germany—and Asiatic Russia much larger still. To achieve comparable devastation to that suffered by Germany in 1943 to 1945 was beyond American capability at the time; it was producing, according to Dr. Ralph Lapp, nuclear fuel for only 100 A-bombs annually.[12] There was, in addition, the problem of delivery—by relatively slow bombers, certain to be challenged by Russia's excellent fighter planes. If the United States, despite such evidence, were foolhardy enough to mount an atomic attack, the ultimate decision would rest on its army anyway. And as George C. Kenney, Commander of the Strategic Air Force, observed: "The United States has no intention of landing mass armies in Europe and slugging it out with the Red Army—manpower against manpower. Napoleon and Hitler both made that mistake."[13]

No one recognized the dilemma of America's position in the first nuclear decade better than the National Security Council. Says NSC-68:

> A powerful blow could be delivered upon the Soviet Union, but it is estimated that these operations alone would not force or induce the Kremlin to capitulate and that the Kremlin would still be able to use the forces under its control to dominate most or all of Eurasia. This would probably mean a long and difficult struggle during which the free institutions of Western Europe and many freedom-loving people would be destroyed and the regenerative capacity of Western Europe dealt a crippling blow.[14]

It was one thing for General Anderson and other rightists to talk about a "preventative war," but quite another to map out a scenario that would bring about an American victory in such a war. Until the mid-1950s, the United States was inhibited from launching a nuclear attack on the Soviet Union by the fact that the Soviets could quickly overrun all of Western Europe. The restraining factor thereafter was a quantum jump in both explosive power and the speed of delivery.

The technological advance from atom (fission) bombs to hydrogen (fission-fusion-fission) bombs in the early 1950s, and from the bomber to the missile in the latter part of the decade, altered the character of the nuclear threat. Before the H-bomb and the missile, it was still possible—at least in theory—to survive a nuclear attack as a viable society. But it was not possible once H-bombs and missiles began to be produced and deployed in large numbers.

"Imagine," wrote Herman Kahn, a weapons and strategy expert who spent eleven years at the Rand Corporation, "that the Soviets have dropped bombs on London, Berlin, Rome, and Bonn but have made no detectable preparations for attacking the United States. . . ." How should the United States respond? "No American that I have spoken to who was at all serious about the matter believed that U.S. retaliation would be justified—no matter what our commitments were—if more than half our population would be killed. . . . Their estimates of an acceptable price generally fall between 1 and 60 million dead."[15]

Assuming that Kahn spoke for the American consensus—which is hard to believe—that casualty toll would be far exceeded in the age of H-bombs and missiles. The atom bomb measured its potency in kilotons—thousands of tons of TNT-equivalent; the Hiroshima bomb was a 13-kiloton bomb, equal in explosive power to 13,000 tons of TNT. But an H-bomb, which is triggered by an A-bomb, can measure its power in megatons—*millions* of tons of TNT-equivalent. The H-bomb detonated by the Russians on October 30, 1961, generated 58 megatons—58 million tons of TNT-equivalent, or 4,500 times more firepower than the Hiroshima bomb. That does not mean it would kill 4,500 times as many people or destroy 4,500 times as much property, but it would leave a vast area devastated and inoperative. H. Jack Geiger, a professor of community medicine, estimated for a Los Angeles audience in 1981 that a 1-megaton bomb dropped on that city would kill 987,000 people and seriously injure 1.4 million, "28 percent of the population. The numbers for a single 20-megaton blast would be 3.8 million killed and 2.5 million seriously injured— 75 percent."[16] Since the two superpowers are believed to have approximately 8,000 megatons between them,[17] an all-out nuclear attack would inflict indescribable losses. President Carter's defense secretary, Harold S. Brown, estimated just before leaving office in January 1981 that "for massive nuclear exchanges involving military and economic targets . . . fatality estimates range from a low of 20 million to 55 million up to a high of 155 million to 165 million in the United States, and from a low of 23 to 34 million up to a high of 64 to 100 million in the Soviet Union." Additionally, said Brown, "secondary and indirect disruptions of the societies attacked, and longer-term fallout . . . would amplify the damage."[18] Those figures are estimates, of course, and could vary up or down, depending on whether the bombs were exploded in the atmosphere or at the surface, which way the wind was blowing, and other factors. But regardless of the variables, it is clear that neither American nor Soviet society could afford such a cost.

After the missile was put into production, the problem was compounded. The cumbersome bomber, dispatched from forward bases in Europe, advanced on its target at 400 or 500 miles an hour; in daytime, every fifth or sixth plane could be shot down. But the pilotless missile, whether fired from an underground silo or from a nuclear-powered submarine, would head toward its objective at 16,000 miles an hour.[19] Though scientists tried to produce an antiballistic missile (ABM) to intercept offensive missiles either in the atmosphere or stratosphere, both superpowers ultimately had to admit that ABMs would not work. For the first time in history, each side possessed a war machine in which offense was absolute, defense virtually nil. Back in 1945, a committee of seven scientists, headed by Nobel laureate James Franck, had warned President Truman that atomic energy was "fraught with infinitely greater dangers than were all the inventions of the past." At other times, science had been able to provide "new methods of protection against new weapons of aggression," but it could not "promise such efficient protection against the destructive use of nuclear power."[20] In the absence of defense, the terrifying power of the Bomb cancelled itself out, since each adversary could destroy the other but could not save itself from destruction. In the nuclear age, said General Eisenhower, "war has become not just tragic but preposterous. With modern weapons there can be no victory for anyone." General Douglas MacArthur predicted such a war would be "double suicide."[21] Even such fervid militarists as Defense Secretary Caspar W. Weinberger, who conceives of the possibility of a "protracted" nuclear war, now admit that such wars are not winnable.

All this is known, of course, to government leaders everywhere. Where military power was once a substantive threat, it is now a charade. Even former President Richard Nixon was constrained to say on a television program commemorating Franklin Roosevelt's 100th birthday that the nuclear threat had become an "empty threat." The race between the United States and the Soviet Union continues not because either side now believes it can win a nuclear war, but because each still hopes to discover the one weapon or strategy that might make victory possible in the future.

For a time, American leaders placed their hopes on civil defense: If enough people and property could be spared while the other side was being leveled, the outcome might be considered a victory. After World War II, a civil defense board under Major General Harold R. Bull formulated a plan to build "blast shelters" where citizens could be shielded in improved versions of the bunkers and air-raid shelters that dotted Germany and Britain during World War II.[22] The experience of Hiroshima had shown that only 15 percent of the immediate deaths were due to radiation; civil defense was needed, therefore, primarily to protect against blast damages. But by 1954, after the first hydrogen bomb tests, it was apparent that radiation affected a much larger area than blast. The deadly dust from the explosion of the Bravo bomb in the Bikini atoll covered 7,000 square miles; the blast affected 300 square miles. Thus, blast shelters were relegated to museums and the new style in civil defense became "evacuation."

Evacuation arrows dotted cities and highways from coast to coast on the theory that in the ten or twelve hours it took for Soviet bombers to reach the United States there would be time for the people of Los Angeles, New York, and Chicago to head for safety twenty-five or thirty miles out of town. But in 1957, after the Russians launched the first space satellite, Sputnik I, it became evident that nuclear warheads would soon be delivered by missiles capable of arriving on target within thirty minutes. The nuclear submarine shortened that time to ten to twenty minutes, and the Pershing II missile, scheduled to be emplaced in Europe by the end of 1983, cuts the time span to a mere five or six minutes from Western Germany to the Soviet Union. Evacuation of cities in these circumstances is obviously impossible – though there are some military people who still believe it could be done during the week or two of crisis meetings that might preceed a nuclear exchange.

With evacuation discarded as a civil defense policy, the Kennedy Administration shifted in 1961 to fallout shelters as the new nuclear defense. Government agencies began designating subways, corridors, and basements as community shelters, and individuals were asked to build private shelters in their homes or yards. With such shelters, said *Life* magazine, then the nation's second largest publication, "97 out of 100 people can be saved" in a nuclear war.[24]

From time to time other proposals for defense were considered. Herman Kahn suggested spending hundreds of billions to build underground cities; once they were completed, the United States could issue an ultimatum to the Russians to "surrender"—since we could kill most of their people and they could kill only a few million of ours. In the 1970s, the Defense Civil Preparedness Agency (DCPA) designed a "crisis relocation" plan to evacuate the urban population to rural areas and mines during the week or two while diplomats were engaged in talks to avert war. Representative Les Aspin called this plan "extremely dangerous nonsense."[25]

Overlapping the efforts for *civil* defense was a search for a *physical* defense. Since 1954, American scientists and engineers had been probing the feasibility of an antimissile missile that would "kill" the enemy's missiles in flight, either in the stratosphere or in the atmosphere. Strategists believed that with an effective antiballistic missile (ABM), nuclear wars might become winnable and the threat to resort to nuclear weapons might become decisive in diplomacy. But the idea, more attractive in theory than in practice, was rejected by both Eisenhower and Kennedy. Lyndon Johnson coaxed $1.9 billion out of an unenthusiastic Congress for an ABM program, and Richard Nixon talked of a more elaborate program costing $7.2 billion. Fully deployed, the Safeguard ABM system would consist of twelve sites in the continental United States and one each in Hawaii and Alaska.[26]

Even Nixon, however, soon realized that physical defense against missiles was not feasible. The Soviets had only to build up their stockpile of offensive missiles, or send up large numbers of decoys, to make the ABM system ineffective. They could also "blind" American radars with high-altitude nuclear explosions; or they could render radar inoperative by placing jamming devices on incoming missiles, or evade it by lowering orbit trajectories. Too much could go amiss, and too much was uncertain. The normal offensive missile was reliable only 41 to 65 percent of the time, according to an estimate by Dr. Daniel Fink, former deputy director of Defense Research and Engineering. Defensive ABMs would be less dependable.[27] President Nixon finally conceded that "although every instinct motivates me to provide the American people with complete protection against a major nuclear attack, it is not now within our power to do so."[28]

Some nuclear strategists today look to outer space to provide a setting for war and victory. The Pentagon's plans call for the reusable space shuttle to place "killer satellites" into the stratosphere. These could shoot down Soviet early-warning, navigational, and communication satellites, leaving the Russian command system blind, deaf, and vulnerable to a surprise attack, a first strike. Soviet missile silos, airfields, and command posts might then be destroyed before Moscow could retaliate. And if Soviet retaliation were attempted, killer lasers aboard a low-orbit U.S. satellite would destroy enemy missiles almost on launch. Senator Malcolm Wallop of Wyoming has claimed that three killer lasers, each capable of firing a thousand "shots," could monitor the entire planet.[29]

In theory, this is a perfect defense, just as a disarming first strike is a perfect offense–defense. With that sort of an advantage, the United States might "Finlandize" the Soviet Union, forcing it to accept American dictates. On the other hand, if Moscow were to outpace Washington for effective space weapons, it would have the means of securing what Nobel laureate Sir Solly Zuckerman calls the best type of victory—surrender without a shot being fired. But many scientists discount the space option. M.I.T.'s Kosta Tsipis calls the laser program "wasted money," certain not to work. Richard L. Garwin, a Harvard physicist and Pentagon consultant, says it will cost too much and only give the illusion of a perfect defense.[39] In a list of "counter anti-satellite capabilities," in a *Bulletin of the Atomic Scientists* article, Garwin included "multiple miniature homing vehicles," pellets, and "small satellites, with low technology" which would follow enemy satellites "around in the sky and be detonable upon radio command."[31] Space war is still an uncharted territory that will, in all likelihood, manifest the same uncertainties and unreliabilities as do other aspects of the nuclear drama. It is, in any case, still decades away.

In recent years, some strategists have talked of a "disarming" first strike—a surprise attack against Soviet missile silos, bombers, and submarines that would disable the enemy's weapons before they could be used. Such a strategy, attractive as it may sound to military planners, would be impossible to carry out. For one thing, there is no way as yet for either side to track down and destroy the other's nuclear submarines. They remain "invulnerable," and would survive a first strike. Second, a disarming first strike would have to depend on weapon and command reliability far beyond any that currently exists. Daniel Fink, former deputy director of defense research and engineering, estimated that missiles are dependable only 40 to 65 percent of the time; assuming those figures may have improved, they still leave too much margin of error for any leader to be confident a disarming first strike would be successful.[32] If even a third of the Soviet Union's 7,500 strategic warheads remained after such a strike, they would annihilate the United States as a functioning society.

The list of uncertainties surrounding the missile issue is long. Scientists are not sure, for instance, whether two American missiles headed in the same direction would destroy each other instead of the Soviet target. They call this risk "fratricide," defined by James Fallows as "the tendency of nuclear warheads to interfere with one another's detonations." To "destroy an enemy's silos," Fallows says, "a lot of missiles have to be aimed at roughly the same area at roughly the same time. When one of them explodes, the blast, debris, radiation, and electromagnetic impulse can destroy or deflect other warheads coming in." One estimate is that a blast by one warhead would "block off the area to other warheads" for twenty or thirty minutes.[33] Optimists in the scientific community believe "fratricide" can be avoided by "perfect, second-by-second coordination" of all launches. But no one really knows.

Think-tank operatives tend to sanitize their calculations. "The seemingly rigorous models of nuclear deterrence," observed Fred C. Ikle when he was director of the Arms Control and Disarmament Agency, "are built on the rule: what you can't calculate you leave out." In a 1981 series for *Science* magazine, William J. Broad gave details of one of the factors usually left out: elecromagnetic pulse or EMP. "In July 1962," Broad wrote,

> the U.S. military detonated a 1.4 megaton hydrogen bomb 248 miles above Johnson Island in the Pacific, and for some time thereafter physicists puzzled over a resulting series of odd occurrences. Some 800 miles away in Hawaii, street lights had failed, burglar alarms had rung, and circuit breakers had popped open in power lines. Today, the mysterious agent is known as electromagnetic pulse (EMP). Physicists say a single nuclear detonation in near space would cover vast stretches of the earth with an EMP of 50,000 volts per meter. . . . Defense strategists today assume that a single Soviet warhead

detonated 200 miles above Nebraska would knock out communications equipment all across the United States. . . . The United States is frequently crossed by picture-taking Cosmos series satellites that orbit at a height of 200 to 450 kilometers above the earth. Just one of those satellites, carrying a few pounds of enriched plutonium instead of a camera, might touch off instant coast-to-coast pandemonium: the U.S. power grid going out, all electrical appliances without a separate power supply (televisions, radios, computers, traffic lights) shutting down, commercial telephone lines going dead, special military channels barely working or quickly going silent.[34]

Some military leaders claim that with enough money and initiative, EMP can be contained and the communications gap closed. But no one is sure, and there is a strong possibility as matters now stand that after the first wave of Soviet missiles — some detonated hundreds of miles high — the president and the generals, not to mention ordinary citizens, would lose all touch with one another. As John D. Steinbruner, a senior researcher at Brookings Institution, notes, "The precariousness of command channels probably means that nuclear war would be uncontrollable, as a practical matter, shortly after the first tens of weapons are launched."[35]

Another factor left out of military calculations, according to physicist Michiu Kaku of City College of New York, is the nuclear reactor. If there had been a reactor in Hiroshima on August 6, 1945, Kaku believes it would still be radioactive today. If there had been a meltdown "rather than a low-yield 13-kiloton uranium bomb, then Hiroshima would still be quarantined," he says. "Because a meltdown releases hundred of millions of curies of relatively *long-lived*, watersoluble radio-nuclides (like strontium-90 and cesium-137), the soil contamination will last for decades, if not hundreds of years."[36] If those calculations are even partially correct, a Soviet strike of one or two warheads for each of the seventy-two American reactors would make the United States uninhabitable for decades. Still another possible consequence of nuclear war not factored into military estimates has been noted by Philip Handler, past president of the National Academy of Sciences:

The depletion of stratospheric ozone resulting from multiple detonations would be global in scope . . . and would persist for years, resulting in such intense ultraviolet irradiation of the Earth's surface as to cause crop failure by direct damage to plants and by major alterations of climate, and to induce intense sunburn in a few minutes and markedly increase the incidence of skin cancer in those exposed. The same global effect would be achieved if one superpower were to use all of its weapons or both were to use half their weapons. . . . "[37]

There are other uncertainties to contend with. For example, it is not at all certain that all the apparently methodical estimates of missile accuracy are correct. Strategists measure the accuracy of a weapon in terms of CEP – "circular error probable." If a weapon is said to have a CEP of a quarter of a mile, that signifies that of twenty warheads launched, ten would be within a quarter of a mile of the center of the cluster, the other ten outside. It does not signify that the warheads would detonate within a quarter of a mile of its target.[38]

Complex electronic gadgets, in particular, are subject to failure. A confidential Pentagon report in the late 1960s, the contents of which were made public by Bernard D. Nossiter in *The Washington Post*, claimed that "of thirteen major aircraft and missile programs with sophisticated electronic systems, only four – costing $5 billion – performed at 75 percent or more of their specifications; five – costing $13 billion – were rated as 'poor' performers, breaking down 25 percent more often than promised or worse. Two more systems, costing $10 billion, were dropped within three years because of 'low reliability.' The last two . . . worked so badly they were canceled after an outlay of $2 billion."[39] A Pentagon report twelve years later makes the point that key weapons are now so sophisticated they don't work well. "In fiscal 1979," reports Bruce Ingersoll of the *Chicago Sun-Times*, "the F–14As were not ready to perform their mission 47 percent of the time, and the F–15s were out of commission 44 percent of the time. . . . "[40] These are not nuclear weapons, but it is reasonable to assume that a similar degree of oversophistication may be causing problems with the more complex nuclear missile systems.

Military leaders are unsure of what would happen if an American missile were fired south to north – as it probably would be in an actual conflict with the Soviets. So far, all U.S. tests have taken the east–west or west–east route, a course whose winds and atmospheric conditions the Pentagon has repeatedly charted. But there is no corresponding data on a south–north route over the North Pole. Furthermore, we have never successfully launched a Minuteman missile from an operational silo; on the four occasions that the Pentagon tried to do so, it failed. This does not mean it cannot be done, but it does inject a note of caution in making judgments on how small or great the toll might be in a nuclear war. To make matters worse, none of this takes into account the human factor: would the nation's leaders and generals remain calm in actual war conditions, or would they be immobilized? These are imponderable elements in the nuclear equation, but it is worth noting, as the Center for Defense Information records, that "about 3,000 U.S. military personnel on nuclear weapons duty have been removed in the last five years because of drug abuse."[41]

As the bombs become more destructive, an element of bluff and bluster comes into play. Each side wants to be perceived as capable of inflicting "unacceptable damage" on the other. In fact, however, so many things are unknown about the behavior of nuclear bombs that even if our government had all the missiles and warheads needed to overwhelm the other side, it would be foolish to try, because just a small number of surviving Soviet missiles and bombs could inflict intolerable damage on us.

There is simply no way to win an all-out nuclear war; hence the threat of one cannot translate into diplomatic gain. Each side knows victory, in the sense of surviving as a functioning and great nation, is impossible. "No threat is stronger," Henry Kissinger once observed, "than the belief of the opponent that it will, in fact, be used." And the only way to convince the Soviet Union under present circumstances that a nuclear threat may in fact be followed by a nuclear attack, is, as Stefan Leader wrote in the *Philadelphia Inquirer*, "to plant a seed in the mind of other countries that we just might be crazy enough" to do so.[42] The game is played, in other words, at the psychological level, where what the other side *perceives* to be our strength and our willingness to use it is more important than what it really is in physical terms. This bizarre development — the replacement of true physical defense that can be measured in the quantity and quality of tanks, planes, and guns by a psychological defense that depends entirely on how leaders on one side assess the *intentions* of leaders on the other — leads to peculiar charges and countercharges. There is, for instance, the claim that "they are getting ahead of us," when in fact neither side can get ahead of the other because each already had the capability of totally destroying the other. There is also talk of fighting "limited" or "protracted" nuclear wars, not because either are feasible options but because the threat of a war in which some (or many) people presumably can survive is more credible than a war in which few or none can survive.

Perceptions, however, can be misleading. Take the concept of Finlandization, which depends on the psychological perception that if the Russians strike first and destroy 90 percent of America's 1,000 Minutemen missiles, eighteen of its forty-one nuclear-missile submarines, and two-thirds of its B–52 bombers, a U.S. president would be immobilized; he would lack the will to order an attack on the Soviet Union for fear the Russian counterattack would result in the death of 100 million Americans.[43] How does anyone know this? Such assertions are based on assumptions formulated in terms of normal human behavior under relatively normal conditions. But an opposite result may occur: The president, either on his Doomsday plane or in a deep shelter, may receive skimpy reports that cannot possibly detail the number of enemy warheads or the amount of damage inflicted. He might not know whether 90 percent or 1 percent of the Minutemen silos have really been hit or whether stray bombs have destroyed cities or fallen on desert areas. He also might not know how many people are dying of radiation that is still spreading. He cannot send inspectors to areas under nuclear attack because they would be dead in minutes; nor is there any mechanical monitoring device that can substitute for human reporters. In this state of affairs, the president may fear the worst, namely, that America is in the process of total annihilation, and, instead of considering submission to Soviet domination, order a full-scale counterattack to devastate the Soviet Union. This is just as likely as the Finlandization scenario. The point is that in the absence of a true, physical, military defense, weird scenarios of psychological defense are spun that are unrealistic and scientifically unsound.

We can only conclude that there is no defense against nuclear weapons, and that the Bomb cannot serve, therefore, as an effective diplomatic instrument. No one is deceived by psychological threats that can only be taken seriously if those doing the threatening have gone temporarily insane. And if the threat is made in earnest, as it was in the October 1962 missile crisis, that simply signifies the adversaries have lost touch with reality to the point where they are prepared to commit double suicide. In any case, empty threats or threats of double suicide can hardly be diplomatic cards that a responsible nation would want to play frequently. "With the advent of atomic weapons," B.H. Lidell Hart has written, "we have come either to the last page of war, at any rate on the major international scale we have known in the past, or to the last page of history."[44]

* * * * * * *

If the nuclear stalemate precludes any significant role for the Bomb, either in an actual war with the Soviets or in diplomacy, some still maintain it could be a factor in preventing total war. The fact that the United States and the Soviet Union both know they can be destroyed may have inhibited them until now from initiating World War III. In strategic jargon, this is called "*stable* deterrence." As defined by Jerome H. Kahan, a former member of the State Department policy planning staff, stable deterrence requires the "assured retaliatory capability" of the United States to destroy "at least 20–25 percent of the USSR's population and over 70 percent of its industrial base," as well as "avoiding weapons and doctrines that pose a threat to the USSR's deterrent. . . . "[45] Until recently, "mutual assured destruction"—MAD—was standard doctrine with American strategists. Kahan and other policy planners credited it with having prevented war for a couple of decades, and hoped it could do so indefinitely.

There is no way to prove this thesis. Certainly the superpowers have been worried about the consequences of a nuclear confrontation (John F. Kennedy said after the 1962 October missile crisis, "even the fruits of victory would have been ashes in our mouths"). Undoubtedly, such anxieties gave them pause on a number of occasions. But there are three factors that more than counterbalance the stated benefits of stable deterrence. One is that there have been at least fifteen situations—and probably others that we have not yet heard about—in which our government seriously considered the use of nuclear bombs, either in an all-out exchange or in a limited attack.

Five of those near-misses were accidental, usually due to the misreading of radar. In the first of these, America's early-warning radar system in Canada picked up what it thought were Soviet aircraft headed southeast and due to arrive over Washington in two or three hours. "All interception and defense forces were alerted," the late Secretary of State Dean Acheson recorded in his book, *Present at the Creation*,[46] and American planes armed with nuclear weapons were actually in the air headed for the Soviet Union. Fortunately, the secretary of defense, Robert A. Lovett, reported a little later that the Soviet "planes" had disappeared from the radar. He speculated that the unidentified objects were probably a flock of geese.

On seven occasions, American leaders seriously considered a limited nuclear assault: in 1953, when President Eisenhower contemplated the use of atomic weapons to force China to end the Korean War; in 1954, when Secretary of State Dulles offered three nuclear bombs to France, one to be used against China and two against the Viet Minh who had French forces surrounded at Dien Bien Phu; in 1958, when the Joint Chiefs advised Eisenhower that the islands of Quemoy and Matsu, near the Chinese mainland, could not be held on behalf of Chiang Kai-shek's nationalists without resorting to nuclear bombs; in 1961, when Kennedy considered dropping the bomb unless the communist Pathet Lao joined a tripartite government in Laos; in 1961, when Kennedy again considered the use of superbombs during the threatened Soviet blockade of Berlin; in 1968, when President Johnson queried the chairman of the Joint Chiefs, General Earle Wheeler, about the possible need for nuclear weapons to hold the besieged Marine base at Khe Sanh in Vietnam; and in 1968 to 1969, when President Nixon, implementing what he himself called "the madman theory," sent the word to Hanoi through intermediaries that he was so "madly" anticommunist he would not hesitate to use nuclear weapons on Vietnam by the end of 1969 unless the communists came to terms.[47] Daniel Ellsberg adds two others to this list: the 1950 nuclear threat by Truman during a press interview on the Korean War, and the 1958 order by Eisenhower for secret nuclear preparations during the "Lebanon crisis."

There have also been three instances of direct confrontation with the Soviets that might have developed into atomic war: the 1946 ultimatum to Moscow to get out of Iran or face nuclear attack; the 1962 October Missile Crisis over the stationing of Soviet missiles in Cuba; and the 1973 DefCon (Defense Condition) alerts during the Yom Kippur War in the Middle East. The latter incident is not well known because the adversaries muted their public confrontation, but the crisis may have been just as acute. After the Soviets and Americans had negotiated a cease-fire in that war, Israel, apparently with Henry Kissinger's secret assent, continued fighting in the hopes of wiping out an Egyptian salient and turning what was until then a stalemate into victory. The Russians sent a ship loaded with nuclear weapons into Alexandria on October 24, 1973, and the Nixon Administration responded with a worldwide DefCon 3 alert, reduced to DefCon 2 in the Mediterranean—just one step from actual war, DefCon 1. Fortunately, the cease-fire was reinstated before the crisis accelerated.[48]

These fifteen—or seventeen—instances of near-war do not attest to the foolproof character of "mutual assured destruction." There is no denying that the prospect of assured destruction weighed heavily on strategists' minds, but in many cases it was luck or some other factor that saved the day: luck, for example, in the five instances where the world came close to nuclear war by accident; fear of the antiwar movement by Nixon in 1969 (as he records in his autobiography); retreat by the Soviets over Azerbaijan; retreat by the Israelis and Americans in the Middle East conflict; retreat by the Soviet Union during the Cuban missile crisis and the Berlin crisis; retreat by the Pathet Lao in 1961; realization by the Joint Chiefs during the Quemoy–Matsu crisis that the medicine was too strong for the disease; failure to win British support for giving nuclear weapons to France in 1954. In any case, a war-avoidance policy that so often brings the parties to the brink of war is a slender reed on which to lean.

Another factor that casts doubt on the concept of stable deterrence is the self-propelling character of the nuclear arms race. As C. Wright Mills once put it, "the immediate cause of World War III" may very well be "the preparation for it."[49] The preparation for a sophisticated war based on modern technology has evolved into a self-propelling system based on (1) a rampant technology, (2) constituencies that promote the technology because they have a stake in it, and (3) a synthetic anticommunism that is used to develop public support for the race. Perhaps a third or more of America's scientists and engineers are engaged in developing new weapons to counter weapons the Soviets are believed to be developing for deployment six to eight years hence. Proprietors of each project seek support, of course, from the Pentagon, industry, academia, the labor movement, think-tanks, local officials, the mass media, and members of Congress. Individually and collectively, this is as formidable an array of power as the world has ever seen.

The Pentagon alone owns more wealth than the twenty or thirty largest corporations in the nation combined. Senator William Proxmire once reported that the military machine had 399 full-time lobbyists, one for almost every member of the House and Senate, as well

as a staff of 6,000 to persuade the public of its needs and ideas.[50]
The 22,000 prime contractors and 100,000 subcontractors similarly
wield great influence, as do other elements of the Military–Industrial
Complex. And such think-tanks as Rand supply erudite rationales
for military strategies, almost always "proving" that the nation is not
sufficiently equipped with the latest and best hardware. These anal-
yses are invariably translated into thousands of popular articles in the
daily press, magazines, tracts. Taken together, the rampant technology and the constituencies that promote it are an immense lobby in
behalf of armaments, moving on its own momentum. This kind of
pressure cannot readily be resisted.

Anticommunism is the mortar that binds America's militarist élan.
Early in the Cold War, the Republican Senate leader Arthur Vandenberg of Michigan argued that if the nation was to be diverted from
postwar pacifism, it would be necessary " to scare the hell out of the
country."[51] A synthetic distrust of the Soviet Union has been persistently cultivated ever since. One hears it constantly in the phrase,
"You can't trust the Russians." To coax Congress into voting for
armaments, the militarists and their allies regularly stir national fear
of the Soviets; they "scare the hell out of the country" with the
argument that Russia is "getting ahead of us" or preparing to take
military action, say, in the Persian Gulf, or that it uses proxy forces
of Cuban and East German troops to intervene in Angola or elsewhere. The American people, bristling with anger and consumed by
fear, thereupon support new weapons and budget increases. This
leads the Soviets to respond with counterweapons to those the Americans are developing, and so the perilous game continues. U.S. militarists demand still another round of new weapons and, to prod them
out of Congress, the hawks denounce the Soviet Union in tones still
more shrill. Distrust breeds distrust, and the arsenal grows in cadence
with that distrust. It is a circle that can be breached only by a public
outcry on an immense scale.

In theory, either side should be able to disengage from the race by
simply stating, "We now have enough weapons to kill the other side
many times over. We will stop producing any more." But both sides
have convinced themselves that to stop will indicate weakness and
will spur the adversary to foment small conventional wars against
friends and allies. And as the stockpiles on each side grow deadlier,
the adversaries conclude that they need ever more and ever better
weapons for a retaliatory strike following a first strike. The situation
clearly does not lend itself to restraint.

A third counterbalancing factor to stable deterrence is the proliferation of nuclear weaponry. The United States was the exclusive member of the nuclear club from 1945 to 1949. It was joined by the Russians in that year, then by Britain in 1952, followed by France, China, and, in 1974, India. for a total of six admitted members. Israel unquestionably has a secret stockpile, South Africa may have one, and Pakistan is on the verge of breaking into the club. In July 1976, President Ford stated that in addition to the six or seven (if you include Israel) that possessed atomic explosives at the time, there were twenty others with the know-how as well as access to the plutonium fuel to make them, and that by 1985 the number would be forty. By the year 2000 it may be 100 — two-thirds of the nations on Earth.[52]

A stable deterrent posture may avert atomic war for a while when there are only two countries that can initiate an attack, or perhaps even when there are six. But there can be no stability when 100 fingers and 100 buttons are involved and when nuclear escalation becomes inherent in any one of the many "little" wars that occur constantly (there have been 140 since World War II and they have collectively exacted a toll almost equal to that of World War II itself — 40 to 50 million dead).

Still another possible channel for proliferation similarly undermines the strategy of stable deterrence. At the moment, only two nations have the nuclear capability to destroy any other state. The British and French arsenal, though dangerous, is relatively small — a few hundred warheads. But if these two powers, as well as Germany, Japan, and perhaps Italy decide to produce cruise missiles on a large scale, they may make a decisive change in the character of the nuclear race. A cruise, carried on an air force plane, is 14 feet long, 26 inches in diameter, and carries a bomb many times more powerful than the Hiroshima bomb. It is slow compared to an ICBM — only 550 miles per hour — and its range is limited to 1,500 miles. But it travels at low levels, is difficult for enemy radar to intercept, and is capable of striking within 100 feet of its target. Equally attractive for militarists is the fact that is is cheap — about $1.5 million per missile.[53] Thus, for $1 or 2 billion, any of the great powers can acquire enough cruise missiles to destroy any other nation on Earth; instead of two superpowers, the cruise missile will create five, six, seven, or more, posing still another threat to the stability of stable deterrence.

Reliance on the atom for security clearly is tenuous: first, because the Bomb cannot be used against the Soviet Union (or against the United States) unless the superpowers are prepared for double suicide, and second because its role as a deterrent is gravely undermined by proliferation and by the self-propelling character of the nuclear race. There remains, of course, the option for the United States to employ thermonuclear weapons in "little" wars, say in Angola or El Salvador. But that, too, is not much of an option, in part because it can change the relationship of forces with the Soviet Union only slightly, not decisively, and in part because the same objective can be achieved, if it can be achieved at all, by conventional weapons or CIA activity. As for using nuclear weapons on a circumscribed scale in Europe, virtually all experts agree such use would inevitably flare into a universal war. "My own judgment," Defense Secretary Harold Brown told a House Appropriations Committee on February 8, 1978,

> is that once one starts to use nuclear weapons, even in a tactical way, it is quite likely that it will escalate, that there is a kind of powder train and even if both sides do not want it to happen—the compression of the time for decision, the lack of information that would be available on both sides, the expected great advantage that a military commander might think would come from being the first to get in his blow, all push for rapid escalation.[54]

Former Secretary of State Alexander Haig, made the same point more tersely before a Senate Foreign Relations Committee confirmation hearing: "Any employment of nuclear weapons represents the most profound change in the character of conflict. . . . It would be very difficult to control."[55]

Retired Lt. General Arthur Collins, formerly second in command of U.S. Army forces in Europe probably expressed the consensus when he told a Washington conference in 1978 that while planners talk of controlling events on a nuclear battlefield, "I doubt very much whether it could be done." In the standard scenario, the Soviets overrun parts of Europe with conventional arms; NATO forces, inferior in such weaponry, respond with tactical nuclear weapons, especially against Soviet tank formations. The Soviets might take a few days to make up their mind, Collins believes, but chances are they, too, would resort to "a massive tactical nuclear attack in depth" and would move into uncontested areas. "The natural reaction for us," says Collins, "would be to strike back with all available weapons. The pressure on the president and Congress would be enormous for a strategic nuclear attack on the enemy's homeland."[56] The "limited" war would become a total one—again, in MacArthur's words, a double suicide.

General Collins's judgment represents the vast majority of expert opinion. "My personal opinion," Vice Admiral Hyman G. Rickover told a House subcommittee on June 19, 1973, "is that there can be no such thing as a limited nuclear war. It is like making a girl partly pregnant. Once you start a nuclear war, it is liable to escalate, as does every war. A country starts using tactical nuclear weapons; after a while, if it is not working out, it starts using something more powerful, and then finally we have ourselves in the swing of things, ending up with a real, all-out nuclear war."[57] Soviet President Leonid Brezhnev agrees. In an interview with West Germany's *Der Spiegel*, he argued that "even though there are some who hope that a nuclear war could be contained on European territory . . . a limited nuclear war is not possible."

If the United States has any military options at all, they are nonatomic – conventional weapons and CIA "destabilizations." But these, too, are limited options today, since they always pose the danger of graduation to larger confrontations – ones with nuclear weapons. The big military breakthrough that the Right and Center in our political spectrum long expected to ensure U.S. predominance in world affairs has turned out to be lame and impotent. Indeed, the policy is so lame that some people, such as former National Security Council director Richard Allen, think of arms escalation primarily as a means of crippling the Soviet economy by forcing the Kremlin to spend more on weapons. What geopolitical purpose this would serve is not clear, but such views are indicative of the confusion in establishment ranks because "the greatest thing in history" is, in fact, of little value on either the military or the diplomatic front.

THE
WRONG 4
ENEMY

The Bomb has been the anchor of our foreign policy since World War II, and the Soviet Union has been the enemy it was intended to restrain. Some writers argue in fact that the Bomb was dropped on Hiroshima and Nagasaki more as a means of bringing the Kremlin into line with American plans for the postwar world than to shorten the war against Japan.[1] "Our possessing and demonstrating the Bomb," Secretary of State James F. Byrnes told scientist Leo Szilard, "would make Russia more manageable in Europe."[2] Though the Soviets had suffered severe wartime losses, they were the only nation with an army and air force formidable enough to challenge the United States either in Europe or Asia; American officials were therefore quite sensitive about the need to inhibit Moscow.

This alone, however, does not explain why the Soviet Union metamorphosed so quickly from ally to enemy. Except in Iran for a brief period, the Russian government certainly was not holding any territory that the United States or the West could consider part of its sphere of influence. Nor was it spawning revolution in order to upset the capitalist status quo; on the contrary, it tried to suppress revolution throughout the Eastern hemisphere. In a talk with the Yugoslav communist leader Milovan Djilas, early in 1947, Stalin insisted that "the uprising in Greece must be stopped, and as quickly as possible. . . . We should not hesitate, but let us put an end to the Greek uprising."[3] This was not atypical. The conventional wisdom that the Soviet Union fomented revolution and class struggle in order to harry the United States does not match the facts of the early postwar period. "Near the end of the war," writes historian D. F. Fleming, "Stalin scoffed at communism in Germany, urged the Italian Reds to make peace with the monarchy, did his best to induce Mao Tse-tung to come to terms with the Kuomintang, and angrily demanded of Tito that he back the [Yugoslav] monarchy, thus fulfilling his [Stalin's] bargain with Churchill."[4]

Communist-controlled Maquis in France and Garibaldini in Italy (the major guerrilla groups in those countries) evacuated the factories they held and allowed themselves to be disarmed. Communist leaders joined "bourgeois governments"; Maurice Thorez, veteran Stalinist, served as vice premier of France for almost two years; and Palmiro Togliatti joined the coalition government of Italy. Stalin's sights were set not on revolution but on Popular Fronts and on closer ties to the United States. This may not have been entirely selfless – Stalin still entertained hopes of receiving economic aid from America to rebuild his country–but it is a fact.

If there is any misconception in the mythology of the Cold War it is that the communists started it by stimulating revolution. On the contrary they held it back. Even in 1947, when in the words of political scientist John W. Spanier, Europe was "on the verge of collapse," the communists made no effort to engineer revolutions.[5] They continued instead to help Europe reconstruct. "Reconstruction comes first" for the communists, Joseph Alsop wrote in 1946, and that held true the following year as well, when the economic situation in Europe became even more bleak.[6] The communists were urging workers to produce more so as to speed economic revival, and they were offering to work with socialist and liberal parties. They were not igniting revolutions.

If the Truman Administration saw the Soviet Union as its enemy, therefore, it was not because Moscow fostered social instability on the six continents. It was the result, instead, of two other factors: first, that communist Russia could not fit in with Washington's plans for reorganizing the world, and second, because a spreading revolutionary wave drove increasingly wider wedges between the two superpowers.

Roosevelt had envisioned a postwar economic order in which the United States would be the linchpin of a *benign* imperialism. American business would enjoy a quantum jump in foreign trade and investment, protected by an international police force that would guarantee the overseas stability required by such ventures. The president was convinced such a program could be carried out with minimal strife and without terrorizing or killing people in underdeveloped countries.[7] "Roosevelt," wrote Richard Hofstadter, "appears to have believed that the ruthless imperialism of the older colonial powers might be replaced by a liberal and benevolent American penetration that would be of advantage both to the natives and to American commerce."[8] FDR wrote passionately of the plight of the Iranian people, 99 percent of whom "do not own their own land and cannot keep their own production or convert it into money or property." He suggested to Secretary of State Cordell Hull that Indochina should become independent because "France has had the country—thirty million inhabitants—for nearly one hundred years, and the people are worse off than they were at the beginning."[9]

Roosevelt's opposition to the old colonialism "was not simply altruistic." He arranged for $100 million in lend–lease funds to Saudi Arabia (an act of questionable legality) to secure oil concessions for American companies in that land—and prevent them from going to British firms—and he planned for enlarged trade and investment in the British empire, China, and other places.[10] From 1939 to 1945, the State Department and the Council on Foreign Relations held joint talks on what American objectives should be after the war. They concluded that if we were to prosper under the present system we would have to control—as recorded by Noam Chomsky—"the entire Western Hemisphere, the former British empire which they [American leaders] were in the process of dismantling, and the Far East."[11] Whether or not that is the exact formulation they arrived at, there is no question the American establishment had visions of a much expanded area for their economic activity. That such considerations were high on the agenda of our strategists is indicated by the comments of Roosevelt's advisers. "My contention is that we cannot have full employment and prosperity in the United States," said Assistant Secretary of State (later Secretary) Dean Acheson "without the foreign markets."[12] Donald M. Nelson, head of the War Production Board, predicted that "unless we can develop a broad export market, for capital goods, I do not see the chance in the reconversion period for the capital goods industries [heart of the American economy] to be prosperous."[13]

After the war, this need for markets was even more pressing. National income had more than doubled between 1940 and 1945; the capital equipment industry, according to the National Planning Association, was "nearly twice the size which would be needed domestically under the most fortuitous conditions of full employment and nearly equal to the task of supplying world needs."[14] America, a market economy, needed outside markets to keep its great economic machine in operation. Under a different kind of social system, Acheson told a congressional committee, "you could use the entire production of the country in the United States," but under the present free enterprise system the government "must look to foreign markets" or "we are in for a very bad time."[15]

The Soviet Union, by its very nature, did not fit into these plans for economic expansion. One of Washington's major demands from those who intended to join Pax Americana was that they open their doors to freer trade and investment. This was a boon for Uncle Sam's entrepreneurs because they then had the most efficient industrial plant in the world by a wide margin. But for the Soviet Union free trade represented a threat; it would mean giving up both its planned economy and its form of government. Under the Soviet system, the state held a monopoly of foreign trade—in part to protect a relatively weak economy. If that monopoly were to be breached and the door opened without restriction to Western imports, American corporations would undersell their less-efficient Russian counterparts and drive them out of business. The East European nations, with the exception of Czechoslovakia, would be even more vulnerable.

The United States, however, kept dangling rewards before Soviet eyes to induce it into an American system, which the Soviets, for their part, could not accept. Back in 1943, Secretary of State Cordell Hull made it clear to the Russians that their chances of obtaining postwar loans depended on agreeing to his foreign-trade program. Later, specific plans were formulated to grant the Soviets a postwar credit of $10 billion at 2 percent a year interest, provided the Kremlin committed itself to supply strategic raw materials to the United States and to "normalize" economic relations. On May 8, 1945, Truman abruptly ended lend–lease to the Soviet Union without offering anything in its place; he made clear that it the Russians were to receive American help they would have to show by good deeds they deserved them—such as honoring property rights of American corporations in Eastern Europe and the Soviet zone of Germany.[16] Still later, a smaller loan was offered Moscow, again with the condition that it open its doors.

There was thus an element of diverging interests between the two superpowers at the outset, and it was made worse by the fact that an overconfident Truman, encouraged by the Bomb, did not feel he had to make conciliatory gestures to the Russians. The differences between the two powers were not insuperable; many people believed that the two economic systems could coexist. But as Secretary of State Henry L. Stimson recorded, the atom bomb project gave Truman "an entirely new feeling of confidence."[17] After eleven days at his White House desk and less than two weeks after he learned that an atomic bomb was being developed, Truman told Charles E. Bohlen that "if the Russians did not wish to join us they could go to hell."[18] Four members of Truman's cabinet, including Stimson and former Vice President Henry A. Wallace, disagreed with this approach. A month after the Bomb was dropped on Hiroshima, Stimson urged Truman to form an "atomic partnership" with the Soviet Union. "Unless the Soviets are voluntarily invited into the partnership upon a basis of cooperation and trust," he wrote the president on September 11, 1945, "we . . . will almost certainly stimulate feverish activity on the part of the Soviet [Union] toward the development of this bomb in what will in effect be a secret armament race of a rather desperate character." As to whether the Soviets could be trusted, Stimson advised Truman: "The chief lesson I have learned in a long life is that the only way you can make a man trustworthy is to trust him; and the surest way to make him untrustworthy is to distrust him and show your distrust."[19] Truman, however, was embarked on an opposite course, and he could not be dissuaded.

Before long, therefore, the antagonism was enlarged by the intrusion of the issue of revolution. The dilemmas of a "benign" imperialism, it turned out, forced the United States into repressive behavior much like that of the older imperialisms, and drove the peoples of what is now called the Third World into resistance. Our government hoped to avoid it, but, given its affinity for the business community at home, it found itself in repeated quandries, and in the end simply succumbed to an old pattern. And the Soviet Union, for its part, ultimately found it more beneficial to take sides with the revolutionaries than to wait for the United States to adopt a posture of coexistence.

This is not to say that there were no moral issues between the two nations or that the criticisms of the Soviet Union by our government had no validity. The postwar elections in Poland were a perversion of democracy, just as our State Department claimed, and the internal life of the Soviet Union itself was certainly totalitarian. But this is not what widened the rift between Washington and Moscow. The Soviet Union was just as totalitarian during World War II when we were aligned with it, and during the 1930s when Roosevelt tendered it recognition despite its forced labor camps and the impending purge and execution of thousands of old revolutionists. Our relationship with the Soviet Union, like our relationships with all countries, is not predetermined by morals (though we, like all nations, try to give our acts a moral flavor). If it were, we never could have entered into compacts with such dictatorships as those of Brazil, Indonesia, Taiwan, Chile, and dozens more. Nor would we have entered into a virtual alliance with Communist China during its harsh cultural revolution. Our relationships are predetermined by our geopolitical interests — and those interests, as defined by postwar presidents, tended more and more to clash with the interests of the Soviets and their allies. Our establishment felt it had to save the status quo; their leadership was ready to help those trying to topple it.

To illustrate the process: On July 4, 1946, consonant with America's anticolonialist posture, the Truman Administration granted independence to the Philippines amid much pomp and ceremony, and pledged $380 million to rebuild the new nation's war-torn economy. Both independence and aid, however, were conditioned on acceptance of the Philippine Trade Act passed by the U.S. Congress. The United States had enjoyed preferential economic treatment in the 7,100 islands on the other side of the international date line ever since they were conquered at the turn of the century; it was understandable, therefore, that American bankers and businesspeople with a stake in the Philippines should want to retain those rights. The Trade Act was passed to fulfill that purpose. Under section 341, Filipinos were required to grant our corporations the same rights as native entrepreneurs — rights denied other foreign businesspeople.[20] Provisions in the Philippine constitution against foreigners owning more than 40 percent of any local company were to be waived in the case of Americans; Philippine currency was tied to the dollar (until 1974); and export quotas were alloted to American firms that had been in foreign trade before the war. In practice, this meant that American corporations would continue to dominate the Philippine economy. Undersecretary of State William L. Clayton conceded that the act deprived "the Philippine government of a sovereign prerogative." *Business Week* called independence "nominal" because it gave "American business a preferential position in exploiting Philippine resources."[21] Testifying to that preferential position, American investments grew by 350 percent.

Not surprisingly, the conditions of the Philippine Trade Act were approved by an administration of questionable credentials. President Manuel Roxas, whose election *Business Week* called a "political farce," had played a double role during the war, collaborating with the Japanese while spying for the United States. After the war, he displayed that same capacity for survival by agreeing to the Trade Act and granting the United States 99-year leases for various naval and military bases. Whether we could have concluded such favorable arrangements with more radical elements is doubtful. We need only envision George Washington granting Great Britain military bases in New York harbour and agreeing to a favored trade position for the British to realize how incongruous such a position is for nationalists.

Nonetheless, this much can perhaps be called the benign aspect of America's new imperial policy—because the U.S. government did provide loans and other aid. But, having entered into the partnership with Roxas and similar elements, we soon found ourselves on the horn of a dilemma. While Roxas was serving the Japanese during the war, the communist-dominated Hukbalahap (National Anti-Japanese Army) was waging guerrilla war against Japan—and receiving U.S. aid to do so. After MacArthur returned to Manila, the Huks disarmed and dispersed, contenting themselves with normal political activities. In the 1946 elections their Democratic Alliance won six congressional seats in central Luzon by large margins, and though the Alliance was only a minority party nationally, it held the balance of power in the legislature. Roxas thereupon used his army—still commanded by American officers—to suppress the movement, remove the six congressmen from office, and outlaw Huk-controlled peasant and labor organizations. The result was predictable. Confronted by the government's iron fist, the leftists returned to guerrilla warfare, and at the peak of their effort, according to Lieutenant Colonel Tomas C. Tirena of the Philippine Air Force, commanded 15,000 armed men, plus "80,000 HMB's [National Army of Liberation], with a mass support of 500,000."[22]

Faced with a popular revolution, the United States was forced to take a position. Theoretically, we could have remained neutral, but we were too involved in Philippine affairs to do so. We could have taken the side of the Huks, which would have assured their victory, but that would have cut us off from friends who had long been helpful to American business interests. Perhaps if someone at the State Department had made the appraisal that this was one of scores of nationalist revolutions soon to take place around the world, Washington would have adopted,a different course—or at least a modified one. But the United States by this time—like the West generally—had a long history of imposing its will on weak countries, especially in the Caribbean, where at one time or another the Marines had been sent in to police, occupy, and pacify Haiti, Honduras, Cuba, Panama, Costa Rica, and others. It did not seem to our leaders in 1946, therefore, that something radically new was happening or that something that would pose a long-term risk was being initiated.

Given this judgment, Washington cast its lot with the conservative Philippine regime against the Huks. Its Joint U.S. Military Advisory Group (JUSMAG) equipped, trained, and advised 54,000 government troops and a similar number of "civilian guards." Despite this superior force and a billion dollars of American aid, there was still a small contingent of Huks in operation sixteen years later, and in March 1964, the government was forced to undertake division-size operations (still under the guidance of JUSMAG) against the Huks in Pampanga and central Luzon. Pax Americana—the favorable trade and business arrangement—could not have prevailed in the Philippines without our help in suppressing the Huks. Nor, on the other hand, could the Philippine congress have remained, as Alex Campbell pointed out in a *New Republic* article, "largely in the hands of big landlords and industrialists."[23] It was, as such arrangements usually are, a quid pro quo rather than a matter of principle. Its corollary was a further strain in the relations with the Soviet Union, for though the Kremlin did not give much material aid to the Huks, it had a political affinity for them, as did communist parties around the world, which predictably espoused the Huk cause.

* * * * * * *

Our presidents spoke in high moral terms but, when faced with a practical choice, invariably came down on the side of what is euphemistically called realpolitik. In an age of revolution, our establishment was transfixed by the past. We failed to develop a new approach or to alter old motivations that pivoted around profit and strategic advantage. We sought out "friends" abroad who were the same kind of "friends" Theodore Roosevelt would have chosen in the age of the Big Stick, and not infrequently we listed our goals in the crass language of material reward—tin, tungsten, raw materials, investment.

"If Indochina goes," said President Eisenhower, "the tin and tungsten that we so greatly value from that area would cease coming." "He who holds or has influence in Vietnam," said Henry Cabot Lodge, "can affect the future of the Philippines and Formosa to the east, Thailand and Burma with their huge rice surpluses to the west, and Malaysia and Indonesia with their rubber, ore, and tin to the south." Latin America, said General Robert Porter, Jr., commander of American military forces in the Panama Canal Zone, "has been a major supplier of approximately 30 strategic materials, including copper, tin, and petroleum." The Latin American counterinsurgents being trained in the Canal Zone, therefore, are needed, said Porter, to "act in conjunction with the police and other security forces . . . to control disorders and riots" and to discourage "those elements which are tempted to resort to violence and overthrow the government." No Leninist could have stated the imperial purpose more forthrightly: to defend established governments from any upheaval that might limit U.S. access to investment or commerce. Secretary of State Dean Rusk stressed the same point in a 1962 statement of American diplomatic purpose: "Our influence is used wherever it can be and persistently, though our Embassies on a day-to-day basis, in our aid discussions and in direct aid negotiation, to underline the importance of private investment." Former Secretary of State Alexander Haig tied the strategic to the economic: "The escalating setbacks to our interests abroad, increasing lawlessness and terrorism, and the so-called wars of national liberation are putting in jeopardy our ability to influence world events . . . and to assure access to raw materials." The effect has been that economic, strategic, and political concerns took precedence over moral ones. Our behavior in Greece, Guatemala, and Iran illustrate this unfortunate duality.

In March 1947, President Truman proclaimed his famous doctrine in support of Greece, Turkey, and other "free peoples who are resisting attempted subjugation by armed minorities or by outside pressures."[24] But the fact that Washington was not entirely guided by such principles was made evident in the first test of the Truman Doctrine—in Greece. There, it was the United States, not the Soviet Union, that imposed the will of the minority upon the majority.

The background for the Greek crisis was this: In October 1944, Churchill and Stalin entered into a secret agreement on the disposition of the Balkan states after liberation. By the British prime minister's account, the Soviets were to have 90 percent influence in Rumania, 75 percent in Bulgaria, and a fifty-fifty status in Hungary and Yugoslavia. In return, Stalin conceded 100 percent preponderance for Britain in Greece, which had been a British sphere of influence for a long time prior to the war.[25] In accord with this understanding, London maneuvered political affairs in Greece decisively to the Right—toward royalism—just as it had done in Italy and Belgium.

The trouble was that popular sentiment in Greece was with the Left. Two resistance movements had emerged during the war—a conservative but antimonarchist group called EDES (National Republican Greek League) and a liberal-radical force dominated by the communists, ELAS (the National Popular Liberation Army) and its political arm EAM (National Liberation Front). By the estimate of British Foreign Secretary Anthony Eden, these leftists constituted three-quarters of the guerrilla movement and commanded the allegiance of 1.5 to 2 million of Greece's 7 million people—easily the largest constituency in the country.[26] That became clear as the German occupation forces withdrew. There was the usual scramble for arms and territory between EDES and ELAS, but the communist-controlled elements prevailed without difficulty, establishing control over most of the villages and cities, except for Athens, Salonika, Piraeus, and a few isolated spots where the British army held sway. While all this was going on, the British installed a monarchist regime headed by George Papandreou and prepared to disarm ELAS partisans. ELAS was not unwilling, for, as historian L.S. Stavrianos points out, it had no intentions of making a revolution—"the current international communist 'line' called for national unity and Allied cooperation. . . ."[27] ELAS refused to disarm, however, so long as rival rightist forces did not do likewise. Almost immediately after liberation, therefore, Greece was plunged into civil war, and, by all accounts, would have turned communist at this point were it not for a British force of 75,000 troops called in to suppress the former guerrillas.

Following an armistice in February 1945, a reign of terror was instituted by the Greek government, resulting in 258 killings and 13,000 imprisonments. "In this manner," writes Stavrianos, "an assortment of rightists, Royalists, and [Nazi] collaborators, unchecked either by their own government or the British, worked their way into control of the armed services and the administration."[28] The *New York Herald-Trubune* reported "a pitiless war on scores of thousands of women and children in a desperate effort to halt a growing rebellion and wipe out not only communists but all democratic, liberal and republican elements."[29] The trade union movement, which had returned a leftist leadership in elections held under the eyes of British laborites, was "reorganized" by the royalist government and placed under a quisling who had served the Axis during the war, Fotis Makris. Half the budget of the regime of Constantine Tsaldaris was spent on police and troops; only 6 percent was spent on reconstruction. Faced with this state of affairs, the communists and EAM—against the wishes of Stalin—retreated to the mountains to fight one more time.

Clearly, the Greece that Britain abandoned in 1947—because it could no longer afford the costs of occupation—and which we were now prepared to shelter under the American umbrella did not in any way fit the Truman definition of free people and free institutions. The president was probably not insincere in hoping for a democratic society in that ancient land. But there were other factors to be considered that were of greater consequence to the American establishment.

Truman's blueprint for the postwar world, like Roosevelt's, envisioned an international climate in which American corporations could operate with a minimum of molestation. Nations that received U.S. aid—economic and military—were therefore required to accept the principle of free trade and a stable international currency, the dollar. Since the United States, as noted above, then possessed the most efficient economy—in fact the only one that was not limping—free trade would allow U.S. corporations to penetrate the market for goods and capital everywhere. An American firm that could produce a ton of steel, for instance, for half or two-thirds what it might cost to produce in Bulgaria, Egypt, Germany, or Japan would swamp the markets of those nations, provided they did not erect high tariff or quota barriers. That was what American policy sought to prevent. As

Truman saw it, only nations that believed in "free enterprise" were compatible with the goals of Pax Americana, and unless "free enterprise" became the world system, the United States would ultimately have to regiment its own economy "to fight for markets and for raw materials."[30]

Given this premise, Truman determined that he had to save Greece from communism. Economic and strategic concerns overrode moral ones. A communist or neutralist Greece would not only have shut the door to American (and Western) commerce and investment, but might have encouraged the Soviet Union to move into the future oil basin of the world, the Middle East. When the British informed Washington they could no longer police Greece, career officers in the State Department openly rejoiced that now they might establish a "Greek–Turkey–Iran barrier" to Soviet penetration.[31] The fear then was that Greece might succumb to communism within a few weeks and that this would inevitably give a strong lift to the Left in Iran, Turkey, and Western Europe. Faced with this imminent threat, the issue of "freedom" in Greece became irrelevant, just as the breaking of a window becomes irrelevant when a fireman has to put out a fire inside the house.

Dwight Griswold, former governor of Nebraska, was sent to Athens in July 1947 to run the American Mission for Aid to Greece. At the head of the Greek government at the time was the former president of the National Bank, M. Maximos, a royalist and a rightist. But Griswold was intent on keeping hands off politics; he would do an honest job so that American dollars would not be siphoned off by corrupt Greek politicians. He firmly believed a line could be drawn between economics and politics. Within two months, however, as the guerrillas grew stronger and the Maximos government collapsed, the United States was embroiled in the internal politics of Greece. Loy Henderson, chief of the State Department's Office of Near Eastern Affairs, was sent to Athens to force the royalists to form a coalition with liberals—on threat that otherwise the United States would withdraw its aid. The new government that emerged—thirteen royalists and eleven liberals—was an American product. It was less objectionable than the Maximos regime, but it lacked the vitality to resolve pressing social problems. The rightists and moderates cancelled each other out. Though the Sophoulis coalition offered an amnesty to guerrillas, it did little else.

Here was the point at which American policy needed razor-sharp definition. There were two opposite methods to deal with the "guerrilla problem." One was to destroy the rebels physically; the other was to weaken their popular support by granting overdue reforms, suppressing the rightists, and conducting democratic elections as promised. Had the United States used its economic aid as bait to effectuate these changes, the guerrilla war might have collapsed quickly. The communists, almost certainly, would have abandoned it, and if they did not, their efforts would have been doomed as they lost the support of village and urban masses. As it was, the war continued until September 1949, and probably would have continued longer if Yugoslavia had not seceded from the Soviet camp, denying the Greek guerrillas a haven.

* * * * * * *

During the first postwar decade, our establishment scored a number of victories such as the one in the Philippines. "Winning" perhaps became too easy, tending to institutionalize Washington's role as the enemy of revolution—nations seldom change strategy when an old one meets little resistance. The greatest success for this policy, of course, was in Western Europe where a combination of $12.3 billion of Marshall Plan aid and a military alliance (the Atlantic Pact) helped thwart an almost certain eruption of social revolutions. Unless Washington provided help, Undersecretary of State William Clayton warned in a talk to a New York audience in December 1947, "the Iron Curtain would then move westward at least to the English Channel. . . ." Such a victory for communism, he said, would mean "a blackout of the European market [and] could compel radical readjustments in our entire economic structure . . . changes which could hardly be made under our democratic free-enterprise system."[32] Even NATO (North Atlantic Treaty Organization) was conceived, as a government interdepartment committee put it, both to deter foreign aggression and "to protect the North Atlantic Treaty Countries against *internal* aggression inspired from abroad."[33] (Emphasis added.) Saving the old order—with some modifications—was clearly the central goal of American policy; and, as noted, it was not too difficult in the early years. In most instances it did not involve military force, and where it did, it was usually of a covert nature under the guidance of the CIA.

The overthrow of democratic regimes in Guatemala and Iran are typical. In the Philippines, our government saw fit to prevent a conservative regime from falling; in Guatemala and Iran, it imposed them on nations that did not want them. What we did, in effect, was something similar to what the old imperial states, specifically Britain and France, did in the nineteenth century when they occupied weak countries and stifled nationalism. The only important difference was that we did not place permanent troops in client states – probably because it was no longer feasible to govern them that way; there were now guerrillas to contend with everywhere. In the nineteenth century, Britain could subdue India with a mere 50,000 troops, and France could seize large parts of Indochina with 2,000; but in recent times, the French had to use half a million soldiers in a losing battle against only 45,000 guerrillas in Algeria from 1954 to 1962. Apart from direct occupation, however, our government was trying to do in the twentieth century what the old imperial states had done in the nineteenth. Communism had little to do with it, except that the word "communist" became a convenient shibboleth for *justifying* intervention.

One of the first manifestations of this pattern was in Guatemala, where a 1944 revolution had ousted General Jorge Ubico, a man who boasted political kinship to Adolf Hitler and claimed to "execute first and give trial afterward."[34] After the overthrow, a former schoolteacher, Juan Jose Arevalo, was elected president by a wide margin and proceeded to legalize unions, abolish forced labor on the plantations, raise minimum pay (to 26 cents a day), and institute other changes that he felt would reclaim his country's economy from the United Fruit Company (bananas constituted two-fifths of the nation's exports) and other foreign firms. When he introduced social security reforms that cost United Fruit $200,000 a year, the company reduced its production by 80 percent, and W. R. Grace and Pan American actively discouraged the vital tourist trade. The tensions with Washington became more acute as attempts were made to oust Arevalo from power, perhaps with the support of Truman's emissary, Richard C. Patterson, who complained about the "persecution of American business."[35]

Arevalo was legally succeeded in the next election by General Jacobo Arbenz Guzman, who, if anything, was considered by our government to be worse. He too was not a communist but, as American pressures increased, he leaned on them – and other leftists – for support. Arbenz's most significant act was the introduction of an extensive land reform (2 percent of the population owned 70 percent of the land) that distributed tracts to 85,000 peasant families. In the process, however, the Guatemalan regime seized 234,000 uncultivated acres belonging to United Fruit. It offered the American corporation $600,000 in twenty five-year bonds – the amount the corporation had listed as its net worth for tax purposes – but United Fruit demanded $16 million. This was the setting when, in the words of a future president of the country, Miguel Ydigoras Fuentes,

> a former secretary of the United Fruit Company, now retired, Mr. Walter Turnbull, came to see me with two gentlemen whom he introduced as agents of the CIA. They said that I was a popular figure in Guatemala and that they wanted to lend their assistance to overthrow Arbenz. When I asked their conditions for the assistance I found them unacceptable. Among other things, I was to promise to favor the United Fruit Company, and the International Railways of Central America; to destroy the railroad workers unions; . . . to establish a strong arm government on the style of Ubico.[36]

Rebuffed by Ydigoras, the CIA fastened on Colonel Carlos Castillo Armas, who had been trained in a military school at Fort Leavenworth. Late in 1953, then, John E. Peurifoy, an old diplomatic hand with experience in the Greek insurgency, was dispatched as ambassador to Guatemala for the purpose of coordinating a revolt against the government to which he was accredited. The action had to be taken, Peurifoy later told a committee of Congress, because "the Arbenz government, beyond any question, was controlled and dominated by communists . . . and the communist conspiracy in Guatemala did represent a very real and very serious menace to the security of the United States.[37] Even if one were to concede that the Guatemalan people had no right to determine their own form of government, this assessment is both far-fetched and puerile. At the time, Guatemala was receiving no aid from the Soviet Union and clearly was not embarked on establishing a communist economic model, unless land reform is construed as "communism." The Guatemalan communist party had perhaps 3,000 members – in a nation of three or four million – and Arbenz inducted some of them to administer a few of his programs, but his principal support came from other leftist forces. In any case, it is difficult to believe that Washington was more concerned about the political coloration of a few thousand of Arbenz' supporters than the $16 million of United Fruit property and the effect that an expropriation in Guatemala would have on governments elsewhere in Latin America.

A few months after Peurifoy arrived, Operation el Diablo was launched. The CIA established a headquarters for Castillo at Tegulcigalpa, Honduras, and not long thereafter, a training camp at Momotobito, a volcanic island belonging to Nicaragua. Meanwhile, Arbenz discovered the plot through intercepted correspondence between Castillo and Ydigoras, and approached the Soviet Union to buy $10 million small arms—putting to work the "the enemy of my enemy is my friend" syndrome. A shipment of Czech weapons aboard a Swedish ship, Alfhem, in mid-May brought charges from Secretary of State John Foster Dulles that Arbenz might be planning to attack the Panama Canal—a thousand miles away. This charge served as a pretext for more-or-less open support for Castillo's invaders. On June 18, the American-inspired colonel led a band of 150 exiled mercenaries over the border from Honduras while four P-47 Thunderbolts, flown by U.S. pilots, bombed the Guatemalan capital. The mercenaries settled six miles inside the border, waiting for the planes to wreak enough havoc for Arbenz to surrender. Unfortunately for the invaders, one bomber was shot full of holes and another crashed. But while our ambassador to the United Nations, Henry Cabot Lodge, was denying the involvement of any American planes or fliers, Eisenhower decided to send in more—enough to tip the scales. Though Castillo did not get as far as the capital, he did not have to. Arbenz, fearful of a bloodbath and deserted by old friends in the army, refused to distribute arms to the unions and peasant organizations clamoring for them. On June 27, he simply gave up.

As an epilogue to the story, United Fruit lands were promptly restored to the company, and a tax on interest and dividends for foreigners was abrogated, saving the company $11 million. Unions were disbanded temporarily (and, when reorganized, were less than a seventh their previous size), the right to strike was abolished, wage increases were held up and, most significant of all, the 85,000 parcels of land distributed to peasants were returned to the *finca* owners, some of whom went on a rampage, burning the crops of their serfs. More than 5,000 people were arrested, and the election law was modified so that illiterates—70 percent of the population—were denied the vote. In the one-candidate election that followed, Castillo was confirmed by what Eisenhower called a "thundering majority."

Twenty-eight years later, Stephen Schlesinger and Stephen Kinzer, authors of a book on Guatemala, reported in the *New York Times* that "land ownership remains in the hands of the few. Social progress is severely limited for most people. Indians, who constitute more than half of the population of 7.2 million, have stayed poor, illiterate, landless. The economy has never recovered; by many measures the people are worse off today than they were under President Arbenz."[38] Since 1954, the regime has secretly exterminated 25,000 opponents, according to Amnesty International, most of them at the hands of "death squads" connected with the security forces.

In the short run, the containment policy worked in Guatemala— though its people paid a fearful price. But one can only wonder whether, in the long run, the next revolution in Guatemala—and in the area—will pose a greater challenge to the State Department. Is the so-called Guatemalan problem solved, or is it only postponed? As of 1982, a civil war was under way in nearby El Salvador, and renewed guerrilla warfare in Guatemala was so worrisome that the Reagan Administration was requesting a resumption of military aid for the regime—aid cut off by the previous U.S. administration because of Guatemala's abysmal human rights record. Tad Szulc, a writer with considerable background in Latin American affairs, was predicting that "Guatemala is on the verge of full-scale civil war between the rightist military government and leftist guerrillas. The U.S. State Department says the army has been unable to control mounting guerrilla activity despite continuing 'search and destroy' operations."[39]

* * * * * * *

What we in the United States see in communism is the totalitarianism of the Soviet government, its lack of civil liberties, its harshness toward dissidents such as Andrei Sakharov, its refusal to allow citizens to travel, and its low living standards compared to the capitalist West. It has been relatively simple, therefore, to create an anticommunist mood here and to use that mood as a shield behind which to pursue the policy of containment. "Our country is now geared to an arms economy which was bred in an artificially induced psychosis of war hysteria," General Douglas MacArthur told the Michigan State Legislature on May 15, 1952, "and nurtured upon an incessant propaganda of fear."[40]

In contrast, what people in developing nations see in communism is something entirely different. They are not shocked by its totalitarianism because they themselves have always lived under totalitarian governments – operated by either foreign powers or native tyrants. Nor are they disturbed by the Soviet Union's low living standards, for theirs is even lower – usually much lower. Eleven hundred and sixty-six million people in the developing nations (excluding China) were living on $4.20 a week in 1980; their plight had improved by less than one percent a year in the previous decade. Far from being alienated, these people see in communism a kindred spirit that professes to oppose imperialism, just as they do, and stands for their own hope for egalitarianism. They often disagree with the communists over tactics and strategy, and they sometimes resent the domineering attitudes of communists they know, but these are differences *within* the revolutionary family, not outside it. When they seek help against the West generally or the United States specifically, therefore, the people in the less-developed countries feel no compunction about calling on the communists – either local ones or those in Moscow. Thus, if the American government wants to apply a communist label on any of the revolutionary forces in the Third World, it is relatively simple. On the principle of "guilt by association," a noncommunist becomes a communist.

Here, for instance, is how Peurifoy, in a report to Eisenhower, justified his conclusion that Arbenz was a communist:

> In a six hour conversation he listened while I counted off the leading communists in his regime, but he gave no ground; many notorious Reds he denied to be communists; if they were, they were not dangerous; if dangerous he would control them; if not controllable he would round them up. He said, in any case, all our difficulties were due to the malpractices of American business. . . . It seemed to me that the man thought like a communist and talked like a communist, and if not actually one, would do until one came along."[41]

Another "destabilization" of a noncommunist government in the name of "fighting communism" was directed against the regime of Mohammed Mossadegh in Iran, who, like Arevalo and Arbenz in Guatemala, was trying to carry out a peaceful noncommunist revolution. Approximately 80 percent of Iran's population at the time was agrarian, almost 25 percent tribal. According to a United States Point Four official, in 1953 nine-tenths of the peasants lived at a subsistence level. Half the population suffered from trachoma, and three of ten babies died before their first birthday.[42] In the capital, Teheran, water ran in open *jubes* along the streets, and was used not only for washing and toilet purposes, but occasionally for drinking. The economy, dependent on oil, was dominated by a British firm, Anglo–Iranian, under a sixty-year franchise granted in 1909. In 1949, the company and the government negotiated a pact whereby Anglo–Iranian would pay Iran 25 to 30 percent of its net profits, but the *majlis* (parliament) refused to ratify the agreement as inadequate. Instead, on May 1, 1951, it appointed as prime minister Mohammed Mossadegh, a leftist who described himself as a social-democrat, and within days the oil company was nationalized.

Mossadegh at this point refused to incorporate the communist Tudeh Party into his National Front (a coalition of nationalist and moderate radicals) because he shared with many leftists an aversion to the Kremlin's brand of radicalism. In fact, in July of that year, the prime minister suppressed a demonstration against the foreign oil companies led by Tudeh, a result of which was scores of people killed and 500 injured.

As Mossadegh explained it to an American writer in 1953, the most urgent need of his country was land reform since 80 percent of the people lived in villages, and land reform could be meaningful, he felt, only if it were accompanied by reclamation projects, electrification, dams, credits for seed and machinery, roads. In Iran, however, the only way to finance such projects was from the profits from oil. If he could sell eight million tons of nationalized petroleum to foreign states, Mossadegh was confident he would solve the nation's basic problems. He would accomplish his peaceful revolution without the help of Tudeh and without calling on the peasants to seize land from the monarchy and feudal lords.[43]

The trouble was he couldn't sell *any* oil; Britain sponsored a world boycott—supported by the United States—that was fully effective. No Western nation would buy Iranian oil or lease tankers to ship it; Mossadegh was mercilessly squeezed. President Eisenhower recorded in his memoirs that "Iranian production fell from 424,000 barrels a day in 1947 to 59,000 in 1954."[44] Appeals by Mossadegh to the United States were met with a dribble of money for agricultural assistance in 1951 and 1952. Later, however, Eisenhower refused economic aid unless Iran reached "a reasonable agreement" with Britain. If Britain, and later the United States, was unable to arrive at an understanding, it was not because of Mossadegh's politics, but because he wanted to use oil for national development whereas they wanted it for the customary reason, profit.

Had the State Department been seeking a counterfoil to the communists, Mossadegh was an ideal choice, being an intelligent noncommunist with a large popular following. Moreover, he was obviously trying to avoid a coalition with the communists, for a time even refusing to legalize their party. "Less than a month before the coup that finally overthrew him," Richard Barnet records, "he received another open appeal to join forces with the communists, but despite the now transparent effort of the United States and its allies to get rid of him and the mounting opposition of the Shah, the army, the landowners, and the middle classes, Mossadegh refused to accept their help. Two days before he fell, his troops turned on communist demonstrators in Teheran."[45] Whatever one may say of the wisdom of this course, or of the alleged right of the United States to intervene, it is obvious that the Iranian prime minister at the time was not a communist.

Despite all that, our government decided to overthrow Mossadegh, for allowing Iran to nationalize its oil might have set a bad example for other oil countries, such as Saudi Arabia or Venezuela. Washington, moreover, hoped to carve out a place for U.S. oil companies in the fourth largest petroleum reserve in the world. The man placed in charge of the CIA project was the grandson of Theodore Roosevelt and seventh cousin of Franklin Roosevelt, 37-year-old Kermit (Kim) Roosevelt. With half a dozen assistants, and in collusion with Fazollah Zahedi, a six-foot-two Iranian general suspected by the British of wartime collaboration with the Nazis, Kim Roosevelt set up operations from a basement office in Teheran. Also on the team was H. Norman Schwarzkopf, who had helped solve the Lindbergh kidnapping in 1932, and had trained a police force for the Shah in the 1940s. He too was close to Zahedi and, according to Andrew Tully, a semiofficial chronicler of CIA history, "supervised the careful spending of more than ten million of CIA dollars," as a result of which "Mossadegh suddenly lost a great many supporters."[46]

The plans went poorly at first. On August 13, 1953, the Shah issued a decree replacing Mossadegh with Zahedi, but the aging prime minister arrested the colonel who brought him the notice and refused to budge. Masses of people sympathetic to Mossadegh and Tudeh took to the streets, and the 33-year-old Shah and his queen, Soraya, fled to Baghdad, then Rome. A few days later, however, Kim Roosevelt's CIA dollars began to work their magic. Countermobs took to the streets, beat up pro-Mossadegh demonstrators, and paved the way for Zahedi to be installed. Summarizing events later, the director of the U.S. Military Assistance Mission, Major General George C. Stewart, stated that the coup was "about to collapse" when the United States began supplying the Iranian army "on an emergency basis – blankets, boots, uniforms, electric generators, and medical supplies that permitted and created an atmosphere in which they could support the Shah. . . . The guns they had in their hands, the trucks that they rode in, the armored cars that they drove through the streets, and the radio communications that permitted their control, were all furnished through the military defense assistance program." He concluded that "had it not been for this program a government unfriendly to the United States would now be in power."[47]

Mossadegh was jailed, the oil properties were denationalized, and five years later, American corporations reaped the harvest. They had previously owned no share of Iranian oil; now the British monopoly was superseded by a consortium in which Anglo–Iranian received 40 percent, Royal Dutch Shell and a French firm, 20 percent, and five American companies – Gulf, Standard of New Jersey (now Exxon), Standard of California, Texas, and Socony–Mobil– the remaining 40 percent. It is impossible not to conclude that oil – rather than communism – had been the issue all along, and that Mossadegh, by refusing to call on the communists when his back was to the wall, probably contributed to his own undoing.

* * * * * * *

It would be wrong to say that our government did not want reform or that it failed to urge it on clients and allies. Chiang Kai-shek in China was repeatedly urged to make concessions to the lowly peasant. As early as 1944, General Joseph Stillwell argued that Chiang's Kuomintang "must be torn to pieces."[48] Thereafter Vice President Henry A. Wallace, Pat Hurley, Donald Nelson, and General George Marshall, all made the pilgrimage to China in a frustrating effort to instill a spirit of social idealism in Chiang's regime. Similar efforts were made with Syngman Rhee in Korea, Ngo Dinh Diem in Vietnam, and others. But when it came to a choice between revolutionaries and old friends with ties to U.S. business, or between nationalist movements and allies such as France or Britain, our government sided with the local conservatives and foreign colonialists. It would have been impolitic to form military alliances with Britain or France, such as the North Atlantic Treaty,and oppose those powers when they deployed half a million troops against the nationalists in Algeria; or 50,000 soldiers, police, and home guards against a ragged group of Mau Mau in Kenya. Nor was it possible to achieve the world order and stability needed for economic expansion by American business and at the same time support neutralist Mohammed Mossadegh in Iran as he ousted and exiled the pro-western Shah. Benign imperialism, it seems, foundered on many shoals.

In laying plans for the future, our administrations from Harry Truman on failed to put the "revolution of rising expectations" in historical perspective—just as they misjudged the role of the Bomb. They tended to brush it aside, pigeonhole it, deal with it on an ad hoc basis. But as Fleming observes, there was a "peasant revolution in the womb of history" at the end of the war.[49] Six dozen nations with more than half the world's population were in the process of shedding colonial and semicolonial status to become nationally independent, and some were going further, toward socialist and communist systems. In point of numbers, this was by far the largest social upheaval in all history. But Soviet communism was not its midwife. It sprang from other causes and as part of a much older historical process.

The revolution "in the womb of history" after 1944 was in fact the fourth phase of a revolutionary cycle that originated in the Netherlands almost 400 years earlier, in 1573. It was hardly something new or—for anyone with a sense of history—unexpected. The first phase of this revolutionary cycle included the capitalist revolutions of Britain (and the American Revolution, which, in the sense that it paved the way for a capitalist economy, was a completion of the British revolutions), the one in France, the unification in Germany and Italy, and the peaceful transformations of Denmark and Japan (during the Meiji Restoration). The cycle can be traced back even further, to the unsuccessful peasant revolts in France (1358), England (1381), Germany (1522), and Spain, Italy, Austria, and parts of Scandinavia at other times. The most important popular goal in all these upheavals was to abolish (or complete the abolition of) feudal or tribal land tenure—goals not much different from those in the Third World today.

The second phase of the revolutionary cycle—a most interesting one—was the *inverted* revolution that took place in many parts of the world during the nineteenth century. Nations that had already made their own capitalist revolutions—Britain and France, for example—suppressed similar revolutions in India, China, Egypt, and many other places, reducing them to colonial or semicolonial status. This was the central design of what became known as imperialism. Taking advantage of the disintegration of the Ottoman, Manchu, Mogul, and Spanish empires, Britain, France, and the others encouraged nationalists to rebel against those empires, then suppressed the rebel forces as they tried to implement land reform and establish democratic capitalist societies.

The suppression of the Taiping Rebellion in China by Britain and other Western states reveals the strange Dr. Jekyll–Mr. Hyde role imperialist states played during the second phase of the revolutionary cycle. In the backlash of the humiliating Opium War, the Manchus were exposed to what the *Times* of London, a hundred years later, called "the World's Greatest Civil War."[50] From 1848 to 1864, the Taipings, led by a schoolteacher, Hung Hsiu-ch'uan, attacked in sixteen of the eighteen provinces of China and held Nanking for more than a decade. Influenced by Christian missionaries, the rebels called Hung "the Heavenly Prince, younger brother of Jesus Christ." In the spirit of "peace" they promised land to the landless and made bonfires of the title deeds of landlords and the promissory notes of moneylenders. The effect on history, had the Taipings succeeded, would have been as significant for the East as the French Revolution had been for the West. In a wily game of divide and rule, however, the Westerners, led by Britain, at first aided the rebels, then turned on them. In 1856, with the dynasty severely weakened, a minor incident—the arrest of a Chinese crew on a British-registered ship—was used as the pretext for a new war against the Manchus. By 1858 the Manchus had been subdued, forced to pay a large indemnity, and expand Western prerogatives in China. But, having suppressed the dynasty, Britain made a volte-face. Major Charles George Gordon, abetted by French and American advisers, attacked the Taipings. A hundred thousand people were killed during three July days in 1864 when Nanking was recaptured for the dynasty. Hundreds of thousands more fled as the city of 500,000 was reduced to 500. All told, the sixteen-year revolution cost millions of lives, by some estimates as many as 15 to 20 million.[51] But a revolution had been suppressed so that the Western states could strengthen their hold—economically and politically—over an ancient kingdom.

The third stage of the revolutionary cycle to which the present wave of revolutions is related began in 1910 with an uprising in Mexico, followed in 1911 by Sun Yat-sen's revolt in China, and finally by the two Russian revolutions of 1917—in March and November. In these upheavals too, the adversary was an old feudal class, usually with links to foreign nations, and the major goals were land reform and democratic rights. True, the early capitalist revolutions displayed few trends toward socialism—though there were men with socialist beliefs involved in almost all of them, for instance, Babeuf in the French Revolution. By the twentieth century, however, nationalism included sizable contingents of populists and socialists, tending to move these revolutions to the Left. The Mexican revolution of 1910, for instance, began as a crusade by the middle classes to win democracy from the 34-year-old dictatorship of Porfirio Diaz. The scope of the revolution expanded, however, as peasants, led by Emiliano Zapata, demanded more radical concessions: "land and liberty." Its momentum was checked, however, as Zapata was defeated, one conservative *caudillo* after another took the reins of government, and the United States applied not only diplomatic pressure to guarantee American oil holdings but, on one occasion, actually seized the port of Vera Cruz by force of arms. The same sort of scenario unfolded in China, where the rebels, led by the physician Sun Yat-sen, quickly disposed of the decadent Manchu Dynasty but were unable to spread the revolution nationwide, evict the foreigners, and abolish feudal land tenure—objectives achieved only thirty-eight years later, in 1949.

The Russian Revolution differed from its two predecessors—those of China and Mexico—only in that it succeeded within a span of eight months to make both a capitalist revolution and a socialist revolution. The first uprising forced the Czar to abdicate in favor of a provisional government broadly dedicated to liberal capitalism. The second one resulted in the ousting of the liberals—primarily because they had been unwilling to deal with the problems of "peace, bread, land"—and the installation of the communist regime. The difference between the Mexican, Chinese, and Russian Revolutions is measured by how quickly (or slowly) each moved along a linear scale from feudalism (and foreign domination) to capitalism and to socialism.

But they had an objective in common: to destroy feudal or semi-feudal social structures and abolish foreign control.

The impulse for the fourth phase of the revolutionary cycle – the present one – differs only in a few respects from that of the other three phases. At its core is the insistent demand of the peasant for a piece of land – land owned by landlords, tribes, or foreigners; the quest of middle classes for democracy and economic opportunity; and, in recent decades, the equally resolute aspiration of city workers for economic security. All these have blended into "an idea whose time has come" – the "revolution in the womb of history" that Fleming refers to. What distinguishes it, in addition to its vastness, is that it seems to have passed the point of no return. The American Right may rail that the new revolutionary societies are not solving the problems of their people – which is true to some extent, just as it was true of the American Revolution in the five "critical years" after 1783. But there is virtually no likelihood the revolution can be terminated – regardless of what steps the United States, the Soviet Union, or any other nation takes. It is a fact of life that we must accept and accommodate to. Early in the postwar period, the Soviet Union was prepared to mute talk of class struggle and revolution in return for material aid for reconstruction. But even if it *had* arrayed itself against the developing revolution, it would not have stopped it. The "revolution in the womb of history" would nonetheless have been reborn – for the fourth time. It might have aborted in some places and been slightly less radical in others, but it would have occurred nonetheless.

It is not likely, for instance, that the Chinese revolution, led by Mao Tse-tung and encompassing one-fourth of the world's population, could have been sidetracked. Whatever aid the Soviet Union gave Mao at the end of the war was insignificant compared to the sums given his anticommunist rival, Chiang Kai-shek, by the United States – $3 billion, plus weapons from a million disarmed Japanese soldiers and a considerable amount of logistic support. But the poor – in and out of the armed forces – came over to communism in droves. Of the four million men in Chiang's army, 1,690,000 defected or were lost from July 1946 to November 1947 alone – their equipment falling to communist hands. Dean Acheson, in an appraisal of the Kuomintang defeat, attributed it to the fact "that the almost inexhaustible patience of the Chinese people in their misery ended. They did not bother to overthrow this government. There was really nothing to overthrow. They simply ignored it throughout the country."[52] Chiang had "overwhelming military power" Acheson said, and the communists were "ill-equipped, ragged, a very small military force"—yet they won. Foster Hailey, a former *New York Times* correspondent, makes the same appraisal in his book, *Half of One World.* The communists came to power, he writes, because they "put their hopes in the political activation of the illiterate peasant and the underprivileged worker by promising him a change. Chiang put his hopes in a military campaign, financed by the United States, that would maintain the status quo. It was inevitable that in the long run the communists would win."[53]

Other revolutions in the postwar period also succeeded with little or no outside aid—in Yugoslavia, Algeria, Cuba, for instance. Some revolutions occurred because imperial powers no longer had the resources to police them—for instance, in India and throughout the British and French empires. London and Paris had no choice but to walk away from most of their holdings. Elsewhere—Eastern Europe and North Korea—a new social order was introduced synthetically, by Soviet occupation forces. (That too is nothing new; Napoleon tried to do the same thing in Europe at the beginning of the nineteenth century, but was less successful than Stalin.) For the most part, however, change came about because hundreds of millions of people were demanding independence and viability and were prepared to fight for it.

Our establishment grossly misjudged the irrepressible nature of the postwar revolution. It dealt with it, therefore, much as imperial powers had done in the past, relying primarily on military force supplemented by what amounted to economic bribes to puppets who "kept order." Again, as on the military front, we pursued yesterday's strategy, evidently unaware—or unconcerned—that history had given birth to a qualitatively different set of circumstances.

THE IRREPRESSIBLE REVOLUTION 5

If revolution has become, by whatever course, the enemy against which our foreign policy is directed, we face three choices for the future. The first is to continue as at present in the hopes that somehow the momentum of social upheaval will spend itself and its alleged sponsor, the Soviet Union, will be weakened, by its own economic ineptitude or our pressures, to the point where it is immobilized. The second alternative is to adopt a program more adventurous than the present one and place American armed forces in half a dozen trouble areas—such as the Middle East, Pakistan, and Central America—and announce that we will use small nuclear weapons wherever the status quo is challenged. The third alternative would be to reverse direction, coexist with the Soviets, and adopt a policy of support for revolutionaries who express the popular will of their people.

Theoretically, we can continue the current containment policy, in the hopes that there will be no more Vietnams or Irans and that perhaps some of these spheres of influence may, with luck, return to the Western fold. But that is taking a narrow view of our predicament. The national and social revolutions that have erupted since 1944 are not accidental or ephemeral. They are linked to a rearrangement of the past such as humankind has never seen before. Except episodically, they are not likely to reverse course.

Since the onset of World War II, our small planet has been engaged in the most far-reaching revolution in all history—a triple revolution, as some have called it, that is technological, military, and social. In each area, the changes taking place are proceeding by geometric progression. Physicist William C. Davidon, formerly with Argonne Laboratories, offers the following guide for measuring the revolution in technology: Burn a teaspoonful of wood, he says, and it provides enough energy to boil one tablespoonful of water; explode a teaspoonful of dynamite and it provides enough energy to boil three tablespoonsful of water; but fission a teaspoonful of uranium-235 and it provides enough energy to boil a million gallons of water.[1]

A similar scale of change is taking place in military science. The largest bomb used in World War II, prior to the Hiroshima bomb, was the "blockbuster"—about ten tons of TNT. The atom (fission) bomb that destroyed Hiroshima was 1,300 times more powerful—a 13-kiloton bomb equivalent to 13,000 tons of TNT—and the hydrogen (fusion) bombs that came on the assembly lines a few years later were hundreds or thousands of times more powerful than atom bombs. A one-megaton bomb (one million tons of TNT equivalent) has almost 80 times the firepower of the Hiroshima bomb; a 20-megaton bomb is 1,500 times as powerful. The kill-capability in weaponry has escalated apace. World War I took a toll of 9.8 million lives; World War II, 52 million lives; but the nuclear stockpiles of either the United States or the Soviet Union can kill billions of people, perhaps everyone on earth.

The third element of the threefold revolution—the national and social upheaval—is the least understood but the most important one. When the American Revolution began in 1776, we were a nation of three million people, 600,000 of whom were black slaves outside the political mainstream. Yet this small revolution had a tinderbox effect on Western Europe. It further undermined the ancient concept of the "divine rights of kings" and implanted in western politics what was then considered a subversive concept: "government by consent of the governed"—democracy. It inspired revolutionaries in many places—including those in France, who in 1789 made the decisive capitalist revolution that sealed the fate of the old feudal system.

Something similar is going on today, but in a shorter time span and over a larger area. Scores of countries, the denizens of which constitute half or more the world's population, have been engaged in a political and social upheaval, seeking national independence or national independence and socialism. If this tidal wave has had any distinguishing characteristic it is that it is *irrepressible*. It tapers off in one place only to burst out in another, or it is suppressed in a particular country only to explode again years or decades later. Sometimes it just simmers for a long time, then "suddenly" boils over. The ongoing or repetitive character of the present spate of revolutions has been apparent from as early as 1944 when the Malagassy people sought independence for their native Madagascar. Britain had occupied this island in the Indian Ocean at the beginning of the war to prevent it from falling into the hands of the Nazis or the Nazi-controlled French government at Vichy. But in 1943, by agreement with General Charles de Gaulle, Free French troops replaced the British, whereupon the Malagassy nationalists demanded self-government – in accord with the promises made by Roosevelt and Churchill in the Atlantic Charter. Instead, de Gaulle offered them a transparent plan that would continue ancient domination: Madagascar would become part of the so-called French union, with the four million Malagassy entitled to three elected members of the French parliament. (The 50,000 French colonists were to be given a similar number.) They would have no independent parliament of their own. When the native delegates arrived in Paris, instead of taking their seats, they denounced the plan as a sham. Tempers flared, incidents occurred, and when the clouds had lifted, the three members of parliament were in jail, sentenced to death – later commuted to life imprisonment in the Comores Islands. The rebellion, however, refused to die. By 1947/48, a full-scale armed revolt was under way in which 11,000 to 80,000 Malagassy people were killed by the French (the nationalist council claimed 220,000). But by 1956, after the emergence of a native Social Democratic Party and a spurt in political activity, the Malagassy Republic became an autonomous country within the French Community and by 1960 was granted full independence. It was simply too costly for France to subdue the local revolutionaries.

Similar outbursts occurred in Algeria, Tunisia, and Morocco – for the same reasons and with the same results. The native peoples demanded independence; de Gaulle, with the assent of Churchill and the less-vocal assent of our government, answered with machine-gun fire. Seven thousand died in Tunisia, where the intervention of an

American consul, Hooker Doolittle, prevented a much worse blood bath, and between 10,000 and 45,000 Moslems were killed in Algeria. Tunisia and Morocco became free in 1956, but the National Liberation Front (FLN) of Algeria had to wage a seven-and-a-half-year guerrilla war, beginning in 1954, to liberate its country. In all three instances, a revolution that seemed to be in limbo succeeded the second time around—in Algeria at a heavy price.

In this first decade after the war, all the empires, except the American and Russian, were falling apart, and revolutionary forces were organizing to step into the breach. Our leaders in Washington were faced with a dilemma. President Roosevelt had promised to liquidate the old imperial system. His bias against British-style colonialism was so evident that Winston Churchill chided him, as already noted, for "trying to do away with the British empire."[2] Roosevelt had a similar reaction to the French empire, as indicated by his comments on French rule in Vietnam. But after the war, the industrial countries of Western Europe became the centerpiece of our government's blueprint for reorganizing the world. Without a stable Western Europe there could be no Pax Americana and no expansion of American trade and investment on the order needed for a robust U.S. economy. Given that situation, it was impolitic to challenge Britain, France, et al., as they strove to save their empires.

Our grudging support for these powers, however, was not an adequate dike against burgeoning revolutionary movements. Almost immediately after Japan surrendered in 1945, there was a wave of strikes and demonstrations in India, and a little later, stoppages by 5,000 naval workers and revolts in the army and air force. *Time* magazine bleakly predicted a historic blow-up because Britain was no longer able to police its colonies. London finally granted independence to India in 1947, after first carving out a Moslem country, Pakistan, as a rival state. Burma and Ceylon won their freedom at approximately the same time. With its reserves seriously depleted, Britain was no longer able to manage its empire—certainly not in far away India.

The pearl of the Dutch empire, the Dutch East Indies—Indonesia—also took advantage of the enervated state of the mother country, though its tie was severed with considerably more bloodshed. During the war, a dogged resistance movement conducted small revolts against Japanese occupation forces on five occasions. After Japan surrendered, Achmed Sukarno and Mohammed Hatta issued a ring-ing declaration of independence, phrased much like the American Declaration of Independence. But British troops soon arrived from India, and the Dutch sent back Dr. Hubertus J. van Mook to act as governor general. Captured Japanese soldiers and the *Kempeitai*, Japan's Gestapo, were enlisted to keep order. The American contribution was to supply guns and equipment to the Netherlands; when the Indonesian rebels protested that military vehicles operated by the Dutch carried American markings, Washington ordered the Dutch to remove the labels—not the vehicles. The United States was not sympathetic to Dutch colonialism but, caught in a quandry between supporting a new nationalism or an old ally, it took the line of least resistance.

A compromise arrangement was worked out between the parties in 1946, but by 1947, when the Dutch military force had grown to 110,000 soldiers, a "police action" was initiated to wipe out the nationalists. Friction mounted until December 1948, when Dutch parachutists descended on Jakarta, arrested Sukarno, Hatta, and other leaders, and virtually restored Indonesia to colonial status. On this occasion the United States sided openly with the rebels, approving a U.N. Security Council resolution that called on the Dutch to release the republican leaders and come to terms. But Holland would have had to leave anyway; in surveying the situation it found itself in an impossible position. It held the major cities in its hands, but the villages where most of the people lived were controlled by the nationalists. The "mother country" faced the prospect not only of alienating world opinion but of engaging in an endless guerrilla war for *merdeka*—independence—that would ultimately lead to Dutch bankruptcy. It decided to cut its losses and submit to the inevitable. In August 1950, after four and a half years of slaughter, in which 100,000 people had died and tens of millions in property had been destroyed, Indonesia was finally granted independence.[3]

While the Dutch were being forced out of their lucrative East Indies and the British out of the linchpin of their empire, India, the French were taking a stiffer attitude toward Indochina. During the war, two nationalist groups had emerged, the Viet Minh (national front) League, led by Ho Chi-minh, a communist, and the Dong Minh Hoi, friendly to the Kuomintang in China. When Japan seized Indochina toward the end of the war, she was challenged by a guerrilla army of 10,000 men determined to smash both "French imperialism and Japanese Fascism." Of the two nationalist groups, the

Viet Minh emerged the more forceful; it liberated six northern provinces and established a broad national government that won the endorsement even of Chiang Kai-shek in China.

France itself recognized Ho's regime in March 1946, but insisted on retaining control over the army, foreign affairs, currency, and the economy, as well as carving out a separate administration for the southern part of Vietnam. This formula for a "free state within the French Union" was rejected by Ho, making a confrontation inevitable. On November 23, 1946, the French cruiser *Suffern* fired on the Vietnamese section of the port city of Haiphong, killing 6,000 people. France seized all of Indochina, just as Holland had done in Indonesia, but was met by a fierce band of guerrillas under General Vo Nguyen Giap. For the next eight years, 70,000 Viet Minh tied down 166,000 soldiers of the French army and cost France $7 billion in cash, 71,500 dead, and 106,000 wounded. In May 1954, the flower of the French army was surrounded and humiliated into surrender at Dien BienPhu. Two months later, the French government negotiated a settlement with Chou En-lai, China's foreign minister, providing for a truce, the division of Vietnam into two temporary segments, and the holding of elections two years later to form a single administration for the whole country.[4]

By this time, of course, Mao's guerrillas had won their war against the American-supported Kuomintang in China, so that by the mid-1950s colonial rule had been expelled from virtually all of Asia. In some of the newly liberated countries, revolutionaries were experimenting with communism, as in China, North Korea, and North Vietnam, and in some with moderate forms of socialism, as in India, Burma, and (temporarily) Indonesia.

Meanwhile, the revolutionary wave was also battering the enervated imperial powers in Africa. In 1951/52, a group of young officers, led by 33-year-old Gamal Abdel Nasser, organized commando attacks against the British who had occupied their country since 1882, and succeeded in driving out their puppet, King Farouk. The British were forced to relinquish their immense military base on the west bank of the Suez — sixty-five miles long and three miles wide — and evacuate the country. In 1956, Nasser went one step further by nationalizing the Suez Canal, long owned and operated by Anglo-French interests.[5]

The following year, hundreds of miles south, Kwame Nkrumah established the first liberated republic in Black Africa. After a decade of riots and protests in which many people were killed, the former schoolteacher was able to wrest independence for his homeland, the Gold Coast, and tenuously weld its fifty-two tribes into a new nation, Ghana. Across the continent, in Kenya, still another guerrilla war against the British raged for six years—the so-called Mau Mau war. Before it was over, the rebels had killed 32 whites, and 1,812 Africans, while losing 10,534 of their own troops and 78,000 wounded. But by 1963, four years after the uprising ended. Jomo Kenyatta, who had been in prison throughout the violence, became the official leader of still another new nation.[6]

In the backwash of so many violent revolutions, the old imperial powers—Britain, France, Holland, and Belgium—granted independence to dozens of other countries either before the uprisings could jell or after brief skirmishes, as in the Belgian Congo (Zaire).

The irrepressible upheaval after World War II was not confined to the old world; there were manifestations of it in the Western Hemisphere as well, though they were usually stillborn. The laboring class, for the first time, gained major status in Argentina, where Juan Peron—for his own purposes—forged a powerful union movement as his base of political power. Peron, no democrat or revolutionary, promulgated a welfare program more extensive than that in the United States—free medical care, vacations of ten to thirty days a year, pensions at age sixty. In the rural areas, landlords were required to provide showers for their laborers and pay minimum wages. The previous union movement, led by socialists and anarchists, had numbered 300,000 adherents, but the new Confederation of Labor, which included agricultural workers, grew to five and a half million.

In 1944, as already noted, the dictator Jorge Ubico was ousted in Guatemala, and a social democrat, Arevalo, was elected in his place. A few years later, in 1952, revolution erupted in the small landlocked country of Bolivia. It was the closest thing to a " proletarian"revolution since Russia's in 1917, in the sense that the proletariat—rather than peasants or intellectuals—were its lightning rod. Victor Paz Estenssoro, a politician of the center, had been elected president while in exile, but was denied reentry to Bolivia by the army when he sought to take his post. A revolt by nationalist supporters of Paz was crushed and their leaders sought sanctuary in every foreign embassy available. At this point, however, the tin miners, commandeering company trucks and, armed with dynamite, descended on the capital and defeated the army. Three to four thousand died as the battle raged on the craggy hills of La Paz, but the generals were defeated — at least until the next round. An interesting feature of this revolution was the prominent role of a small group of Trotskyists, who provided ideological leadership for the movement and devised the plan for arming workers and peasants. Unlike typical palace revolutions in Latin America, this one brought about real — though temporary — changes. The tin mines, backbone of the economy, were nationalized. Indians, formerly prohibited even from walking the main streets of La Paz in native clothes, were given land belonging to the large landholders and armed with rifles. Fifty thousand workers were formed into a labor militia.[7]

Some of the enthusiasm for overthrowing dictatorial regimes spilled over from the old world to the new world after the war. A democracy of sorts was reestablished in Venezuela, and though it lasted only three years, after which General Marcos Perez Jimenez executed a coup with American assistance, reform-minded militarists ousted the dictator a decade later and installed something approximating a capitalist democracy under Romulo Betancourt. Even so, and despite Venezuela's wealth in oil (U.S. owned), conditions for the mass of people remained so poor that guerrilla warfare rocked the nation throughout the 1960s.

The assassination of a radical liberal leader, Jorge Eliecer Gaitan, in Bogota, Colombia while an Inter-American Conference was being held there in 1948 led to a bloody civil war in which 180,000 people died between 1949 and 1962. Civil war or guerrilla war flared at one time or another in Paraguay, Bolivia, Cuba, Ecuador, Argentina, Uruguay (city guerrillas), Chile, Guatemala, El Salvador, and Nicaragua. Revolutions in this hemisphere, however, did not often succeed because they were in the back yard of the United States, which had sufficient resources to suppress them or help rightist Latin American allies do so themselves.

Our government operated a School of the Americas in Panama, where 35,000 Latin American officers were trained at one time or another in the art of counterinsurgency, as well as schools in continental United States where 200,000 other Latin Americans received military training.[8] Military aid to the region increased from a mere $200,000 in 1952 to $11 million in 1953 and $92 million in 1961 — in order to improve "internal security capabilities," as Defense Secretary Robert S. McNamara put it.[9] The generals in one country after another invariably used the aid to establish or strengthen military dictatorships.

On March 30, 1963, Colonel Enrique Peralta overthrew the government of Guatemala because it was obvious that former president Arevalo, a moderate socialist, would easily defeat his rivals in the impending election. On April 1, 1964, General Humberto Castelo Branco executed a coup d'état against the elected government of Joao Goulart in Brazil because Goulart proposed to introduce land reform and establish normal relations with the Soviet Union. In June 1966, president Arturo Illia of Argentina was overthrown by a military clique headed by General Juan Carlos Ongania. With the help of the AFL–CIO leadership, the CIA subsidized strikes in Guyana that ultimately led to the ouster of Cheddi Jagan's leftist government and the installation of a more moderate one under Forbes Burnham.[10] Our arms and money also helped a military clique overthrow a left-wing socialist, Salvador Allende, in Chile. After secretly funding opponents of Allende in three elections prior to his 1970 victory, the CIA gave aid to the assassins of a democratic-minded army chief, Rene Schneider, and then helped General Augusto Pinochet install a harsh dictatorship and kill Allende in 1973.

The pattern of American intervention was sometimes bewildering. About the time of the 1961 Bay of Pigs fiasco in Cuba, the CIA supplied machine guns to conspirators in the Dominican Republic plotting to assassinate Rafael Trujillo, the rightist dictator who had ruled their land for thirty-two years. The State Department presumably had become disenchanted with Trujillo for overplaying his hand. After the assassination, with the encouragement of the Kennedy Administration, an honest election was held in that troubled country and a writer with democratic socialist leanings, Juan Bosch, assumed office on a program of agrarian reform and economic development. He didn't last long. Within months, Bosch was deposed by the Dominican generals for refusing to outlaw the Communist Party and failing to denationalize hundreds of millions of dollars of property that had once belonged to Trujillo. The coup was actively encouraged by the American labor attache in Santo Domingo as well as the American military mission.[11]

Two years later, on April 24, 1965, young officers led by Lieutenant Colonel Francisco Caamano Deno arrested their superiors and announced their intention to restore Bosch to the presidency. The next day, as police stations were invaded, guns distributed to 20,000 civilians, and gasoline handed out to those willing to make Molotov cocktails, the rightist government supported by the United States disintegrated. But four days later, President Johnson ordered the first contingent of 22,000 American troops onto the island, on the grounds that what began "as a popular democratic revolution" had been "taken over and really seized and placed into the hands of a band of communist conspirators."[12] The rebels were forced to yield. In an election held a year later during a period of terror, an associate of Trujillo's, Joaquin Balaguer, defeated Bosch, who justifiably feared for his life and left his home only sporadically during the campaign.

But despite many setbacks for the Left such as this, the Americas were not a subdued area by any means. Leftist uprisings usually failed, but a few did succeed – in Cuba and Nicargua, for instance – and there were always others in the process of gestation.

* * * * * * *

Faced with an expansive revolution, the American establishment has by no means been monolithic on how to deal with it. Not a few of its leading figures recognized that we were living in a turbulent period requiring a new approach both to military power and toward other countries. As noted earlier, even before the first nuclear bomb was produced, Secretary of War Henry L. Stimson told an elite "Interim Committee" that the atom bomb must be considered not only as a new weapon, "but as a revolutionary change in the relations of man and the universe."[13] After the Bomb was dropped, he urged an "atomic partnership" with the Soviet Union to avoid a "desperate" arms race, and pleaded with Truman that "the only way you can make a man trustworthy is to trust him. . . ."[14]

General Dwight D. Eisenhower opposed the use of the Bomb on Hiroshima, as did large numbers of scientists who had produced the weapon. All nine top scientists on the General Advisory Committee of the Atomic Energy Committee wrote a report in 1949 opposing development of the hydrogen bomb.

There was also dissent from the policy of containing revolutions. A Win-the-Peace conference in 1946, sponsored by two liberal groups, opposed loans to Britain "until sufficient guarantees have been made that these materials and funds will not be used for the exploitation and oppression of the colonial people."[15] This conference, chaired by Paul Robeson, was infiltrated with communists, but there were many respected noncommunists as well, such as former Secretary of the Interior Harold Ickes, who was the chairman of one of the sponsoring organizations, and two other former members of Roosevelt's cabinet, Henry Morgenthau, Jr., and Henry A. Wallace. When the Truman Doctrine was proclaimed a year later it was denounced by many of these people as an "invitation to war."

Like the French with the Maginot Line, however, the core of American decisionmakers decided on a foreign policy that mimicked the past — reliance on military force, suppression of revolution. To implement that policy, they soon found they needed a host of new governmental institutions and a new approach to their constituents, the American public. Thus was born what has been called the National Security State. New agencies were incorporated into government — and other greatly strengthened — that *predisposed* Washington in an antirevolutionary and militarist direction. The National Security State virtually froze the American government into a particular stance and deprived it of flexibility. It also severely constricted the countervailing power of the American public, making it far more difficult for that public to correct the course of its officialdom.

At the heart of the National Security State, of course, was the military machine. After previous wars, the military had always been reduced to a skeleton, but this time — despite the atom bomb, which presumably should have awed any adversary and therefore made traditional armies redundant — the armed forces were reorganized under a unified command, with millions of troops, hundreds of billions in land holdings, munitions, and property, and thousands of public relations personnel (2,700 as of 1950, according to Senator Homer Ferguson)[16] to spread its philosophy. The number of troops retained after the Spanish–American War had been 53,000; on the eve of World War II we had only 139,000 men under arms, but as of 1969 the Pentagon had at its disposal 3.5 million (today about 2 million) and was ensconced in 470 major bases and installations as well as 5,000 lesser ones at home and 429 major bases and 2,972 minor ones overseas.[17] It was a formidable force, with far greater weight in the councils of government than it had ever before enjoyed.

At the hub of the new institutional arrangement was the National Security Council (NSC), the most wide-ranging command structure in American history, charged under the National Security Act of

1947 with coordinating "domestic, foreign, and military policies." Covert, secretive, and removed from popular controls, NSC formulated long-term policy and sanctioned, as Senator Frank Church's committee reported in 1976, literally thousands of covert undertakings around the world—for example, a coup d'état in Brazil, the financing of friendly political parties in Italy, disruption of a union in France—carried out by its subordinate body, the CIA.[18] In effect, the NSC was a second government, a dual state, not subject to the checks and balances inherent in the U.S. Constitution. "Since the Council meets without publicity," Blair Bolles observed, "the American people cannot challenge its thinking directly."[19]

A third feature, made necessary by the fact that the CIA and sister agencies were engaged in covert action that violated existing treaties as well as domestic and foreign laws, was the institution of a blanket of secrecy on many government documents and activities. Under the McMahon–Douglas Atomic Energy Act of 1946 it became a crime punishable by prison, and in some cases death, to disseminate "restricted data" concerning atomic energy—the first such law ever in peacetime. Presidential executive orders by Truman and Eisenhower permitted—in fact instructed—agencies of government to withhold information vitally necessary for an informed electorate. Scores of millions of documents in due course were designated "classified," "secret," "top secret," and closed off to public review. "Secrecy," noted a Library of Congress report prepared for the Senate Foreign Relations Committee in December 1971, "has been a factor in making foreign policy since the first days of the nation's history. . . . It is only in the period since the Second World War, however, that the problem of classified information has grown to its present dimensions."[20]

A fourth feature of the National Security State tended to block off domestic opposition to the strategy of containment. At the outset of the postwar period, when pacifist and isolationist moods seemed to be setting in, the Republican leader of the Senate, Arthur Vandenberg, argued—as previously noted—that it was necessary to "scare the hell out of the country."[21] The Atomic Energy Act of 1946 required a rigorous screening of employees for "character, associations and loyalty." A year later, President Truman invoked a loyalty program for *all* people in the federal employ. In the first five years, the FBI, according to its director, J. Edgar Hoover, investigated and processed four million applications for government jobs.

People considered suspect were either denied positions or fired from existing ones.

The Attorney General of the United States, Francis Biddle, prepared a list of 200 "subversive" organizations, many defunct, as a guide for checking the loyalty of federal employees. When the House Committee on Un-American Activities (HUAC) made that list public, it became a blacklisters' "bible" for ferreting out alleged subversives in private occupations as well. Soon, there was a cascade of measures to check loyalty everywhere, and a corresponding fear on the part of liberals and radicals that some off-hand remark might be interpreted as an apology for communism. A Magnuson Act was passed providing that merchant seamen and specified longshoremen be cleared for "security." State and local governments took over where the federal government left off: hundreds of thousands of teachers, professors, and other employees were required to sign loyalty oaths attesting that they were not communists or "subversives." Under the Taft–Hartley law, union officials were obliged to execute noncommunist affidavits or lose the right to represent their union before the National Labor Relations Board.

Applications for passports were screened, and leftists were denied the right to travel. HUAC, the Senate Internal Security Subcommittee, and later Joseph McCarthy's Government Operations Committee used their facilities as a means of punishing dissidents. Hiding behind congressional immunity, these committees publicly stigmatized alleged "subversives" and in hundreds of instances caused them to be discharged. In addition, of course, such committees functioned as blacklisting institutions. HUAC admitted in 1948 that it had compiled dossiers on 300,000 individuals; a year later the figure was a million, little of it kept secret.[22] The committee furnished derogatory information concerning 60,000 individuals and 12,000 organizations to inquiring employers.

The result of all this was that a mood of quiescence and conformity spread across the nation—one that was altered only after the civil rights and antiwar protests of the 1950s and 1960s began, by which time, our foreign policy was fully hardened. Before someone joined anything as innocent as the American Civil Liberties Union or the National Association for the Advancement of Colored People he might ask himself whether it was on the proscribed list and whether such membership might someday surface to reduce his chance for job advancement. Additionally it muted opposition to the State Department's foreign policy; anyone publicly defending Arbenz or Mossadegh might be termed politically suspect, with all the attendant consequences.

Thus, with the partial curbing of dissent, a circle was squared: an undemocratic foreign policy antithetical to the traditions of self-determination proclaimed by our forebears was supplemented by institutions that aborted democratic expression. That, too, could only predispose government officials to be diffident about supporting radicals in foreign countries—even if they were noncommunist—since the anticommunist hysteria at home made little distinction between rival forms of Leftism.

In its totality, the National Security State became the operative agency for an imperial policy—and an imperial presidency—that acted in thousands of instances without either the advice or consent of Congress, and more often than not, without its knowledge. The National Security Agency, which breaks codes and monitors foreign communications, for instance, was established by executive order, without a vote of Congress, even though its expenditures—kept secret—have run into billions of dollars. "Within the branches of government," observed Robert Borosage, "a realignment of power took place. The executive pre-empted many of the legislative functions. In the area of national security, the executive became sovereign; the legislature, except for its powerful committee heads, who are satraps of the security bureaucracies, was rendered impotent."[23] The executive, by way of example, entered into treaties—called "contingency agreements"—with forty-two nations without seeking the approval of the Senate, as required by the Constitution. The presidency, in addition, took unto itself the right to make war without congressional sanction, as required under Article 1 Section 8. When Truman sent troops to Korea in 1950, Secretary of State Acheson argued that the president's "authority may not be interfered with by the Congress. . . . "[24] The war in Vietnam, too, was prosecuted under presidential authority, with the Justice Department claiming that the Tonkin Gulf Resolution, authorizing retaliation for an alleged act of agression by North Vietnam, was the "functional equivalent" of a declaration of war.

The National Security State, reversing George Washington's policy of "no entangling alliances," entered into nine security agreements from 1947 to 1955—with twenty Latin American nations in 1947 (the Rio Pact), with fourteen Western European countries and Canada in 1949 (the North Atlantic Pact), with Japan in 1951, with the Philippines the same year, with Australia and New Zealand (the ANZUS Pact) also in 1951, with South Korea in 1953, with Spain in 1953, with "Nationalist China" in 1954, and with seven other nations for the defense of Southeast Asia (SEATO) also in 1954. All the treaties included language to the effect that an attack on one would be considered an attack on all, requiring each to come to the aid of the others, and virtually all underscored America's commitment to help allied governments against native revolutionaries. The security treaty with Japan, for instance, provided for the United States, if so requested, to use its army "to put down large-scale riots and distrubances, caused through instigation or intervention by an outside power or powers."[25]

As of 1964, the United States was supplying weapons to sixty-nine nations, half the sovereign states in the world, and training most of their armies. Since then, the figure has been cut, but is still significant. "Military assistance," Defense Secretary McNamara told the Foreign Relations Committee in 1966, "provides essential arms, training, and related support to five million men in allied and other friendly forces. ... "[26] In effect, as political analyst Amaury de Riencourt has observed, we assumed a "protectorate" over dozens of nations, on behalf of whose governments we could intervene from thousands of bases and installations overseas.[27]

The scenario envisioned for imperial control runs something like this: The United States gives military and logistical support to a friendly government to help it stay in power. If that is enough to defeat potential or actual rebels, as in Europe or in Iran during most of the Shah's reign, the matter ends there; if it isn't, as in Vietnam or the Dominican Republic, we send in our own forces—sometimes called "advisors," such as the 22,000 "advisors" sent to Vietnam by Kennedy—and if that too fails to hold off the insurgents, we ourselves take over the major share of the fighting. A Pentagon lecturer at one of its national security seminars listed four "U.S. options in insurgency situations," which accurately reflect what our government has been doing:

1. Military advice and assistance to the country's military establishment.

2. Training by American officers and enlisted men.
3. Adequate and suitable material for this kind of war.
4. If necessary, direct support by U.S. forces of combat missions launched by government troops, and *unilateral U.S. operations against the insurgents.*" (Emphasis added.)[28]

This is obviously not the noninterventionism that we are committed to, but it is justified on the grounds that it is done in the name of "freedom." Dr. Herbert I. Schiller, editor of the *Quarterly Review of Economics and Business*, has noted in an article on "The Use of American Power in the Post-Colonial World," that "The association of the objectives of American expansionism with the concept of freedom, in which the former are obscurred and the latter is emphasized, has been a brilliant achievement in American policy. Rarely has the word 'freedom' produced so much confusion and obtained so much misdirected endorsement."[29]

* * * * * * *

The National Security State has commanded more resources and power than the world has ever seen in the past. It was inevitable that it would score many victories, particularly in the first quarter of a century after the war, when our economy was in a buoyant upward spiral. The vision of a Grand Area under U.S. control – the Western Hemisphere, the former British Empire, and the Far East – was fleshed out reasonably well. American investments abroad jumped by 2,000 percent from 1950 to 1980, from $11 billion to $213 billion, and exports jumped by nearly as much. Had it not been for American power, the revolutions beyond our border would have been more successful – certainly in Latin America – and many of them would have swung further toward one of the many forms of socialism or communism.

In the late 1940s and early 1950s, Americans talked about a "line" – a line beyond which we would not permit the Russians to "expand" – and seemed to be congratulating themselves that they had done well in containing the Soviet bear behind that line. John Fischer, editor of *Harper's* magazine, wrote in 1951 that "the Line of Containment has held, under great pressure, in Korea, Greece, Indochina, Turkey, Berlin and Yugoslavia."[30] Secretary of State John Foster Dulles pronounced his "massive retaliation" doctrine in January 1954, warning in effect that if the Soviet or Chinese communists strayed beyond that line they might have to contend with an atomic attack against their own territory. He pointedly cautioned the Chinese not to engage in "open aggression" in Vietnam or there would be "grave consequences which might not be confined to Indo-China."[31]

But despite the awesome might of the National Security State and the menacing rhetoric of containment, the line has not held as anticipated. It has been breached repeatedly and at opposite ends of the world – in China, Libya, Cuba, Indochina, Angola, Mozambique, Ethiopia, Afghanistan, Iran, and Nicaragua, not to mention the many countries, called "neutralist," that straddle the line. Initially, the impulse for this revolutionary wave was World War II, which gravely weakened all the leading powers except the United States. The subsequent impulses came from a variety of sources – the momentum of hundreds of millions of people in open defiance of the past; the inability of small imperial powers like Belgium, Spain, and Portugal to continue financing counterrevolutionary armies in such places as the Congo, Spanish Sahara, and Angola; and the continuing and worsening economic difficulties of the Third World. Most of all, there is now a worldwide constituency for revolution that while inspiring popular forces to form guerrilla movements or other types of resistance in the developing areas, also inspires people in the industrial states to vigorously oppose plans by their governments to intervene against such countries. Given this set of circumstances, the revolution, though sometimes held in abeyance or set back, has been irrepressible.

Cuba is an example of the tendency for revolutionary renewal. The Cuban people fought a desperate but futile "Ten Years War" from 1868 to 1878 to liberate themselves from Spain. Seventeen years later, they rose under the leadership of their "apostle," Jose Marti, only to be frustrated again as they neared victory when the United States joined the war against Spain and imposed what amounted to a protectorate over Cuba. For the next half a century, Washington made and unmade governments on the island to suit U.S. commercial interests – primarily in sugar. One of those who served with its blessings was Fulgencio Batista, an army sergeant who had engineered the "Sergeant's Revolt" in 1933, and another revolt in 1952 when it became obvious he could not win the presidential election that year.[32]

On July 26, 1953, however, Batista was challenged by a charismatic young lawyer, Fidel Castro, who led an assualt on the Moncada army barracks in Santiago in a futile effort to ignite a rebellion. Jailed, then amnestied, Castro reorganized his forces in Mexico and, in December 1956, landed back home surrepetitiously aboard an overcrowed 58-foot yacht with eighty-two men—only ten of whom reached the Sierra Maestre to carry on their revolution against Batista. Though never numbering more than 1,200, Castro's army defeated the American-trained Batistiano army of 43,000 men and rode to power on New Year's Day 1959.[33]

In another day, Washington would have had little trouble disposing of, or coopting, the young rebel. It had done so with others; it tried this time too. On the very day Batista was preparing to flee, U.S. ambassador E.T. Smith was still attempting to form a military junta to forestall Castro. Afterward, there were innumerable raids on Cuba by right-wing exiles from Miami and half a dozen attempts by our CIA to assassinate Castro, sometimes in collaboration with mafia gangsters.[34] Outright occupation of Cuba by American troops would have been risky. Hundreds of thousands of ordinary Cubans were doing guard duty every night to intercept counterrevolutionary or foreign forces. Unless we were prepared to contend with a guerrilla war for years to come, as in Algeria or Vietnam, intervention by our own troops was out of the question. This was not the kind of situation Washington had previously confronted in Latin America, where a few hundred or thousand Marines were enough to enforce North America's will, say in Nicargua, with minimal danger of a public outcry at home. But Castro had built up a sizable constituency in the United States itself. An editor of the *New York Times*, Herbert L. Matthews, had visited him in the mountains and publicized his cause when most people thought him dead. Public sympathy here in the United States for the bearded revolutionary was something that could not be brushed aside by the Eisenhower or Kennedy Administrations. Neither tried to send in the Marines; instead, they operated through the exiles.

Castro, like so many of today's revolutionary leaders, was not as vulnerable to the communist label as the State Department might have hoped. His guerrilla tactics did not fit the Stalinist or Trotskyist mold; indeed, after the attack on the Moncada army barracks, the Cuban Communist party labeled him a "putschist."[35] The CIA's judgment was that Castro was an independent leftist but not necessarily pro-Soviet. Deputy CIA Director General C.P. Cabell told the Senate Internal Security Committee in November 1959 that the

Agency's "information showed that the Cuban communists do not consider him a Communist Party member, or even a pro-communist. . . . The communists consider Castro as a representative of the bourgeoisie. . . . We believe that Castro is not a member of the Communist Party, and does not consider himself to be a communist."[36] After an interview with the Cuban leader during his first year in office, CIA's political action officer for Latin America, Frank Bender, concluded that "Castro is not only not a communist, he is a strong anti-communist fighter."[37] Moreover, there was little question that despite the flight of large numbers of Cubans to the United States, the man who ousted Batista had the support of a majority of his people. "All intelligence reports coming from allied sources," wrote CIA Inspector General Lyman Kirkpatrick after the ill-fated Bay of Pigs invasion, "indicated quite clearly that he was thoroughly in command of Cuba and was supported by most of the people who remained on the island."[38]

What is so striking about Washington's attitude toward Castro — and others in the same political stance — was that it made so little effort to win him to the American camp. The National Security State seemed to lack the disposition to compromise or coexist. Its approach was stiff necked and, in historical perspective, myopic. On taking the reins in Havana, Castro had requested a $4 million loan for road-building equipment and a $1 million barter exchange of Cuban chrome for American corn to meet a food shortage; both were turned down. A mission headed by Dr. Justo Carillo came to Washington in February 1959 and returned empty handed.[39] Washington was willing to provide military advisers but no economic aid and no support for land reform that would have gravely affected U.S. corporate holdings. Small planes, based in Florida and piloted by Cuban exiles, made repeated raids on Cuba's cities and sugarfields, but the State Department offered no apologies and the Justice Department took no steps to enforce the neutrality laws, which specifically forbade such acts.

In April 1959, Castro came to the United States to address a meeting of journalists. Eisenhower refused to see him. Secretary of State Christian Herter did, but only in a hotel room so as not to dignify the event as formal negotiations. Castro offered indemnity for American property similar to the arrangement Mexico had made after seizing American-owned oil fields a generation earlier. That was rejected.[40] Instead, President Eisenhower adopted the suggestion made by Vice President Richard Nixon — after a private meeting with Castro — to organize (and fund) a military invasion of the island by Cuban exiles based in Miami.

In an effort to prevent a revolution from succeeding in a small country of seven or eight million people, we drove a non-Soviet radical into the Soviet camp. Former Congressman Charles O. Porter of Oregon recalls when he introduced Castro to editors at the National Press Club during that visit:

> he said he wasn't a communist and would hold elections in the near future, and would abide by the charter of the OAS (Organization of American States) and welcome private investment. I believe he meant what he said but that when the multinational oil companies cut him off because he confiscated their refineries, just as he confiscated every other business which had been paying off Batista, Castro had no choice but to make a deal with the Soviet Union for oil from the Baku fields and accept the ideological tie-in. The Cuban economy without oil would have gone belly-up in three months.[41]

It is difficult to understand the Eisenhower–Kennedy bellicosity. They certainly knew the state of affairs in Cuba — one-third of the work force unemployed; a work year for three-quarters of the sugar workers of only three to four months (during the *zafra*, harvest, season); more than a third of the population totally illiterate and another third partially so; 90 percent of the people in rural areas suffering from worm diseases, such as dysentery, or from anemia; 91 percent of the rural homes without electricity; 98 percent without inside piping for water; and 97 percent without indoor toilets.[42] Unless they were more cold hearted than commonly believed, Eisenhower and Kennedy must have recognized these were legitimate grievances crying for resolution. Even from a business point of view, an understanding with Castro would have been mutually beneficial. The Cuban leader made an offer through an American writer on the eve of Kennedy's inauguration to pay for the seized sugar, oil, mines, and banking properties from the two or three cents a pound subsidy that we then paid for sugar imports.[43] Such an arrangement would have been beneficial to Castro because it would have allowed him to continue buying vital necessities from the United States and selling his sugar — 80 percent of the island's exports — to the United States. It would also have been beneficial to us. Our businesspeople would have been reimbursed for their property, and our trade would have continued. But the offer, relayed to Kennedy through U.N. Ambassador Adlai Stevenson, was rejected.

What worried the president was probably that if he showed "weakness" in dealing with Castro it would encourage other client states to seize American property. This sort of thinking soon would become known as the "domino theory," but if that theory was valid there was also a *reverse* domino theory. By opposing the Cuban revolution we forced its leadership to turn toward the Soviet Union—the only other place where help was available. And it paved the way for Cuba later to send troops to Angola, Ethiopia, and elsewhere to buttress revolutionary forces our government was opposing. It also paved the way for the 1962 October missile crisis, in which the two superpowers came closer to nuclear war than they ever were before or have been since.

* * * * * * *

There has existed since World War II a revolutionary impetus, a disposition by young people in yesterday's colonial areas to give up their lives, if necessary, to achieve social change. It is not exactly the automatic process envisioned in the domino theory; rather, it is a spreading confidence that "we can do it" because other young people have already succeeded on behalf of hundreds of millions of people in so many other places. There is also the feeling that "we are not alone," that there are now many countries to which to turn for economic and military help—not only the Soviet Union, but China, Cuba (which has helped the rebels of Angola, Ethiopia, and probably Nicaragua and El Salvador), Algeria (which gives aid to the Polisario forces fighting in the deserts of Northwest Africa), Mexico (which is often a haven for Latin American revolutionaries), and others. Added to all this is the self-assurance that came to would-be revolutionaries when the most formidable power on earth—the United States—was beaten by one of the least formidable—Vietnam.

All these factors combine to make the "revolution of rising expectations" irrepressible—in the same way that the capitalist revolution became irrepressible at a certain stage in its development, sometime between the late eighteenth and mid-nineteenth century. That is not to say that no national or social revolutions have been set back. They have been, of course, in such places as Malaya, Indonesia, Thailand, the Philippines, and in much of Latin America, to name only some. But there is everywhere a feeling that the play is not over; the evidence of Ethiopia, Nicaragua, Vietnam, Iran, Cuba, and Angola are firm indications that none of the rightist dictatorships can be deemed stable.

To illustrate: As of 1960, few Third World governments seemed more safely entrenched than that of Emperor Haile Selassie in Ethiopia. One of the few independent nations in Africa, with a heritage going back thousands of years, Ethiopia had been seized by Mussolini in 1936 but was recaptured in 1941 by Britain and South Africa. The monarch was restored to his throne and thereafter ruled with little overt opposition—despite abysmal social conditions. Only 5 percent of the people of this ancient land were literate. Venereal disease was rampant. There was barely one doctor for every quarter of a million inhabitants outside the big cities. Fifty-five percent of the land was owned by the crown, church, and nobility; millions of peasants were landless. Yet there were no major uprisings and the Emperor was able to forge a strong alliance with Washington. On May 22, 1953 he signed an agreement with the United States allowing it to operate the largest military base in Sub-Sahara Africa, the Kagnew Station. As of June 1970 Ethiopia had received, as a quid pro quo, $400 million in military and economic aid—the largest such program in Africa south of the Sahara—and 2,800 Ethiopian officers had been trained at American military bases. "Our program," said George W. Bader of the Defense Department, "is authorized for and keyed to their internal security problem."[44] In December 1960, in fact, when Haile Selassie was temporarily overthrown by a revolutionary group while traveling abroad, he was ferried back to his country by the U.S. Air Force, and troops loyal to him were transported to Addis Ababa to put down the rebellion.

The denouement for the emperor came when he suppressed peasant demonstrators pleading for bread while 100,000 to 200,000 people were dying of famine following the 1972/73 drought. Student demonstrations, a general strike, and an army mutiny finally swept the regime aside and, in due course, Colonel Mengistu Haile Marian came to power and declared Ethiopia a "socialist state." It was a natural step, since so much of the wealth of the country had belonged to the emperor, his cronies, and foreign corporations. It was also natural for Mengistu to turn to the Soviet Union rather than Haile Selassie's ally, the United States, for help. Later, when a war broke out between Ethiopia and Somalia over the Ogaden desert,

Mengistu drew closer to Moscow and invited Cuban troops to help in his nation's war effort.

A similar drift from the West toward the Soviet Union occurred in Angola, which had been a Portuguese colony for hundreds of years. Despite worldwide condemnation of Portugal for medieval-type brutalities in Angola, Mozambique, and three other African holdings, Washington continued to supply it with military and economic assistance after World War II, and trained 3,000 of its troops in the United States.[45] Inevitably, when liberation came to the colonies there was little love for our country, and it was made worse by our secret collaboration with South Africa against Angola.

Angolan nationalists were divided into three groups. The oldest one, the Popular Movement for the Liberation of Angola (MPLA), was a multiracial organization headed by a medical doctor, Agostinho Neto, who was neither an avowed Marxist nor a Soviet communist—a circumstance that made the Russians sometimes waver in their support of him. The National Front for the Liberation of Angola (FMLA) was equally committed to independence but its leader, Holden Roberto, brother-in-law of the Zairean president, Mobutu, had been courted by the CIA and for a period of seven years had been on its payroll at $10,000 a year. The youngest group, headed by Jonas Savimbi, a complex and charismatic man who received help from China as well as the United States, went by the acronym UNITA (National Union for the Total Independence of Angola) and was strongly based in the Ovimbundu tribe, which accounted for 30 percent of the population.[46]

Angola's liberation came as a surprise to the American government. A memorandum prepared by Henry Kissinger's office early in the Nixon Administration (NSSM 39) said of southern Africa—including the Portuguese colonies, South Africa, and Rhodesia—that "the whites are here to stay and the only way constructive change can come about is through them. There is no hope for the blacks to gain the political rights they seek through violence which will only lead to chaos and increased opportunities for the communists." As for Angola specifically, "the rebels cannot oust the Portuguese and the Portuguese can contain but not eliminate the rebels."[47]

Kissinger obviously misjudged matters. On April 25, 1974 a group of Portuguese army captains, disenchanted by the costs of colonialism in money and men—12,000 Portuguese dead, 40,000 wounded—toppled the rightist regime of Prime Minister Marcelo Caetano, and nine months later offered the Angolan nationalists free elections, a constituent assembly, and independence.

Perhaps if the superpowers had not been so heavily involved, each with its own faction, things might have gone smoothly. But in July 1974—a few months after the coup in Lisbon—the CIA began contributing more money to Roberto, and the Mobutu government in Zaire (an American client state) supplemented it with armaments. All told, according to a Senate Committee on Intelligence, more than $62 million was funneled to FNLA and UNITA, a figure that may have been twice as much if Zairean, Chinese, and other moneys are included. Washington estimated Moscow's support to Neto at $200 million, a figure also disputed by the other side. In any case, the three constituent groups of a government presumably dedicated to unity had the military wherewithal to fight a civil war and were soon embroiled in one. In March 1975, Roberto's FNLA, aided by 4,000 Zairean troops, drove its way into the town of Caxito, thirty-five miles from Angola's capital, Luanda.

Neto called on help from the Soviet bloc and was supplied with 12,000 Cuban soldiers. Savimbi and the United States called on South African forces, which drove within 300 miles of Luanda from the south before being set back. It was a pathetic performance by the CIA and State Department, particularly since the Soviet-backed forces carried the day. Kissinger denied involvement with South Africa, but Pieter Botha, the defense minister of the racist regime in Pretoria, complained to his parliament that Washington had encouraged the invasion but then "recklessly left us in the lurch."[48] John Stockwell, a CIA agent assigned to Angola, confirms the collaboration in his book, *In Search of Enemies*: "Without any memos being written at CIA headquarters saying 'Let's coordinate with the South Africans,' coordination was effected at all CIA levels and the South Africans escalated their involvement in step with our own."[49] Our narrow containment policy not only helped precipitate a civil war that might have been avoided, but also isolated us from a potential friend and reduced our stock of good will when we allied ourselves with a government the rest of Africa hates.

* * * * * * *

The reincarnation of the revolutionary spirit always seems to surprise Americans, perhaps because our mass media seldom publicizes developments below the surface. Even within "monolithic" rightist regimes there is usually some kind of revolutionizing process at work. Socially conscious priests lead peasant protests (as in Brazil or Colombia), lower rank officers form dissident clubs (as has happened in Argentina), fissures widen within the ruling elites (as happened in Nicaragua). This too is part of the irrepressible contemporary revolution, but little of it is reported until it attains civil-war status. Thus, what seems to be a "sudden" revolution in Cuba, Nicaragua, El Salvador, or Iran is not sudden at all—it is simply a subsurface phenomenon coming to the surface.

We have seen a number of such "sudden" revolutions lately in Central America. An insurgency in 1979 toppled the Somoza dynasty which had ruled Nicaragua since 1936. It was a unique and unexpected development because North American interests had been in control of that poor land since 1849, when Cornelius Vanderbilt was granted a contract to transport gold-hungry Easterners across the isthmus to the Pacific. From 1912 to 1933, except for a few months in 1925, American marines ran the country through the National Guard (a combined constabulary and army), which they trained to enforce law and order.[50]

It was as commander of this *guardia* that Anastasio Somoza, a former shopkeeper and mechanic, founded the Caesarian dynasty in 1936, three years after the marines were withdrawn by Franklin Roosevelt. On his death, he was succeeded by his older son, Luis, and later by the West Point-trained younger son, Anastasio, Jr., who liked to be called "Tachito." During this long saga, the family accumulated a vast fortune by bribery, extortion, and simple seizure of property that suited their tastes. But as Canadian author Gerald Clark observed in a 1962 book, "fully half the people are either unemployed or underemployed, selling soft drinks at street corners, shining shoes for two cents, or just begging. Lord knows how they live. . . ."[51] Behind the Somozas was the United States, which supplied tens of millions of dollars in economic aid and military equipment. What was unique about the 1979 revolution, therefore, was that it took place at all, and that in the end Washington was forced to disassociate from its long-time ally, Tachito, and let him fall.[52]

The Sandinista National Liberation Front (FSLN), which more than any other force was responsible for Tachito's defeat, had been formed by radical students in the 1960s as a rural-oriented guerrilla movement that executed quickie attacks on military installations. But its campaign made little progress until the late 1970s when, as the *New York Times* put it, there was a "national mutiny in Nicaragua."[53] Rich and poor, radicals and conservatives joined with the FSLN to stage a national two-week strike, and though this effort failed, they established a joint Opposition Front which succeeded the following year, when the Carter Administration finally withdrew its support from the Somozas. The Government of National Reconstruction, which was established in July 1979, included two representatives of commercial and business interests and three Marxists; though it did not last long — the non-Marxists withdrew — it punctuated a tendency in many parts of Latin America for members of the middle and upper classes to join peasants and workers in a common venture against dictatorship. Two years later, something similar happened in El Salvador, where a segment of Christian Democrats, and others of the middle class, joined with the peasant-based guerrillas.

A second defection from Pax Americana in this hemisphere — a small one — took place in the tiny island of Grenada (population 110,000) a former British colony that gained its independence in 1974 after a general strike. Five years later, Maurice Bishop, a friend of Fidel Castro and leader of the People's Revolutionary Party, ousted the regime of Eric Gairy, an ally of General Augusto Pinochet in Chile, and incurred the wrath of both London and Washington.[54] The United States may yet reverse the tide in Grenada and Nicaragua, as it did in Chile in 1973 when the CIA successfully "destabilized" the regime of left-wing socialist Salvador Allende. But the volcanic social eruption is not likely to be capped.

While the Reagan Administration in 1982 was cutting off aid to Nicaragua and allowing remnants of Somoza's *guardia* to train in Florida, California,[55] and Honduras for a future attack on their homeland, a guerrilla war was raging in El Salvador and another one was pending in Guatemala. The Salvadorian conflict had already reached the proportions of a civil war, with 5,000 to 8,000 well-trained guerrillas of the Democratic Revolutionary Front engaging forces of the military-dominated junta with three or four times their number. It was a civil war that could have been avoided with some help from Washington, for in October 1979, when young officers overthrew the right-wing regime of General Carlos Humberto Romero, there were great hopes to end repression and redistribute land to the great mass of Salvadorians who were landless. But the dreams died within months as the old clique reestablished its dominance, forced the representatives of the young Turks out of the five-member junta, stalled the land reform, and reinstituted a reign of terror. The result was civil war, with the United States again buttressing the Center and Right—even in the face of thousands of flagrant assassinations initiated from within the army and government itself. In Guatemala, the number of guerrillas was smaller—estimated by Penny Lernoux at 2,000—but the insurrection was "coalescing faster" because, for the first time, it was winning support of the Indians, who constituted a majority of the population.[56] In both countries conditions were so dire, with thousands of people being assassinated by the right-wing terrorists each year, that increasing numbers of ordinary people, not necessarily leftists to begin with, joined the rebels because they felt they must make a literal choice between "liberty or death."

* * * * * * *

Two other narratives are worth recounting to illustrate the tenacity of the revolutionary élan in our contemporary world—those of Indochina and Iran. They constitute the gravest defeats for American policy since World War II, shattering our image of invincibility and encouraging an economic revolt by the oil-producing nations from which the Western industrial nations are still reeling. The benefits of empire used to be that wealth drained from the colonies to the mother countries through what economists call "favorable terms of trade"—goods sold to the colonies went up faster in price than raw materials bought from the colonies. The post-Vietnam result is that the thirteen members of the Organization of Petroleum Exporting Countries (OPEC) have drained away hundreds of billions of dollars *from* the rich, industrialized states since 1973 simply by raising the price of their product by 1,500 to 2,000 percent. Thirty years ago, our government would have responded to such actions by overthrowing the errant regimes—say, in Saudi Arabia or Venezuela—just as it overthrew the Mossadegh regime in 1953. But after the U.S. defeat in Vietnam—even more, after the defeat in Iran—that was no longer possible.

No greater miscalculations have ever been made by Washington than in the instances of Vietnam and Iran. Our economic stake in Indochina—Vietnam, Laos, Cambodia—was negligible: less than $10 million in exports in 1950 and $11 million in imports; a decade later, when we were heavily committed to the Ngo Dinh Diem government, it still accounted for only $60 million of our exports and a much smaller amount of our imports. But Secretary of State Dulles was convinced, as he stated in March 1954, that "if the communist forces won uncontested control over Indochina or any substantial part thereof, they would surely resume the same pattern of aggression against other free people in the area."[57] This "domino theory," used to justify the war, implied that if Indochina fell to the communists, Burma, Thailand, Indonesia, and others in the area would follow suit.

When the French army was surrounded by the Vietminh at Dien Bien Phu, Dulles and Admiral Arthur Radford, chairman of the Joint Chiefs of Staff, proposed a joint U.S.–French–British offensive that would include air strikes by 200 planes and, according to French Foreign Minister Georges Bidault, the possible "use of . . . one or more nuclear weapons near the Chinese border against supply lines," and two against the Vietminh at Dien Bien Phu.[58] The plan was vetoed by Eisenhower only because Britain demurred and leading figures in Congress, among them Lyndon Johnson, gave it a lukewarm reception. After France signed the Geneva Accords ending hostilities in 1954, however, the Eisenhower Administration replaced France as guardian of the Vietnamese regime. At our behest, Ngo Dinh Diem was installed as premier, then as president after a rigged 1955 referendum. (He claimed 98.2 percent of the vote.) Diem now refused to discuss the elections agreed to at Geneva, because, as columnist Joseph Alsop wrote, "anywhere from 50 to 70 percent of the southern Indochina villages are subject to Vietminh influence or control. French experts give still higher percentages, between 60 and 90."[59]

Fortified by hundreds of millions of U.S. dollars and American training for his troops and police, Diem turned to repression in order to stay in power. In 1956 he eliminated the elected village councils, substituting his own appointees. In 1959 he introduced a decree to regroup peasants into "relocation centers" or "agrovilles," which were surrounded by barbed wire and spiked moats. Manhunts against communists and anyone else who had previously opposed French rule began in 1956 and, according to Philippe Devillers, France's leading expert on Indochina, as many as 75,000 people may have been killed in this campaign, and by the government's own admission 48,250 were incarcerated.[60] The prevailing landlord system in the rural areas remained untouched. In the face of all this, tribesmen and former Vietminh guerrilla fighters retreated to the forests, regrouped into the National Liberation Front of Vietnam in December 1960, and initiated a new guerrilla campaign. Our response was to send in 22,000 soldiers, euphemistically called "advisors," during the Kennedy Administration, and when it became apparent in 1964 — after Diem had been removed and assassinated — that the Viet Cong were only months away from victory, President Johnson escalated to full-scale war.

The American commitment then steadily grew from 23,000 troops in South Vietnam in 1964, to 185,000 the next year, 385,000 in 1966, 485,000 in 1967, and peaked at 542,000 in 1968. From 1965 to early 1970, four and a half million tons of TNT were dropped on Vietnam, and another couple of million tons were dropped before the fighting finally stopped. It was inconceivable to American leaders that a band of guerrillas in a backward country that even today has a GNP of only $8 billion (one-quarter of one percent of ours), could inflict a defeat on the combined forces of the United States and a million troops of its allies. Johnson felt certain that his soldiers would sweep through Vietnam, like a bulldozer. But we were destined to defeat.

The guerrilla, we soon found out, was deficient in firepower but had other advantages that made up for it. He combined rudimentary military tactics with revolutionary nationalism, making him next to invincible. The regular soldier could easily be identified, the irregular one wore no uniform (until his forces were large enough); he could hide among the people because in fact he was part of them — their friend. As an Italian writer put it, he could "hide into yesterday or tomorrow."[61] In the beginning, the guerrilla was a part-time soldier. At night he blew up bridges and disarmed regulars. By day he worked in his normal occupation. But when he and his comrades had captured enough materiel and money, they turned into full-time soldiers, supplementing the part-time "saboteurs and diversionists." This factor of being able to hide into yesterday and tomorrow was so harrowing for a traditional army that, American strategists concluded, it would take ten to fifteen regular troops to dispose of one irregular on the other side.

Our forces in Vietnam never attained that strength; even if they had, it is not sure they could have won. One of the factors that bedeviled the Johnson and Nixon Administrations was popular revulsion *at home.* Beginning with small demonstrations of a few hundred people in mid-1965, the antiwar movement – at first led by Gandhian pacifists – was able to bring millions of protesters into the streets by 1969 (two to three million for instance in hundreds of cities and towns on Moratorium Day, October 15, 1969, and 780,000 in Washington a month later). Johnson and Nixon both pretended these actions were irrelevant (Nixon used to insist he was watching a football game while the demonstrations were going on a few hundred yards from the White House), but, in fact, it became impossible to rule under these circumstances, as Nixon himself now admits in his memoirs. (Johnson was forced to renounce his ambitions for a second elected term as president because of the determined demonstrators who followed him everywhere.) Behind the thousands of demonstrators were tens of millions who shared their antiwar views, some out of conviction that the war was wrong, others because we were losing and the affair seemed hopeless. When Congress began to bend to the popular mood, Nixon was forced to end the war – on Hanoi's terms. American troops withdrew while North Vietnamese troops remained in South Vietnam to help the Viet Cong achieve total victory by 1975.

A second, and in some respects even more remarkable miscalculation by our leadership, took place in Iran. With the overthrow of Mohammed Mossadegh in 1953, the revolutionary spirit in this oil-rich country seemed to be in suspended animation for a quarter of a century. Few people believed that a leftist rebellion was in the making – or, for that matter, possible. As late as the summer of 1978, half a year before Shah Mohammed Reza Pahlavi departed from his country, a CIA assessment was that "Iran is not a revolutionary or even a pre-revolutionary situation. Those who are in opposition, both violent and nonviolent, do not have the capacity to be more than troublesome."[62] A few months previously, on New Year's Eve, President Carter had offered a toast to the monarch while in Teheran, proclaiming that "Iran under the great leadership of the Shah is an island of stability in one of the most troubled areas of the world. This is a great tribute to you, your Majesty, and to your leadership and to the respect, admiration, and love which your people give to you."[63] Neither Carter nor his subordinates probed beneath surface trivialities, and thus did not gauge the latent bitterness of a nation of 35 million people in which half a million had been imprisoned and 2,000 executed for political dissidence in the twenty-five years after Mossadegh.[64] Under pressure from the Kennedy Administration for social reform, the Shah had instituted what he called a "White Revolution" and distributed some of his estate, but it was not enough to mitigate significantly either poverty or popular discontent concerning the reign of terror by SAVAK, the American-trained secret police. With leftist groups functioning underground, the clergy mobilized anti-Shah sentiment. On June 5, 1963 – according to the opposition – 15,000 protesters were shot by the Shah's forces in Teheran, Shiraz, and Qom; their leader was the man who would come to power at the head of a unique Moslem revolution sixteen years later, Ayatollah Ruhollah Khomeini.[65]

Washington's assessment from 1950 on, as stated by a congressional committee, was that "Iran needs an army capable primarily of maintaining order within the country, an army capable of putting down any insurrection – no matter where or by whom inspired or abetted."[66] Military aid by the United States from 1946 to 1972 amounted to $1.5 billion in loans and grants. Kennedy had been lukewarm to the Shah's request for armaments, but Nixon – under the Nixon Doctrine of supplying weapons to allies in the developing world so as to relieve the United States of the necessity of doing the fighting itself – agreed to sell the Shah $20 billion in modern equipment, including some planes that the Pentagon had not yet acquired for itself. Iran was viewed as the linchpin of American policy in the vital Persian Gulf – a solid ally to police the oil area against revolutionary instability.

That this powerful and heavily reinforced government should fall before a revolution led by a religious leader then living in France is testament to the vigor of popular movements in our times. That it should fall to a group that did not have any military force at its disposal – neither guerrillas nor a platoon of regular infantrymen – until the very end, is even more remarkable. Almost every day, Khomeini's followers (including leftists of a dozen varieties) demonstrated in the streets, confronted police and soldiers, and died in large numbers for their cause. But in the end, the Shah and two moderate prime ministers were displaced by one of the strangest revolutionary groups in history. Whatever one may think of Khomeini's subsequent brutalities and his outdated moral code, he undoubtedly, at least at the outset, had a strong popular mandate. By failing to evaluate correctly the storms brewing below the surface, the United States lost its anchor in the Persian Gulf. It had viewed the country in pragmatic, strategic, and financial terms, disregarding and downplaying human and social factors. "Iran," said Senator Abraham Ribicoff, "is one of the most important allies the United States has. When you realize that 50 percent of the world's oil comes through the Staits of Hormuz and the only armed forces to protect it are Iran's, to refuse him [the Shah] arms would be sheer stupidity on the part of the United States."[67] History proved that giving the Shah arms was an even greater stupidity.

Summarizing the postwar saga, the late Professor Hans Morgenthau — by no means a leftist — stated that "with unfailing consistency, we have since the end of the Second World War intervened on behalf of conservative and fascist repression against revolution and radical reform. In an age when societies are in a revolutionary or pre-revolutionary stage, we have become the foremost counterrevolutionary status quo power on earth. Such a policy can only lead to political and moral disaster."[68]

* * * * * * *

If our destiny is to be arrayed against social revolution, we are clearly on a toboggan sliding downward. Sooner or later the irrepressible tide of social revolution will engulf pivotal nations in our camp — perhaps Saudi Arabia, Pakistan, Brazil — and the worldwide relationship of forces will almost certainly change decisively. We would then either have to go to war to defend areas that neoconservatives like Norman Podhoretz consider "ours," or watch helplessly as Pax Americana disintegrates and our entrepreneurs are cut off from vital raw materials and markets. We are in the unhappy situation that we cannot enlarge our sphere of influence — except in the unlikely circumstance that the communist countries turn to capitalism — but can only see it contract. One of the striking features of our containment policy is its defensive character. Most of its successes consist of holding on to bastions already considered "ours," not gaining new ones. The overthrow of the neutralist Goulart regime in Brazil, for instance, did not add a new nation to the Western camp; it simply prevented further contraction. Similarly, the defeat of the Caamano uprising in the Dominican Republic added nothing to the American empire; it merely halted a defection to neutralism or communism. If the gains made were often pyrrhic, most of the losses, such as Cuba or Vietnam, were real in the sense that they constituted secessions from what we deemed to be our sphere of influence. Moreover, even such negative successes will become increasingly difficult to attain unless we can improve our own economic health – the bedrock on which Western capitalism has rested for seven decades.

In the wake of World War I, revolutions and general strikes broke out in a dozen countries, but succeeded in only one, the Soviet Union. Where they failed it was due to a combination of mistakes by their leaders and judicious aid from the exchequer in Washington. Had it not been for the $13 billion in loans from the United States from 1918 to 1929 (a large sum then) it is doubtful that Western Europe could have survived as a capitalist society. Germany was saved by $2.5 billion of American money, plus the paring down under the Dawes and Young plans of the $32 billion owned in reparations.[69] The wealth of the United States helped put the old order back on its feet, confining the socialist revolution to a single state.

Fortunately for the Western establishment, the United States enjoyed a booming prosperity in the decade after World War I and was therefore capable of spending the sums needed to achieve stability overseas. When that prosperity drained away in the 1930s and the world could no longer lean on the United States for support, schisms developed among the Western powers that led to war.

In the wake of World War II, revolutions broke out in six dozen countries, and independence of one kind or another was achieved in almost all of them. This time the United States spent some two hundred billion in economic and military aid, to prop weakened societies everywhere. Had that money not been available, the old order would have disintegrated not long after the end of hostilities.

Fortunately for the West, the United States enjoyed an even greater prosperity after 1945 than after 1919 – and it lasted considerably longer. Our citizens had been forced to save their money during the war, and when it was over they had billions to spend on automobiles, road building, housing, business investments. Some of the technological innovations developed during the war were used as the basis for new industries – e.g., air transport, computers, and electronics. And with the Korean War we steadily expanded military production. Thus, we enjoyed a long period of affluence. The world was our customer; the dollar was good as gold; we could undersell all competitors, and we could therefore underwrite the recovery of our industrial (and some preindustrial) allies – which was indispensable to our own recovery. To some extent, this prosperity was synthetic because it was based on vast expenditures on a nonproductive military machine. It also carried within it the seed of crisis because it rested largely on steadily pyramiding debt—government debt, business debt, consumer debt. But with all that, the United States was the keel that kept the capitalist ship from capsizing.

In the last twelve or fifteen years—especially since 1971, when Nixon froze wages and prices and divorced the dollar from gold because we faced an astronomical balance of payments deficit—our economy has lost its resiliency. Everything seems to be in limbo—the auto and housing industries are in decline, technological innovations are not spawing as many lucrative industries as in the past, not even President Reagan's arms buildup is enough to sustain prosperity. "From 1964 to 1968," records John Buell, associate editor of the *Progressive*, "the unemployment rate dropped from slightly more than five percent to less than four percent—a level that would be considered 'full employment' today. In the same period, the annual inflation rate never exceeded five percent. . . . [But] during the period from 1967 to 1980, despite chronically sluggish demand and persistent unemployment, prices rose by 125 percent." Some economists blame this combination of stagnation and inflation (stagflation) on special circumstances such as the Vietnam war or the Soviet grain purchases, "but history," argues Buell, "is, after all, a succession of special events, and an economic system must be capable of coping with them." [71] Evidently we are not capable of coping with them. To make matters worse, we are under great pressure by other industrial giants, Germany and Japan in particular. Our recessions are turning into small depressions; unemployment reaches new highs each downturn; the economy suffers from stagflation; and our debts—in all three categories—have become mountainous and threatening. The large additional sums for the military are being paid for by trimming equal amounts from the social benefits of the poor and less affluent.

To put it bluntly, though the United States has twice saved the established system from revolutionary upheaval, it no longer has the reserves for doing so a third time. This being the case, the irrepressible revolution beyond our borders is bound to become less and less amenable to control by our National Security State. We are heading, as professor Morgenthau put it, toward "political and moral disaster."

WILL
THE
SOVIETS 6
DISAPPEAR?

One segment of the American establishment wants to continue the policy of containment in its present form, bracing itself for what Henry Kissinger expects to be a long-term "competition" that "will remain a permanent feature of our foreign policy."[1] Soviet power, in this scheme of things, would erode only gradually. But there is another segment of the establishment, typified by the neoconservatives, that believes containment is limping because it is being implemented too timidly. This segment wants to strike out with greater determination. Michael T. Klare of the Institute for Policy Studies calls this group the "Prussians" because they urge "a more vigorous U.S. 'police' presence abroad plus a massive expansion of America's nuclear arsenal."[2] The Prussians are not content to wait it out for what might be decades; they want a direct and unyielding confrontation with the Soviet Union and those revolutionary forces who look to it for aid as quickly as possible. They seek to place the Soviet Union in a position where it would have no option but to submit to Washington's dictates — to be Finlandized, in other words.

In a major article for *Foreign Affairs*, Robert W. Tucker defines the differences this way: "Our alternatives today are either a policy of a resurgent America intent once again on containing wherever possible the expansion of Soviet influence — as well as the expansion of communism generally — or a policy of moderate containment that may prove inadequate to sustain the power and discipline even to protect interests on which our essential security depends."[3] Under the first, more aggressive, alternative the United States would not hesitate to place troops in areas it felt vital to its welfare, such as the Middle East, and would use them quickly if an ally were threatened by external enemies or revolution. Norman Podhoretz makes the point with emphatic directness: "If the United States [is] not prepared to use force to ensure its access to oil for the sake of what could it be expected to do so?"[4]

The militant policy is a reflex against what has become known as the Vietnam Syndrome. As *Business Week* describes it:

Vietnam caused a loss of confidence in the ability of the U.S. to defend non-Communist regimes in Third World countries against subversion and military takeovers by Moscow's allies. This perception of paralysis was confirmed when the U.S. stood by helplessly as Russian-backed insurgents, aided by Cuban troops took over Angola. And it was enhanced when the Soviet-aligned Ethiopian government crushed separatist movements in Eritrea and the Ogaden.[5]

Not only did a War Powers Act, passed in the wake of Vietnam, impose restraints on the president's right to use American forces in "police" actions, but there was a pervasive mood in the nation itself, as Michael Klare points out, of "opposition to a 'go anywhere, do anything' stance," most Americans preferring that "surrogate gendarmes" be used for fighting in the Third World rather than our own forces.[6]

But a drift away from the Vietnam Syndrome was already evident in the last years of the Carter Administration. President Carter boasted that military spending, which had "dropped by one third" in the "eight years before [he] became President," had "been increased every year" since.[7] Approximately $15 billion had been cut away from what otherwise would have gone for social and domestic programs, in order to hike the defense budget by $12 billion. A 1979 Presidential Directive (PD–18), kept secret from the public until revealed in the *New York Times*, called for a special force to fight "brush-fire" wars in the Third World.[8] As originally conceived, the "quick-strike-force," later called the Rapid Deployment Force, would consist of 100,000 troops ready to be transported at an instant's notice to fight in the Persian Gulf, the Middle East, or anywhere else outside of Europe where there was "instability." This was nothing new—in 1965, Defense Secretary McNamara had proposed "a mobile 'fire-brigade' reserve . . . ready for quick deployment to any threatened area in the world"[9]—but it seemed out of place in the period of detente that had existed since the early 1970s. Nor did it seem compatible with the SALT II treaty that Carter and Brezhnev had signed in Vienna just four days before PD–18. The treaty itself was flawed by the fact that it allowed each side to add approximately 4,000 warheads to its stockpiles, but the mere fact that it had been negotiated left the impression with many people that it might be the precursor to a thaw in relations between the superpowers. However, a sense of national frustration, carefully exploited by such groups as the Committee on the Present Danger (to which Ronald Reagan and thirty-two of his future staff members belonged),[10] prevented the treaty from being ratified and moved sentiment to the Right still further.

Carter yielded to that sentiment. Naval forces in the Persian Gulf were strengthened as a warning to Iran not to play fast and loose with the American hostages, seized at the U.S. Embassy on November 4, 1979. Then, after Russian troops marched into Afghanistan on December 27, 1979—ostensibly to protect a recently installed communist government that was wracked with factionalism and facing attack by conservative Muslim forces—he cut off exports of grain and high-technology equipment to the Soviet Union and prevented American athletes from participating in the summer Olympic games held in Moscow that year. In his State of the Union address, less than a month after the Afghan invasion, Carter proclaimed a "new" doctrine reminiscent of the one proclaimed by Truman in 1947. Any attempt by "outside" forces to control the Persian Gulf or Mideast oil supplies, he said, "will be regarded as an assault on the vital interests of the United States of America, and such an assault will be repelled by any means necessary, including military force."[11] To punctuate the point, the president dispatched additional warships to the Indian Ocean.

The election of Ronald Reagan in November 1980 signaled a further toughening, or, as some called it, "revitalizing" of American foreign policy. *Time* magazine caustically commented that "the Reagan Administration came into office with stubborn, simple-minded prejudices against arms control, unrealistic ambitions for massive rearmament, and a propensity for bellicose rhetoric that has frightened its allies and its own citizens more than it has restrained its adversaries."[12] The diplomatic language of detente was superseded by the harsh verbiage of confrontation: "Let's not delude ourselves," Reagan had told the *Wall Street Journal* a few months before the elections, "The Soviet Union underlies all the unrest that is going on. If they weren't engaged in this game of dominoes, there wouldn't be any hot spots in the world."[13] This kind of attack on Moscow as the source of international deviltry continued, even intensified, after the new administration took office. "The Soviet Union," said Secretary of Defense Caspar Weinberger in his fiscal 1983 report, "poses a greater danger to the American people than any foreign power in our history. . . . [It] is embarked on a sustained effort to encourage and arm totalitarian forces in various parts of the world, so as to expand its political influence and military reach."[14]

Central to the revitalized containment policy was its all-or-nothing, last-ditch character, as if the administration were preparing for one desperate last throw of the dice. The Soviets were to be confronted with military and economic pressures that would make them helpless—leaving their allies and "proxies" equally helpless. On the military front, the contemplated build-up was the most far reaching in all history, outstripping those of previous administrations by a wide margin. The annual outlay was scheduled by 1987 to be twice what it was in 1982. In the five year period, fiscal 1983 to 1987, the administration expected to spend $1.6 trillion ($1,643 billion) on its war machine, including $222 billion for new strategic weapons and improved command and control facilities.[15] That latter figure may have been underestimated by $80 billion, according to the Joint Economic Committee of Congress.[16] Enormous sums were to be expended for a variety of wonder weapons—the advanced technology "stealth" bomber (capable of avoiding Soviet radar), 100 B-1 bombers, 3,000 air-launched cruise missiles, one Trident submarine a year, the Trident II missile, hundreds of sea-launched cruise missiles, and 100 MX missiles (each with ten warheads).[17] Billions more were designated for neutron bombs, civil defense ($4.2 billion), a fleet for the Indian Ocean, a new transport plane for the Rapid Deployment Force, the space shuttle, an orbital laser battle station, and an advanced new antiballistic missile system, the Low-altitude Air Defense System (LoADS).[18] Within a decade, 17,000 nuclear warheads were to come off the assembly lines—6,500 to replace old ones, 10,500 as new additions to the stockpile—making a total of some 20,000 strategic warheads, plus a slightly larger number of tactical warheads.

The operating fleet of the Navy was to be expanded from 569 to 640 ships by the early 1990s — at a cost of $96 billion plus inflation — and 572 tactical Pershing II and cruise missiles were to be completed and deployed in Western Europe by the end of 1983.[19]

To convince the American public that all this was necessary — particularly in the face of tens of billions in cuts from social programs — the Reagan Administration relied on a fear psychology. The nation was told that the Soviets have far outspent us in recent years and had not only achieved parity, but were forging ahead. We were simply trying to catch up, in order to overcome "the severe inadequacies in the realm of strategic and other nuclear weapons."[20] This claim — made by an editor of *Air Force* and others — was disputed by such men as former Defense Secretary McNamara, who charged that the Pentagon has consistently exaggerated Soviet advances. "Go back to 1960," McNamara said, "when many believed there was a missile gap favoring the Soviets. With hindsight it became clear that there wasn't any missile gap. But Kennedy had been told there was."[21] The Center for Defense Information, headed by retired Rear Admiral Gene R. La Rocque, once a nuclear strategist for the Pengagon, was specific:

> The Soviet Union does not have military superiority over the U.S. The U.S. and its NATO allies have outspent the Soviet/Warsaw Pact military forces for many years — $215 billion to $175 billion in one year alone. The massive U.S.Navy exceeds the Soviet's in warship tonnage and nuclear-powered submarines and ships, and outnumbers the Soviets in aircraft carriers by 13 to 0. Now we are building 110 new warships. Our submarines carry 5,000 nuclear weapons — 3,000 of which are always aimed and ready to fire at the U.S.S.R. The Soviets keep 400 nuclear weapons at sea, ready to fire at the U.S. The U.S. has 410 strategic bombers, compared to the Soviet's 145. More than half the Soviet bombers are still propeller-driven. We have *always* had more strategic nuclear weapons than the Soviets. Today we can explode 12,000 nuclear weapons on the Soviet Union, while they can explode 7,000 on us. Neither we nor the Soviets can build a defense against nuclear weapons, no matter how much we spend.[22]

The Reagan Administration was able, however, to deflect the claims of men like McNamara and La Rocque; fear of the Soviet Union has become so endemic in American life that presidents can play on it like a magic flute. The huge increase in the military budget was approved with little challenge in the Congress. When the Reagan arsenal is in place during this decade, the Soviet Union will be surrounded by fire power such as no nation has ever confronted in the past. It will have to contend with thousands of first-strike weapons able to hit its soil within six to thirty minutes.

In the Reagan scenario, the United States will have stationed in Western Europe (by the end of 1983) 108 Pershing II medium range ballistic missiles with a range of 1,000 miles or more and capable of reaching targets in the Soviet Union within five or six minutes.[23] Our 464 ground-launched cruise missiles will similarly be emplaced in Europe. The cruise, assuming everything that is claimed for it is true, is the weapon of the future because it is cheap to produce, mobile, able to fly below radar, and extremely accurate. Powered by a 130-pound fanjet engine, it cruises at 20,000 feet for most of its journey, then drops to tree-top level (50 to 100 feet) to avoid Soviet radar, and is guided by a sensor called TERCOM (terrain contour matching) to a target 1,500 miles away. By 1984 the Tomahawk cruise missile will be carrying a 200-kiloton warhead, fifteen times as powerful as the Hiroshima bomb, and will hit its target within thirty yards. In addition, current plans are to place 3,000 air-launched cruise missiles on B–52 and B–1 bombers within a few years, and thousands more on thirty destroyers, twenty-two cruisers, and even two mothballed battleships.[24]

The cruise poses many problems, apart from the havoc it can inflict. Its accuracy makes it a good first-strike weapon—though not ideal because it travels slower than a ballistic missile. It is also so cheap and relatively uncomplicated that any industrial country will be able to produce it (certainly Germany, Japan, France, and Britain), thus magnifying the problem of proliferation and contributing to international instability. Worst of all, its position and numbers are difficult to verify—how can you tell, even with the best surveillance from space, whether a B–52 is carrying twenty, ten, or *no* cruise missiles? "If both sides were to engage in massive deployment of long-range, nuclear armed cruise missiles at sea," says Republican Senator Charles Mathias, "then President Reagan's search for an arms control agreement incorporating verifiable cuts in nuclear arsenals would become a practical impossibility."[25]

Of similar urgency for the Russians would be the MX missile. The race-track basing mode, by which 200 MX missiles were to be transported on an elliptical roadway to twenty-three shelters each (a total of 4,600) to make them invulnerable to Soviet attack has been given up. A hundred such missiles are now planned, to be positioned in a more orthodox manner. Even so, the thousand warheads on these launchers, each twenty-seven to thirty-nine times as powerful as the Hiroshima bomb and having a 95 percent chance of "killing" a Soviet missile in its silo, will offer the most effective first-strike challenge yet devised.[26]

The Soviets would also have to keep a wary eye for half a dozen Trident submarines expected to be deployed in the next few years, each with 192 warheads capable of hitting within 800 feet of a target 4,000 miles away—accurate enough, in other words, to destroy almost any medium-sized city. These ships, and their successors, the Trident II, will be virtually invulnerable to attack because their range gives them much more ocean to hide in.[27] (Soviet submarines are also invulnerable—for the time being—but the United States is believed to be much further advanced in developing an antisubmarine weapon.)

To all this must be added stepped-up CIA activity; the Rapid Deployment Force, now scheduled to have 300,000 troops and bases in Oman, Somalia, Egypt, and perhaps elsewhere; a space shuttle that in time will be able to place in space "killer satellites" designed to render inoperative Soviet communication, navigational, early warning, and other command satellites; and finally the orbital laser battle station, with high-energy lasers that the Pentagon hopes some day will be able to destroy Soviet missiles either on launch or in their early orbit.[28] Few people expect lasers to be operative soon—many scientists, in fact, believe they never will be—but if the Pentagon is right, the laser, MX, and some of the other new weapons will give American strategists a capability that has eluded them for decades—a capability for a "disarming first strike."

Parallel to the new weapons, the administration has formulated a new doctrine for "protracted" nuclear war lasting days, weeks, or even months. Though its provisions are still secret, the *New York Times* was leaked a copy of the 125-page document called "Fiscal Year 1984–1988 Defense Guidance," and published a summary of its provisions. Coming on the heels of President Carter's Presidential Directive 59 (PD–59), which called for targeting Soviet nuclear, command, and industrial facilities rather than cities—a first-strike stance to eliminate Soviet war fighting ability—the latest "defense guidance" punctuates the fact that the Reagan Administration is thinking seriously of actually using nuclear weapons, though it insists, of course, it will not do so except in reply to a Soviet attack. "The armed forces," summarizes the *New York Times*, "are ordered to prepare for nuclear counterattacks against the Soviet Union 'over a protracted period'. . . . The civilian and military planners, having decided that protracted war is possible, say that American nuclear forces 'must prevail and be able to seek earlier termination of hostilities on terms favorable to the U. S.' "[29] This, says *Time*, is "a policy shift from the traditional imperative of deterring nuclear war to a new, or at least more explicit, preparedness to wage such a war if necessary."[30]

It does not seem likely that Washington will retreat from this hawkish stance unless forced to by public pressure or by major reverses, such as a depression. In 1982, prodded in good part by the large antiwar demonstrations in Europe and at home, the administration agreed to two sets of arms negotiations with the Soviets — one dealing with medium-range weapons and the other with the more vital strategic ones. The positions taken by the State Department seem to preclude the possibility that these talks will lead to meaningful reduction in arsenals or that the essential Reagan strategy will be dropped. In the tactical-weapons negotiations, State was asking the Soviets to give up many hundreds of medium-range missiles, such as the SS-20, that it has in place, whereas the U. S. would forego 572 Pershing II and cruise missiles *not yet* built or deployed. In the strategical-weapons talks, State was seeking large cuts in the heavy weapons on which Soviet defense relies most, such as the SS-18, and an equalization of throwweights — in which they enjoy a large advantage.[31] "There is a considerable suspicion in Europe," writes Alan Wolfe, a member of the editorial board of the *Nation*, "that the talks are a trick designed to lull the antinuclear movement into a false sense of security. . . . The assumption is that once the demonstrations in Europe quiet down, a pretext will be found to disband the talks"[32] — or put them in abeyance. Whether or not that is true, there is little doubt that President Reagan is making a last-ditch effort to roll back Soviet power and has no intention of permitting arms control negotiations to stand in the way.

Tacked on to the new offensive is a plan to increase economic pressure on Moscow with the same intensity as in the 1950s. To begin with, our own increased military expenditures will cause Soviet expenditures to go up in cadence, thereby imposing an additional strain on Moscow's economy. There are people at high levels in the State and Defense departments who believe that one way to force the Soviet Union into bankruptcy is to expand our own military spending, forcing Moscow to keep pace, and since it cannot match our resources or GNP, it is bound to succumb.[33] Beyond such indirect pressures, Washington has cut off high-technology exports; succeeded in having its allies increase interest rates charged the communist bloc; and forbidden sale of equipment, by American corporations or their subsidiaries abroad, vital to the 3,700 mile natural-gas pipeline that the Russians are building to supply Germany, France, and other states with a sizable part of their energy. This could delay a project that the Soviets hope will soon bring them $5 to $10 billion a year in hard currency.

"Some opponents of East-West trade seem to hope," Henry Kissinger writes, "that a total denial of economic benefits would force the collapse of the Soviet system." Kissinger himself does not agree: "This theory is disproved by history. The Soviet system survived several decades of economic isolation and did not crumble."[34] But each addition of pressure is another straw on the proverbial camel's back, and there seem to be people in the Reagan Administration who believe that withholding trade and credits can greatly hasten Soviet disintegration.

* * * * * * *

Fierce and threatening as the Reagan program appears to be, however, it does not change anything fundamentally. With a clear superiority in nuclear arms, administration officials may be more tempted to use them in "small" wars, like Vietnam, or against lesser opponents, like Cuba. But that might be counterproductive as world and domestic opinion turns against Washington. The essential point is that no set of military circumstances foreseeable before the end of this century can make the Soviet Union pliable to the demands of the American establishment. A decade or two from today, the State Department will be in no better position to issue an ultimatum to Moscow than it is now—probably less so. The Reagan build-up will cause difficulties for the Russians but it will also exacerbate our own problems.

It is revealing that our strategists now talk of surviving a "limited" nuclear war, or a "protracted" war; they are conceding thereby that for the conceivable future they have no way of bringing about a disarming first strike, and short of that, there is no threat, no matter how intimidating it appears, than can Finlandize the Soviet

Union. The arithmetic of the nuclear race is such that the Pentagon would have to be sure of "killing" almost every land-based missile, submarine-based missile, and bomber of the Soviet Union to assure that the United States would be viable after a counterattack. If only 10 percent of the Soviet force were to escape destruction—an understated figure in view of uncertainty about the effectiveness of nuclear weapons—the Soviets would have 700 warheads with which to strike back. That would be more than enough to dispose of our urban centers. The Defense Department has estimated that if 400 one-megaon bombs were to burst over Soviet cities it would lay waste more than two-thirds of its industry and kill one-third of its population; that figure is undoubtedly valid—give or take a few million—the other way around too.[35] For American leaders to contemplate allowing the death of 70 or 80 million of its citizens, not to mention two-thirds of its industrial resources, in an all-out first strike, would be lunacy. No American (or Russian) leader would seriously consider it. Even with the expanded Reagan arsenal, the threat remains empty. It is likely to harry the Soviets, but not terrify them into submission. There have been other times when the United States enjoyed a wide margin of superiority in numbers of firepower. In 1960 the United States had 1,702 launchers (missiles and bombers) as against 150 for the Soviets. It had 6,500 warheads, as against 300 for the Soviets, and an edge of twelve to one in firepower.[36] That disparity did not cause the Soviets to yield; it is unreasonable to assume that the present, lesser disparity will cause it to yield now—to get out of Afghanistan, break its pact with Cuba, stop supplying arms to Ethiopia, reduce its influence in Poland, and so on.

As new American armaments—the cruise, the MX, the Trident, and others—are deployed in this decade, the Soviet Union will take countermeasures. Brezhnev has warned that if the 572 cruise and Pershing II missiles are deployed in Western Europe, he will put the United States in comparable jeopardy. What that means is not clear, but he might place missiles in Cuba or, more likely, maintain a small fleet of nuclear-armed submarines in international waters off California and New York. Soviet defense minister Dimitri Ustinov has announced that Moscow might change its "launch under attack" policy to one of "launch on warning." This would mean that a nuclear attack could be initiated almost automatically, based on computer readouts; and since the United States itself has had hundreds of computer false alarms that lasted from a few seconds to as much as six minutes, this is a frightening prospect. "The aggressor, too, should know that the advantages of the preemptive use of nuclear weapons will not assure victory for it . . . ," Ustinov warned. "The aggressor will not be able to evade an all-crushing retaliatory strike."[37] It is fairly certain that Moscow will try to match the Pentagon build-up with one of its own. Exactly what the arithmetic of that build-up will be, or whether it will encompass technological breakthroughs not yet anticipated by our side, is difficult to predict. But we can be all but certain that at the end of the process there will be a nuclear stand-off just as at present — with the one difference that in the meantime half a dozen or a dozen more countries will become members of the nuclear club, making *both* superpowers less secure. In their 1981 posture statement, the Joint Chiefs of Staff expressed the fear that a dozen or more nations will have "some military nuclear capability" by 1990.

If the military aspect of the latest version of containment offers little solace to those who are implementing it, other aspects are even less heartening. The hawkish policy is viewed by its promoters in a one-dimensional fashion — how much pressure does it put on the Soviets. But there is another dimension that counterbalances the first — namely, the problems it poses for us. As happens now and then in medicine, the side effects of a so-called remedy can be worse than the disease.

There are to begin with, the economic side effects at home. For the first time since 1940, living standards have begun to fall in the United States. Reagan's enlarged military expenditures exacerbate the problem, for we no longer can afford guns and butter both as we did years ago. The $34 billion increase in military spending in the first Reagan budget was managed by cutting approximately the same sums from social expenditures — welfare, food stamps, and the like. The administration — and part of its opposition — seems intent on continuing this kind of tradeoff, despite the dire effects on the lower classes. What the social costs will be remains to be seen. The poor tended to be complacent from 1979 through 1982 as their real earnings were slashed by government fiat, but there is no guarantee they will remain that way. After the stock market crash of October 1929 there was a hiatus of three or four years before protest movements exploded in militant action. That may happen again, but the lull is likely to be followed by intensified resistance.

A second side effect is that the program has, strangely, manufactured its own opposition. The economic corollary to the Reagan foreign and military policy — Reaganomics — has hurtled many millions of formerly inactive people into the political process. Men and women whose only participation was to cast a vote every two or four years have been made aware, by economic reverses such as their own unemployment or the bankruptcy of their small businesses, of the impact of government actions on their lives. They are questioning the justice of diverting billions of dollars to the military—dollars that otherwise might be used to relieve unemployment and revive the economy. In the past, these people were content to let the politicians decide such matters but, as they began to worry about their own economic insecurity, more and more opted for curbing the military. Out of this frustration has emerged a revived antiwar movement. In just one year, advocates of a bilateral freeze drew so many people to their cause that, according to all leading polls, they represented a majority of public opinion. The freeze proposal has been embraced by the Democratic Party, the House Foreign Affairs Committee, almost half the members of Congress, a segment of the AFL–CIO, and many feminist, medical, black, Hispanic, and other forces that had not previously been active on the peace issue. It peaked at a New York demonstration June 12, 1982, when 800,000 to a million people marched through the city calling for disarmament—the largest protest in American history. The growing antinuclear mood forced Reagan to tone down his rhetoric and start arms negotiations with the Russians sooner than had been intended. The President stopped referring to antiwar activists as dupes of the communists; instead he praised their sincerity and even used their terminology. He kept repeating he too was in favor of a freeze—but only after the United States catches up with the Soviets.

The Reagan forces were waiting for the antinuclear mood to spend itself in the summer and fall of 1982 so they could proceed with their program unchallenged. But while the opposition may taper off for periods, it probably won't go away. Unless the economy can be brought back to its previous expansiveness and prosperity, the confrontation between those who want more guns and those who want more butter is bound to intensify.

Another ill effect from our toughened foreign policy is the fissures it is creating within the Atlantic Alliance, both at government and popular levels. Coincident with the Marshall Plan in the late 1940s, Western Europe accepted without challenge the American regulation against trading in strategic materials with the Soviet bloc. But in mid-1982 there was a stormy outburst against the Reagan order banning the sale by American firms of gas turbine blades for the pipeline the Soviet Union was building from Siberia to Western Europe. Even Margaret Thatcher, the conservative prime minister of Britain, closest in ideological bent to the Reagan Administration, joined in decrying the embargo. Other fissures between the United States and its industrial allies were surfacing with greater frequency and intensity—over high interest rates in the United States (which drains away potential investment capital from other members of the alliance), over attempts to restrict imports into the United States of Japanese automobiles or European steel. "We have some really serious economic problems dividing us and Europe coinciding all at once," Trade Representative William E. Brock told *Business Week* in July 1982.[38] Such breaches over economic issues make it difficult to unify the Western alliance for a foreign-policy assault on Moscow.

The European leaders too have been caught in the whirlwind that affects us. Their economies, closely linked to ours, have been experiencing similar trauma—inflation, rising unemployment, stagnation. On the political front, they are under antinuclear pressures similar to ours. Until the United States and NATO agreed to place 572 cruise and Pershing missiles in Europe, antinuclear sentiment on the old continent was muted. American weapons stationed there had short ranges, so that they were no direct threat to the Soviet Union; hence, they were only a minimal target for nuclear reprisal from Moscow. But the cruise and Pershing II missiles changed that. With a range of 1,000 to 1,500 miles, capable of hitting the Soviet Union itself, they were destined to be live targets for Moscow's military machine. Thus, a nuclear danger that seemed distant suddenly became real for Europeans, and a public that was apathetic about the issue suddenly began to express itself vigorously. The antinuclear movement that burgeoned in 1981 was broad based, with the Church—especially in Holland—playing a major role. The demonstrations of hundreds of thousands of people in 1981 to 1982 reflected European sentiment and were another factor in mitigating the hawkish policy in Washington. It had to be taken into account.

In the tug of war, then, between the militant containment advocates on the one hand and the American, European, and Japanese publics on the other, the Reagan Administration has had to give some ground. It was unable (or unwilling), for instance, to reinstitute a grain embargo against the Soviet Union after the Polish government declared martial law in December 1981, because our farmers—and the public generally—would not have tolerated it. When the administration sought to aid the rightist junta in El Salvador, it was restrained by a burgeoning anti-interventionist movement like the one that arose during the Vietnam War. This time, moreover, the opposition formed quickly, grew to the point where it attracted demonstrations up to 100,000 people, and enjoyed major public support. It reflected majority opinion almost immediately, by contrast to the resistance movement formed during the Vietnam War, which attracted small numbers to begin with, and took years to galvanize.[39] The administration was able to send a few dozen military advisors and some money to El Salvador, but it was patently aware that escalation of that aid might lead to determined opposition not only in the streets but in Congress.

Considering all the economic difficulties, the fissures in the alliance, and the spreading antinuclear forces here and abroad, the Prussians—to use Michael Klare's term again—were either forced to proceed slowly or give ground on this or that issue, thus incurring criticism even from their own legions. Reagan's reprisals against the Soviet Union after Polish martial law was declared were too harsh for the European allies, who value trade with Moscow beyond what we do, but it was far from adequate as far as the American Right was concerned. Norman Podhoretz, who had pledged fealty to Reagan at the outset, now berated him for being more timid than Carter. According to Podhoretz, the president should have taken "decisive action" in Central America—meaning, presumably, that he should have sent the Marines into El Salvador and perhaps Nicaragua, entirely cut off credits and technology to Moscow, made an "all-out effort" to halt construction of the pipeline from Siberia to Western Europe, and perhaps reinstated an embargo on grain. Podhoretz laments that Reagan, who "even said that he welcomes the signs of an impending breakup of the Soviet empire from within and . . . has looked forward to a time when communism itself will disappear," evidently lost his nerve. He could not bring himself "to go even as far as Carter had gone."[40] A few disenchanted conservatives accused Reagan of loving business more than he hates communism.

Reagan as president obviously could not do what Reagan the candidate or Reagan the private citizen had espoused a few years before, any more than Truman, Eisenhower, or Nixon could do whatever they pleased without paying heed to public clamor. Reagan undoubtedly would have preferred a total embargo of trade and credits on the Soviets, and military action against El Salvador and probably Cuba, but with pressure both from abroad and at home, his options were more limited than his rightist supporters would have liked. That too must be deemed a brake on the latest containment strategy. Along with the others, it doomed it to sterility, as some advocates of a "Resurgent America" reluctantly conceded.

* * * * * * *

The ability of the Soviet Union to survive all these years, then, reflects in some measure the weaknesses, divisions, and illusions of its adversaries. "If there is a single factor which more than any other explains the predicament in which we now find ourselves," Senator John W. Fulbright wrote in 1958, "it is our readiness to use the specter of Soviet communism as a cloak for the failure of our own leadership."[41] The other side of this self-justification is that we overstress Soviet communism's weaknesses—its lack of democracy, its totalitarianism, its difficulties with East European allies, its constant problems with agriculture, and the like—but fail to understand its strong points or its resiliency. For instance, we note that the Soviet standard of living is much lower than that in the West, but we don't stress that the gap was much wider before communism. The Soviet gross domestic product in 1981 was about $1.6 trillion as against $2.6 trillion for the United States.[42] Considering that the Soviet leadership had expected to catch up with capitalism long before now, this is a criticism of its efforts, but considering, on the other hand, that they have taken an undeveloped country, ravaged by two wars and a costly counterrevolution, and have built it into the second richest economy in the world, their efforts have been a success. Noting the dire predictions that are being made of Russia's future, Stuart H. Loory, former managing editor of the *Chicago Sun-Times*, who spent a number of years in the Soviet Union during the 1960s, wrote the following on his return from a seven week stay in Moscow in June 1982:

> There are no signs that Marxism–Leninism will soon end up 'on the ash heap of history' as President Reagan predicted in a speech to the British parliament in June. Neither are there any signs that the Soviet leadership has cynically put the country 'literally on a starvation diet of consumer goods,' as Mr. Reagan charged in his June 30th press conference to support the biggest military building in history. The crisis is manageable, and the regime under Soviet president Leonid I. Brezhnev has been coping, if not making headway.[43]

We need not overlook the lack of civil liberties or other vices in the Soviet orbit to recognize that, even if it were justified, the liquidation of the Soviet Union is beyond our means. A mature nation cannot base its foreign policy on wishful thinking; it must face reality. The reality is that, short of a nuclear holocaust, Soviet communism is destined to survive. It will change and be modified, and if there is a lessening of world tensions, it will be moderated—as has happened in Yugoslavia, Hungary, and China. But it will not disappear.

There are secessionist tendencies among the Soviet Union's client states (China and Yugoslavia actually seceded from Moscow's sphere of influence). There are also serious weaknesses in the Soviet economy—for example, its continued dependence on imports of foreign grain and the slowdown of its rate of growth. There are long lines for food, the quality of goods is poor, and so forth. But, on the other hand, it is not as dependent on foreign trade, foreign investments, and foreign raw materials as is the United States. It can adjust easier; it is more adaptable. Whatever the defects of its planned economy, it can better tailor its production to available resources; if it is short of foreign valuta, for instance, it can cut back on imports—in a way that a "market economy" cannot; if it lacks a particular raw material, it can use a substitute that may reduce quality but at least keeps production going.

As for the turmoil within the Soviet orbit, that too must be worrisome for the Kremlin; but whereas turmoil in the capitalist orbit has often led to a repudiation of capitalism, no communist states have yet repudiated communism. The East Germans who went on strike in 1953, the Hungarians who erupted in revolution in 1956, the Czechs who ousted their Stalinist government in 1968 were not seeking to restore capitalism but to establish a democratic form of socialism—"socialism with a human face." Whether that was also the objective of the Polish Solidarity movement in 1980/81 is not clear because of the enigmatic role of the Catholic Church in that movement. But millions of its members (some of whom carried cards in the Communist party) hoped to resolve their difficulties within the context of a humanistic socialism, not capitalism. That was also true, for the most part, of Polish dissidents of 1956, 1968, 1970, and 1976. What this suggests is that communism is more likely to be modified than to disintegrate. No social system in history that has expanded as much as communism has, ever returned to older social forms.

Suppose, therefore, that instead of dying or "eroding," Soviet communism changes form. That would not be surprising, for all social systems are of great diversity. There are enormous differences, for instance, between capitalism in Greece and capitalism in the United States, between capitalism under Hitler, Mussolini, Franco, and Salazar, and capitalism under Schmidt, Mitterand, Reagan, and Thatcher. Soviet communism too has undergone many transformations: from a multiparty system for a year or two after the revolution, to "war communism," to the "new economic policy," to Stalin's totalitarianism, to Malenkov's "new course," to the Khrushchev and Brezhnev brands. The communist social system has ranged from Stalin's centralism (what may be called "war communism") to decentralized communism in Yugoslavia, with other forms in between.

Each of these forms of communism is the product of specific circumstances. What shaped the Soviet Union in its Stalinist stage were such mundane factors as a shortage of capital, the failure of socialist revolutions elsewhere, the bitter factional conflicts within the Party involving Bukharin, Stalin, Trotsky, Zinoviev, and Kamenev, the refusal of the West to grant long-term credits, and the privations after the war and civil war. What will shape it in the next few decades is another set of circumstances, now in the gestation stage – economic slowdown due to a rigid form of planning, an inadequate labor supply, the pressures of a sophisticated young generation demanding reform.

The two foremost problems Soviet communism had to contend with since its revolution have been the threat of intervention by the Western powers and the need to acquire capital for reconstruction and development. It was from these earthy concerns, more than from ideology or the character of its leaders, that the communist system took shape. At every juncture it could have taken a different turn; it had humanistic as well as totalitarian options open to it. It was not inherently destined to take the course it did, for there is nothing in the writings of Marx, Lenin, Trotsky, or Stalin that calls for abolishing free speech, introducing forced labor camps, or depriving citizens of the right to travel. On the contrary, their books and tracts stress the opposite: freedom, democracy, humanism. But their dreams fell asunder in the crucible of reality.

In November 1917, when the Bolsheviks came to power, they inherited an exhausted country that had suffered almost ten million casualties – dead, injured, or captured. Railroads were operating only sporadically, bread was in short supply, inflation had reached a rate of 400 percent during the previous two years, and scarcely a month later, a civil war began, led by four rightist generals who had the support of Britain, France, the United States, and fourteen foreign armies stationed on Soviet soil.[44] Russia, observed Walter Duranty of the *New York Times* was "a wilderness of disorder, disease and hunger."[45] By the time the civil war ended in 1920 the situation was catastrophic—millions had died from hunger and typhus alone (not less than a million during Admiral Kolchak's retreat from Siberia), and many thousands had perished on the battlefield. The grain harvest of 1920/21 was only 40 percent of prewar levels, industry only 15 percent, pig iron and steel less than 5 percent, coal less than 10 percent. Three-fourths of the locomotives and two-thirds of the freight cars were out of commission. To add to the difficulties, a crop failure in 1921 caused widespread famine. Had it not been for the daily food rations supplied by Herbert Hoover's American Relief Administration to 10 million children and adults, as well as the aid of the Soviet Relief Committee, to an equal number, millions more would have died of starvation.[46]

When they disposed of the civil war and foreign intervention the communists turned to their second problem: capital. Lenin and Trotsky had not really given this matter much thought; they had expected capital to flow into the Soviet Union from Germany and other developed countries after successful socialist revolutions in those lands. "The work of construction [in Russia]," Lenin said in 1919, "depends entirely upon how soon the revolution is victorious in the most important countries of Europe. Only after this victory can we seriously undertake the business of construction."[47] But the revolution failed "in the most important countries of Europe," notably in Germany, and the Soviet Union was left to its own devices; the capitalist West, particularly the United States, was unwilling to grant Moscow long-term loans.

In this state of affairs, Russian leaders finally realized that the capital they needed would have to come from sacrifices by their own people. For a brief time in 1922, Trotsky urged that the working class adopt a policy of "self-exploitation"—forego improvements in living standards, so that the moneys saved could be used for industrialization. But Russian laborers, who had already suffered excruciating privation, were in no mood for further sacrifices.

In the three-way dispute that ensued, Nikolai Bukharin proposed an annual rate of capital formation of 7 percent of the national income, (it was 9.5 percent before the war). Bukharin's policy had the merit of leaving ninety-three cents of every dollar (or ninety-three kopeks of every ruble) for personal and public consumption. Industrial development admittedly would proceed slowly, and most of Russia's imports would be consumer goods rather than capital goods, but neither the working class nor the peasantry would have to be "squeezed" to provide development funds.

Trotsky argued that the flaw in Bukharin's thinking was that the peasant would refuse to bring his grain to the market unless the state could provide finished goods. In fact, in 1926/27, when agricultural output was close to prewar levels, only 14 percent of harvested crop was being brought to the cities as against almost twice that percentage in the prewar years. To deal with this "scissors," Trotsky urged doubling the rate of capital formation to about 14 percent so that consumer-goods factories could be built to satisfy rural demands for cloth, seed, plows. The extra money would be exacted by a compulsory grain loan on the richest 6 percent of the peasantry; this "kulak" class would be squeezed, but the rest of the population would enjoy improved living standards, and the pace of industrialization would be respectable.[48]

Whether Bukharin's or Trotsky's formulas were workable, neither would evoke great popular opposition or require extraordinary police measures. Both were consistent with a limited degree of internal democracy; both, and certainly Bukharin's, would have been conducive to what the Czechs in 1968 would call socialism with a human face.

The third position, that of Stalin—who originally had agreed with Bukharin and had predicted that rapid industrialization "will certainly ruin us"[49]—was predicated on fears of a second Western intervention. The Sixth Congress of the Communist International, meeting in Moscow in June 1928, proclaimed that the Western nations, "with England at their head" were preparing an invasion of the Soviet Union.[50] This prognosis was eleven years wrong, but it was not all fantasy, for there *had* been a war scare in 1927. In this circumstance, Stalin decided that *no matter what the cost* the Soviet Union would have to industrialize rapidly, concentrating on those heavy industries, such as steel, that form the backbone for a military machine. Though there was no war as yet, this was in fact a war economy—one that diverted resources and energies from consumer goods to producer-goods industries, from light industry to heavy industry, from human needs to military needs. No matter what sacrifices the Soviet people made, it just had to be done, in Stalin's view, since there no longer was any hope for successful socialist revolutions in Germany, Britain, or anywhere else at that time.

The new capital was exacted from the whole population in the form of heavy taxes, forced loans, low wages, speed-up, rationing, high prices, a staggering inflation, the seizure of crops and livestock, and forced collectivization. The government printed four billion paper rubles from 1928 to 1933, tripling the money in circulation and reducing the purchasing power of money to 40 percent of what it had been in 1926.[51] Since the state needed grain for export—so as to buy industrial machinery abroad—the recalcitrant peasant, who balked at selling because there was so little to buy, had to be divested of his grain by compulsion. Stalin forced him to give up his land, his cattle, and his tools and join a collective farm managed by Party members and supported by the police.

As might be expected, peasants joined sullenly. Instead of placing their animals into the common pool, they slaughtered them or sold them to neighbors not yet collectivized. They ate the seed put aside for next year's crop; they destroyed equipment. It was a long time before Russia recovered from this silent war. "These years are a nightmare," wrote French author Victor Serge, who lived in the Soviet Union at that time. "Famine comes to the Ukraine, the Black Lands, Siberia, to all the Russian granaries. Thousands of peasants flee across the frontiers to Poland, Rumania, Persia, or China." The government responded with repression to the hostility that enveloped it. In the sixty-five days after December 27, 1929 alone, for instance, two million peasants were deported to remote places. Scores of small uprisings were suppressed, and tens of thousands of former Trotskyists and Bukharinists were unceremoniously jailed, held without bail or trial, and sent to forced labor camps.[52] Factionalism within the Party was outlawed, workers were required to carry internal passports and punished with jail terms for breaking work discipline. The secret police, tightly controlled by Stalin, became a power unto itself. There were other, less onerous, options opened to the Russian people (a slower and more balanced rate of industrialization, for instance, probably would have resulted ultimately in a richer economy), but Stalin took the most extreme and most painful course.

Thus was born a version of communism that may properly be called war communism. It was overcentralized, the state determining virtually everything—prices, wages, production quotas, foreign trade, personal living conditions. It was also, as all war economies are, a shortage economy. In an economy under rigid state control—particularly a poor one—it was not always possible to direct goods in the right quantities to where they were most needed. Thus, even today, two-thirds of a century after the revolution, one still sees long lines in Moscow for various commodities. Without a market mechanism, it was also difficult to control the quality of products—the plant manager had little incentive to produce better goods since he was judged, under the five-year plans, by the *quantity* of his production; and the consumer had no means by which to penalize the producer since there was only one source from which to buy: the State.

The Stalinist economic model continues in the Soviet world, with modifications, even now, a third of a century after Stalin's death. But both before and after Stalin's death there were opposition tendencies to "war communism."

* * * * * * *

The Western world did not create Stalin, nor is it responsible for his crimes. But by isolating the Soviet Union, denying it credits, and imposing embargoes on it, the West contributed to the emergence of Stalin*ism*. Inevitably, in this integrated world, capitalism and communism have affected each other's development, and in the critical period, Western capitalism contributed to the evolution of Stalinism. A different policy from Washington, London, and Paris might have influenced the emergence of a softer form of communism—a theory supported by what happened in Yugoslavia after its break with Stalin. Had the West taken a similar attitude toward Tito as it took to the Soviets in the 1920s, Yugoslavia would either have been driven back into the Soviet fold or, at the very least, re-adopted the Stalinist system of war communism. But the West did not; it did not invade Yugoslavia (as it had invaded Russia in 1918 to 1920), and it did not cut off economic contact; instead, it made available hundreds of millions in credits and other forms of aid. Yugoslavia, therefore, was able to develop differently from the Soviet Union and today probably points the direction toward which the communist world as a whole will ultimately be moving.[53]

Tito's quarrel with Stalin began over the issue of national autonomy—with the Yugoslav leader insisting that Moscow cease efforts to dominate his country—and evolved from there into a broader dispute on how a socialist state should function. In June 1948, the Titoists were ousted from the Communist Information Bureau (Cominform) and found themselves isolated from former trading partners. If Yugoslavia were to survive it had to turn to the West and the Third World to market its exports—one-sixth of everything it produced.

Changing from one market to another, however, was not just a matter of soliciting new customers. The Yugoslavs could not compete with Austria or Italy for the markets of the West because its machinery was less modern, its workers less efficient, and the quality of its goods inferior. To catch up it had to call on its people to be more efficient, which was impossible without tapping the initiative of managers, workers, and peasants. In the limited confines of the parallel market in which the Soviet bloc functioned (Comecon), price, quality, and unit cost could be partly disregarded by applying the heavy-handed methods of state manipulation—what Tito called "administrative socialism" or "bureaucratic centralism." Additional costs could be absorbed by manipulating wages and living standards.

"Administrative socialism" was no longer feasible in Yugoslavia, not only for economic reasons, but for military ones. In the early years after the break, Tito had to worry about a possible attack by the Red Army (as was to happen later in Hungary and Czechoslovakia). In that case too he would need the initiative and allegiance of the Yugoslav people to fight back. Out of these concerns was born the system of "self-management"—based on the checks and balances of a market system, competition, and popular involvement—that was to become the cornerstone of a different kind of communism.

Under the principles of self-management, the enterprise—mine, mill, factory, department store, hotel—is deemed to be under the collective operation of those who work it, not the nationalized property of the government. It is managed by the workers themselves, much like the producer cooperatives organized by the American labor leader, William H. Sylvis, in the nineteenth century. In each Yugoslav enterprise the workers elect a Workers' Council, which in turn chooses a Management Committee to decide matters of policy, as well as hire, fire, and set the salary for the director. The Management Committee determines what products to manufacture, how much and from what bank to borrow, the sales and advertising budgets, price ranges, what to export and import, and whether to merge with or arrange for pooling agreements with other enterprises.

Since the Management Committee is charged with earning a profit, it enjoys autonomy in sales as well as in production. Unlike the Stalinist system, in which a state planning institution determines the price as well as the retailer in advance, the self-managed enterprise in Yugoslavia can sell to anyone at whatever price it can get. A yard of cloth or a pack of cigarettes may sell for a certain price in one store and a different price in another. The enterprise hires salespeople, makes marketing surveys, places advertising on radio, television, billboards, and in newspapers — all aimed at increasing sales and profits. If this mode of operation seems similar to that of free-enterprise capitalism, it has the fundamental difference that the surpluses earned (profits) go to workers and society as a whole, not to individual entrepreneurs or shareholders. At the end of the year the government takes its share of the profits and the workers take theirs. Until the mid-1960s, the division was about two-thirds for the state, one-third for the workers. With the reform of 1965, however, the percentage was reversed so that the workers get more than twice as much as the state. The profits can be used by the Workers Council in one of three ways: for new equipment, for social improvements such as housing or medical facilities, or for employee bonuses. In effect, the members of the Workers' Collective do not receive wages as such, but rather, a share of the earnings.

There are other novel features to the self-management system. Economic planning is decentralized. Without spelling out the minute details, the government sets targets for new industrial facilities, such as steel mills; but instead of giving direct orders to individual ministries to carry them out, as in the Stalinist centralized planning, the Yugoslav federal government turns the matter over to the republics and their local administrative agencies to plan construction and operation. An enterprise may expand its plant or purchase new machinery without government permission. If the national regime is not satisfied with either the quantity or quality of production of an enterprise, it sometimes imports products from abroad to compete with its own enterprises, thereby pressuring them to become more efficient. To force its own soda water industry to improve it may import soda water from Italy, for instance. But it doesn't tell the enterprises what to do, what to charge, or what to pay.

The national government is kept in the background. So is the Party — the League of Communists — which usually allows members to disagree with each other on enterprise issues and run against each other for the management committees. It is a loose arrangement with relatively little compulsion—though what exists is more than critics like Milovan Djilas feel is necessary. (Djilas, once the second or third most powerful figure in Yugoslavia, supports the concept of self-management, but feels it cannot work well unless more democratic prerogatives are permitted than at present. A group of professors who started publishing an opposition magazine called *Praxis* in 1964, and have suffered reprisals but not jail, has a similar position.)[54]

There has been a steady rise in living standards in Yugoslavia despite periodic slippages. In 1960, Denis Healey, a leader of the British Labor Party, acclaimed Yugoslavia's rate of economic growth in the previous five years as exceeding that of any nation anywhere with the exception of China. "But unlike China," he noted, "Yugoslavia has also enjoyed a staggering increase in personal consumption."[55] It continued throughout the 1970s when per capita income rose to $2,300 according to Yugoslav statisticians, and $3,000 according to American analysts, as against $500 in 1963. A 1981 government paper, generally considered to be accurate, boasts that "in 1976 36 percent of all families owned a private car, compared to only 8 percent in 1968. . . . The share of food expenditures in total personal consumption declined from 54 percent in 1952 to 39 percent in 1973, per capita consumption of foods having been doubled in the meantime."[56] What is important in this saga is not the rate of growth but the way it was achieved. "South Korea and Taiwan," says a Yugoslav economist, "may have a similar rate of growth, but they have reached it by an intense exploitation of their labor force. We have done it while greatly improving the living standards of our people."[57]

Self-management has not been without its flaws, but it is proof that a different kind of communism—more decentralized and more humanistic—is possible, and that it can be helped along by a more judicious attitude on the part of the West.

* * * * * * *

No communist country has as yet widened the process of decisionmaking or extended personal freedom as far as Yugoslavia, but Hungary and China have moved part of the way toward self-management, and Poland, for a year prior to the institution of martial law in December 1981, was preparing to take similar steps. Four factors are nudging the communist world toward what the Czechs in 1968 called "socialism with a human face." First, the Soviet Union itself can now provide modest amounts of capital to its allies for economic development and offers a measure of defense against possible Western intervention. Second, there is the insistent demand of the ordinary citizen, especially as material hardship eases, for a better life. A third factor is the continuing demand of lesser members of the Soviet bloc for autonomy. Though Stalin and his successors were able to quash aspirations for greater independence in Bulgaria (which at one time hoped to form a Balkan Federation with Tito's Yugoslavia), East Germany, Hungary, Poland, and Czechoslovakia, the bonds have loosened somewhat recently—as indicated by Hungary's drift from the Stalinist model and Rumania's independence in international affairs.

The fourth and most important factor has been the exigencies of economics. Soviet planning has been overcentralized, stringently controlled, wasteful, and relatively inefficient. According to Isaac Deutscher, "as late as the mid-sixties Russian output per man-hour was estimated at only 40 percent that of the American."[58] This was considerable progress from the 1920s, when it was only 10 percent, but it was still a good distance from closing the gap. Up to a point, the disparity was not alarming because the communist countries (except for Czechoslovakia) could draw on a reserve of labor in the villages. Two people operating at 50 percent efficiency presumably could produce as much as one person at 100 percent. But the redundant labor in the villages is not inexhaustible and, as it dwindles, the communist countries find they can improve matters only by importing better labor-saving equipment and liberating the initiative of managers and workers, which has been dammed up for a long time. If the Kremlin hopes to continue its economic ascent, it will soon have to relax the reins of state domination and cater more urgently to the wishes of its people.

Communist leaders have not been unaware of this problem. Immediately after the death of Stalin in 1953, hundreds of thousands of people in forced labor camps were freed, and the camps as an institution, operated by the hated GULAG, were for the most part abolished. The secret police were deprived of some of their power, and a semblance of legality was introduced. This was not yet freedom, but it was a relaxation of repression. Georgi Malenkov, Party leader for a time, introduced the "New Course" in August that year. There was to be, Malenkov said, a "sharp rise in the production of consumer goods," a termination of the compulsory buy-up from collective farmers, and an increase in agricultural income of two billion rubles.[59] For the worker he held forth the prospect of lower prices and higher wages. The New Course in Russia invited emulation elsewhere. In East Germany, after the Berlin revolt of June 1953, the Socialist Unity Party voted to reduce investments in heavy industry by 1.7 billion marks and to reduce prices and taxes. Imre Nagy, just installed as premier of Hungary, also committed himself to curtailment of investments for heavy industry and a simultaneous improvement of living standards. His program envisioned a controlled withdrawal of peasants from collectives, more religious tolerance, and the closing of internment camps. The New Course, adopted in one form or another by the whole bloc, meant that communism was ready to slow the pace of capital investment in heavy industry so as to better meet the needs of its people. Typically, the Polish plan slashed the capital accumulation budget from 25.1 percent of the national product in 1953 to 19.8 percent in 1955. In those two years it was expected that retail trade for the consumer would rise by a fifth.

The New Course was aborted by Khrushchev after he eased Malenkov out of office. But the internal struggle within the communist camp continued, manifesting itself by the revolts in Poland and Hungary in 1956. Probably the clearest augury of what may be communism's future was the introduction of "socialism with a human face" in Czechoslovakia in 1968. Two currents came together to bring about this revolutionary development: writers and intellectuals who had been demanding democratic freedoms for a long time; and economists, like Ota Sik, who insisted that the country was at the end of the line unless it revised its economic system. A Czech leader recalls:

> Already in 1956 we began to feel something was wrong. Countries in the West began buying high quality goods from other Western countries, instead of average quality goods from us. Our orientation on heavy industry, it became obvious, had been a mistake since we were poor in raw materials such as iron ore. Our strength in the past had been our skilled labor in glass, wood, ceramics, shoes, textiles, leather, and the Skoda Works. But after the war those fields were neglected. We operated along 'extensive' lines, drawing in new people to the labor force from agriculture and women from the homes. But that supply of labor reached its peak in 1960 and after that we were in trou-

ble. We needed 'intensive' development through efficiency and automation; instead we thought we could solve our problems by adding more manpower. It didn't work.[60]

One of the reasons it didn't work was that only 18 percent of the Czech population lived on the farm as against 40 to 60 percent in other communist countries.

The dilemma of Czechoslovakia can be expressed in the following way: since there no longer was a reserve of labor to be drawn from the villages, it was necessary to rationalize industry, but to do so the country needed machinery and computers of a more advanced type than were available from the Soviet bloc. To pay for such equipment from the West, Czechoslovakia had to sell more goods *to* the West. But since its product was of inferior quality, it could not adequately compete on the world market. It could improve that quality and become cost efficient only if it stimulated the initiative of workers and managers. The economic problem, in other words, boiled down to a political one: either grant democratic freedom to the populace or stagnate.

Freedom of assembly and speech were revived; censorship was abolished. The unions expelled their old leaders (they refused to permit them to resign), reasserted the right to strike, and established a fund to pay strike benefits. Minority elements, such as the Slovaks, were granted a considerable degree of autonomy, and it was generally assumed that Czechoslovakia would become a federation of Republics on the Yugoslav model. Most important, the Party removed itself from day-to-day control of mass organizations, confining itself to policymaking, and leaving the implementation to those at the grass roots. Scores of new organizations blossomed to express divergent interests and views — thirty new youth groups alone. These political changes, it was generally assumed, were to be a prelude to an economic overhaul resembling the indicator planning and self-management in Yugoslavia. The mood in Prague that spring was to make communism work, not abolish it.

The Czech renaissance collapsed when Soviet tanks marched into Prague that August but, since like causes bring like effects, it is fair to assume that other communist countries, including the Soviet Union, will ultimately have to consider the Czech example. The Stalin model, though different from what it was in Stalin's day, cannot fit the needs of communism itself at its present stage. A relaxation of world tensions would induce the transformation more quickly. Continued tensions and a continued partial embargo on credits and trade will, of course, have the opposite effect. The United States, in a true sense, has the power to influence the course of Soviet development. But it does not have the power to "gradually erode" or destroy it.

* * * * * * *

Impeding a change in our policy are a number of "conventional wisdoms" we have imbibed in the course of decades of embitterment: "you can't trust the Russians," "they intend to take us over," "better dead than red," and so on.

It is true that we cannot trust the Russian government. It promised honest elections in Poland after the war but didn't live up to that promise. It promised self-determination to all peoples but used force to deny that right to the people of Hungary, Czechoslovakia, and Afghanistan, and used great pressure to deny it to the people of Poland and East Germany. It is also true, however, that we cannot trust *any* government, including our own. Nor should we, since we believe in "government by consent of the governed," a system in which the people are the watchdogs over their governors.

The United States, like the Soviet Union—like all governments— has also reneged on many promises. We pledged at the end of World War II that Germany would never be permitted to remilitarize and that the Ruhr would never be permitted to become an industrial base for militarism, but we not only encouraged Germany to rearm and provided it with the materiel, but have been nudging it to arm more rapidly in recent years. We made similar promises relative to Japan, forcing it, in fact, to write into its constitution that it would not reestablish a military force beyond that which was needed for domestic security. But we have been urging Japan also to devote a larger share of its GNP to armaments. We gave a solemn pledge in the United Nations charter and in many treaties not to intervene in the internal affairs of other nations, but that too has gone by the boards. Our CIA intervenes every day, and all too frequently goes so far as to overthrow governments it doesn't like. No government honors its promises unless it suits its purpose to do so, and we have been no better than the rest. To aver then that "you can't trust the Russians" is no more meaningful than to say that "vigilance—against all governments—is the eternal price of liberty." The Russians need not be singled out.

It is also true that the Soviet leadership would welcome the death of capitalism. Khrushchev may have been overdramatic when he exclaimed "we will bury you," but the Soviet hierarchy is not neutral on the question of capitalism's survival. It wishes for and works for its death. But why should that surprise anyone? Capitalist states, including ours, have repeatedly tried to strangle the communist system. It is in the nature of rival systems to fight each other, especially if they are both dynamic.

Nor is there anything dire about the charge that the Soviet Union would like to expand its sphere of influence. That is inherent in the very character of the nation-state. All nation-states have the same failing, none more so than the United States, which since 1945 has grown in power and influence more than any other nation-state in history. Morally, it may be right to question whether the Soviet Union should determine the destiny of Poland, or the United States that of El Salvador. But this is a problem that will remain with humanity until the nation-state itself is supplanted by an inter-nation state.

There is an undeniable divergence of interests between the American and Soviet governments. But what is unique about the present period is that there is one *convergence* of interests on an overriding issue, namely, the survival of the human species. The species itself is in jeopardy—not figuratively, but literally. We are much like two fighters flailing at each other, who suddenly discover that the ring is on fire. Unless they jointly put out the fire, neither can win the contest; both in fact will die.

Almost imperceptibly in the last third of a century, the Soviet Union and the United States have acquired a mutual enemy: technology. For the first time in history, the human species can destroy itself, and for the first time in history the institution of war has become obsolete. It can no longer be the final arbiter in international disputes between the superpowers; it can only be the final death trap. We can shout ourselves hoarse that "you can't trust the Russians" and we can flatter ourselves with macho slogans such as "better dead than red," but common sense dictates that we somehow join hands to save the human species.

We have no other choice anyway; no matter what we do, Soviet communism will not disappear.

STRATEGY FOR SURVIVAL 7

This is the fourth traumatic moment in American history. The first culminated in the revolution of 1776. Had we not made that revolution we might have remained thirteen colonies or thirteen nation-states limited to the Eastern seaboard, our economy underdeveloped and perhaps still dependent on the British. Or, some of the colonies might have joined Canada, some might have been incorporated into the Spanish empire (which then owned the Floridas and Mexico), probably to be seized later by either France or Britain. We certainly would not have made the Louisiana Purchase in 1802, which added 828,000 square miles to our territory. A third possibility is that the colonies might have evolved into thirteen small nations no more significant in world affairs than Guatemala or Colombia, living side by side perhaps with a British-sponsored Indian nation to the West, with California, New Mexico, and Texas still provinces of Mexico, Alaska part of the Soviet Union, Oregon and Washington a province of Canada or a separate British colony, and Hawaii a small independent state in the Pacific. There would have been no *United States* as we know it, and what did exist would certainly not be number one in the firmament of nations.

The second traumatic moment reached its apogee with the civil war of 1861 to 1865. Again, the nation was unable to continue in the old direction, with two hostile social systems — capitalism in the

North and slavery in the South—living within the same political body. Had Northern capitalism not overwhelmed the Southern Bourbons, we might have split into two countries. We certainly could not have developed the industrial structure or living standards we now have. Despite the robber barons and the corruption and heartlessness of the "gilded age," we expanded more rapidly in the ensuing decades than ever before.

The third traumatic moment, in the 1930s, coincided with the most debilitating depression in our history. It was no longer possible to continue with laissez-faire capitalism unless we were prepared to accept as its successor either communism or fascism. Roosevelt, as he himself boasted on more than one occasion, saved the system by introducing a form of state-controlled capitalism, including Keynesian economics and the welfare state.

There may have been other options at each of these historical flash points. Karl Marx and American socialists believed in 1861, for instance, that the Civil War would pave the way for socialism here. But the paths that were taken at each turning point were adequate to give our nation a new thrust. Had they not been taken we could not have resolved the crises of 1775, 1861, or 1933 without either stagnation or disintegration.

We are now at a fourth traumatic moment in our history, more critical than the other three because the stakes are higher, and if we do not take a quantum jump toward a prorevolutionary and antinuclear policy we face extinction. If we remain wedded to the strategy of containment, we will face a Hobson's choice: continue to challenge each revolution or leftist insurrection as it surfaces, hoping that eventually, by a reverse domino effect, the revolutionaries and their supposed sponsors—the Soviets—will become demoralized and give up; or, launch a "disarming first strike" against the Soviet Union in the hopes of winning a nuclear war. The first alternative dooms us to one little intervention and war after another, until we are enervated, like Rome, or until a "little" war evolves into the big one. The second takes us directly to the big war. Neither of these courses is a feasible policy.

Our true security lies in joining the revolution of rising expectations and in undertaking the complex task of disarmament. Unfortunately, these are not minor, schematic changes, like adding a few billion dollars to our economic aid program or cutting a few thousand warheads from our nuclear arsenal. They involve a change in our way of life so drastic that our past will be virtually unrecognizable — just as were the changes after the revolution, civil war, and Great Depression. Our biggest handicap may be our inability to recognize the dimensions of our problem and the drastic nature of the needed change.

* * * * * * *

The broad objective of a strategy of survival should be what professor Saul Mendlovitz calls "demilitarization"— the ultimate abolition of three systems that now threaten human existence. Those include: the war machines and auxiliary institutions on which the nations of the world now expend almost $600 billion a year; and the systems of local tyranny (dictatorships) and hegemonism (domination of weak nations by strong ones) that those military machines were designed to perpetuate. That of course is a tall order; it moves us into a period of the unknown as awesome as the one our forebears faced when they made the historic pilgrimage from a nomadic society to an agrarian one, or from feudal stagnation to the dynamism of industrial capitalism. To implement such an objective as demilitarization is, in effect, to reverse thousands of years of history. It involves not only political but psychological and cultural changes, the dimensions of which cannot be fully forecast. But the starting points are obvious: (1) we must disarm; and (2) we must help the revolution of rising expectations reach fruition.

We cannot, of course, make revolution in another country — nor should we — but we can help it with judicious aid, or hinder it, as we often do now. The criteria we have been using since the 1940s for granting aid to other countries has been whether it helped our business interests and furthered our strategic objectives. Nations that received our Marshall Plan aid had to pledge they would loosen restrictions on our commerce and investments and, in some instances, give opportunities for our private entrepreneurs to expand — the Rockefeller interests, for instance, were allowed to purchase 600,000 shares of Tanganyika Concessions in the Belgian Congo as a condition for aid to the mother country. We were never averse to having the poor in recipient countries benefit from our aid, but the overriding concern was profits for our own businesspeople. In the majority of cases, that meant forming an alliance with the rich in our client states to help them repress the poor — thereby scuttling any hopes for social improvement. If now we are to join the revolution of rising expectations we must adopt the opposite criteria: how our aid will help the lower and middle classes complete their revolution. To put it differently, we would exchange aid and know-how for pledges of social reform and international integration.

There are a variety of ways such a policy could be implemented. We could carry it out by ourselves unilaterally, or we could form a compact of the wealthier nations, including the Soviet Union, to set aside a certain percentage of their GNPs for international aid—administered either by an existing world agency or one to be created. The supranational approach is preferable because the donor agency would not be under the same kind of pressure from establishment interests at home. It could concentrate more readily on its prime objectives: alleviating hunger, disease, illiteracy and poverty; and creating the rudiments for democracy.

The specific details obviously are complex and would have to be elaborated by experts and technicians in each instance, but their general thrust is apparent. We—and the other developed nations— would terminate military aid to regimes in the developing countries since, as things now stand, most of that aid simply helps military dictators suppress their own people. For the same reason, we would withdraw our CIA agents from foreign lands, and pursue a policy of openness.

On the economic front, our aid would carry conditions, as it does now, but of a different nature. Recipient states would be judged on: how well they were implementing a fair and viable land reform; village development; education; health and housing programs; whether they were reducing the gap between the upper and lower classes; whether they were muting or increasing dissent. Such a program obviously can be abused but as with everything else in politics, vigilance and political participation are the ultimate guarantors of social justice.

Money is not the only requisite for economic development. One of the problems faced by poor countries has been that foreign corporations warp the economies of their hosts. They buy farm land, for instance, to produce cash crops for *export*, rather than foodstuffs for the home market. They withdraw profits to their home country instead of reinvesting them at the source. The petroleum industry in Mexico illustrates the point. For decades before Lazaro Cardenas nationalized it in 1938, oil did little to enhance the native economy. Standard Oil—and a few others—brought the "black gold" to the surface, put it in tankers for shipment elsewhere, and sent the profits to New York. After nationalization, however, oil became a fulcrum for economic development at home. Placing the industry under the aegis of the Mexican government made it possible to use oil for developing the *Mexican* economy. The nationalized company, Pemex, used its resources to launch fertilizer, petrochemical, insecticide, paint, and other industries. It encouraged electrification and spurred the building of 25,000 miles of modern highways. "By supplying fuel below cost," the First National City Bank of New York said, "Pemex has played an important role in subsidizing agriculture, industry and public transportation."[1] Standard Oil would not have done that; it was interested in taking out, not putting in.

To reorient foreign investment to serve native economies, one suggested technique is the "fifty-fifty company." The United States would put up the venture capital for a new enterprise (or buy out one of our own companies in that country), provide the supervisory help, and operate the undertaking. The native government would own 50 percent of the stock—with no investment—and enjoy no management prerogatives for some time. We, the United States, would manage the facility and withdraw a certain amount of the profits each year to cover our investment. We would train local engineers and administrators, and after ten, fifteen, or twenty years, turn over the company to our hosts, free and clear. Hopefully our allies and the Soviets would adopt a similar program. This is a better system of aid for industrial development than that of using private enterprise for the job because (1) it can be coordinated with the economic plans of the developing nation, and (2) it leaves most of the profits at home for further investment. It is not a system that has been tried extensively, but at one time Israel and Ghana had an arrangement of this sort for the shipping industry of Ghana. Britain and Burma also had one for the mining industry of Burma.

Another program to help along the revolution of rising expectations might be the formation of customs unions, common markets, and eventually "internations." Most of the countries that have attained independence are either too small or too weak to survive on their limited resources and limited markets. They are hindered by unfavorable terms of trade, tariffs, quotas, and other restrictions placed on their exports by stronger states. Self-interest dictates that they take steps to amalgamate with nearby nations in similar plight; but they cannot do so without temporary dislocation of their economies. The long-term value of customs unions and common markets, as the European common market has shown, can be negated unless weaker industries are given support. For instance, assume that a cusoms union is formed in the Caribbean and that the beer industry of country A is less efficient than the one of country B; lifting tariffs between them will mean that the beer companies in A will fall behind those of B and perhaps go bankrupt, leaving employees out of work, facilities unused, and so on. To prevent that from happening, the nations in the area need scrupulous planning (with which we can help), economic support to renovate the closed plants so they can be used for other purposes, and work for the displaced workers. Customs unions and common markets are not yet sure-fire steps toward economic viability, but they are, as Shakespeare might have said, consumations devoutly to be wished.

None of these proposals should be taken as panaceas in themselves. They simply indicate direction—the direction our government ought to take in its relations with revolutionary countries. The specifics lend themselves to endless variety and innovation so long as the purpose remains to cast our lot with popular revolution rather than with counterrevolution.

* * * * * * *

A more pressing problem—because we are racing the clock—is what to do about the Bomb. Revolutionary progress will take time, but the Bomb is an immediate threat that becomes increasingly dire. Unfortunately, too much time has already passed for there to be easy solutions. When the nuclear age began in 1945, it would have been simpler to do what has to be done now. Our thinking patterns were not so frozen; our intelligentsia was avidly discussing proposals for world government and pointing to long-term perils unless the nuclear menace was capped. "The secret of the atomic bomb," Albert Einstein said in a *Newsweek* interview March 10, 1947, "is to America what the Maginot Line was to France before 1939. It gives us imaginary security and in this respect it is a great danger."[2] Many people were making the same point, arguing not just for modification of official policy, as liberals are doing now, but for reversal. The number of bombs to be disposed of then could be counted on the fingers of both hands; they were owned by a single power, and, in the view of the White House, no other nations were likely to get them for many years. A radical revision of policy thus would not have had to contend with as many obstacles or clash with as many entrenched interests.

In point of fact, fundamentally new approaches to the future were occasionally expressed even in the higher echelons of government. Returning from the San Francisco United Nations Conference in the spring of 1945, President Truman implied to a Kansas City audience that he favored the idea of world government:

> It will be just as easy for nations to get along in a republic of the world as it is for you to get along in the republic of the United States. Now when Kansas and Colorado have a quarrel over water in the Arkansas River they don't call out the National Guard in each state and go to war over it. They bring a suit in the Supreme Court of the United States and abide by the decision. There isn't a reason in the world why we cannot do that internationally.[3]

Truman did not pursue this objective, but the idea that more than a hundred nations might give up their individual sovereignty to become a single supranation was certainly a revolutionary one.

There was a strong feeling in the 1940s—held by a sizable and influential minority—that humanity was at a crossroads at which drastic alterations in goals and lifestyle had to be made. In a memorandum to Truman on September 11, 1945, urging an "atomic partnership" with the Soviet Union, Secretary of War Stimson—who, ironically, had only the month before ordered the dropping of nuclear bombs on Japan—put his finger on the problem with remarkable clarity. If "the atomic bomb were merely another though more devastating military weapon," he said, we could "follow the old custom of secrecy and nationalistic military superiority." The Bomb, however, is "too revolutionary and dangerous to fit into the old concepts. I think it really caps the climax of the race between man's growing technical power for destructiveness and his psychological power of self-control and group control—his moral power."[4] We were at a climactic moment, in other words, where humanity had to either adopt a moral policy or ultimately see itself destroyed. Stimson urged, as a step toward avoiding this catastrophe, atomic partnership with the Russians. Even Bernard Baruch, in presenting his plan for atomic disarmament to the United Nations on June 14, 1946, spoke in apocalyptic terms: "We are here to make a choice between the quick and the dead. We must elect world peace or world destruction."[5]

The openness to new ideas, however, closed off within a few years and was extinguished entirely when McCarthyism arrived on the scene in 1950. It still has not been fully revived; we consider suspect, for instance, many proposals on which there has been no (or only superficial) national discussion—ideas such as economic planning or unilateral initiatives for disarmament. In an era of revolution we are hesitant about adopting even liberal ideas, and we often backslide on some already adopted. By way of example, in 1964, with prospects for disarmament dim, the thought occurred to some people at the United Nations that perhaps the superpowers might at least agree to a "freeze" on nuclear weapons.[6] Lyndon Johnson accepted the suggestion, adding the word "verified" to "freeze," and thus was born the Strategic Arms Limitation Talks that began, after years of delay, in 1969. The SALT agreements subsequently negotiated, however, did not "freeze" the number of strategic weapons on both sides; they allowed them to rise by many thousands, in tandem. Then, in 1982 we reinvented the wheel—a "freeze" movement caught popular fancy and its theme was translated into a resolution in Congress signed by 200 representatives and senators. We were back, in other words, to an idea that had been born eighteen years before, except that this time another president, Reagan, vehemently rejected the resolution.

Although it is more difficult for Americans to formulate and execute a strategy for survival now than it would have been in 1945, the rudiments of such a strategy are approximately what they were then. On the immediate agenda, today as yesterday, is the matter of disarmament—beginning with nuclear weapons, biological weapons, chemical weapons, and finally conventional arms. Disarmament by itself will not guarantee permanent peace; if we were to dismantle all the nuclear bombs in the world there would still be innumerable people who know how to produce them, as well as stocks of plutonium and uranium–235 to fuel them. If all uranium-enrichment plants and plutonium reactors were torn down, it would be possible nonetheless for scientists and engineers to assemble fission bombs—like the kind terrorists may be making soon—and, thereafter, more sophisticated ones. We cannot delude ourselves that disarmament is a final goal but, on the other hand, we must recognize that without it there is no possibility whatever for developing the structure for peace.

Dozens of nations are at the threshhold of the nuclear club today. Some can produce the super weapon within a few months after they decide to do so—for instance, Japan or Germany. Others may already have secretly stockpiled a supply—Israel and perhaps South Africa. Still others are perilously close to a breakthrough—Pakistan, Taiwan, Brazil, Argentina, and others. By the year 2000, says the Committee for Economic Development, a prestigious group of business leaders, "the total plutonium expected to have been produced as a by-product of nuclear power would be equivalent in explosive potential to one million bombs of the size that destroyed Nagasaki."[7] The longer we tarry in reversing the arms race, the greater the likelihood of a nuclear war either in a direct confrontation between the superpowers themselves or one ignited by a smaller nation that may soon enter the nuclear club.

In any case, once we concede that containment cannot work—that the Soviet system will not disappear and the revolution of rising expectations will not be curbed—armaments become an expensive anachronism that can do little to enhance either our own or the planet's security. A demilitarized world, uneasy as we all are about something so alien to our experience, becomes an indispensable first step toward survival. The question can no longer be whether to demilitarize; it must become how and when to do so.

The superpowers can, if they wish, begin this process of disarmament where they left off in 1955, when the Soviets accepted in principle a British–French scheme, approved by Washington, for step-by-step disarmament. Under its terms the superpowers agreed to prohibit the use of nuclear weapons "except for defense against aggression"; to reduce their conventional forces to certain levels—a million or a million and a half each for the United States, the Soviet Union, and China, and 650,000 each for Britain and France; and to terminate the manufacture of nuclear weapons after the first half of the scale-down of conventional arms has been completed.[8] That was an encouraging beginning, but it was vitiated when our government withdrew its own proposal.

If the 1954/55 disarmament plan is no longer feasible, the superpowers can try another formula, beginning with a freeze on the production, testing and deployment of nuclear weapons and proceeding to a timetable for dismantling present stockpiles and reducing conventional forces. It is a drawn-out, but not an overtaxing, process; any number of experts can work out the details in short order. Critics on the Right might object that during this interim period we would be leaving ourselves vulnerable to Soviet mischief. But we —

and they—have so much overkill capability that we would retain a deterrent capability even after reducing stockpiles by as much as 95 percent. Should the Soviets become uncomfortable with a "disarmament partnership," they would be lunatics to attack us whether we had 9,200 strategic warheads in our silos, submarines, and on our bombers, or just 5,000 on our submarines; the threat of retaliatory annihilation would be virtually the same. Former Defense Secretary Robert S. McNamara once stated that one hundred nuclear weapons dropped on the Soviet Union would cause the death of at least 35 million people and the destruction of almost two-thirds of its industrial capacity.[9] That should be more than enough to give them pause. There is so much overkill in both arsenals, so large a so-called margin of safety, that the dangers in reversing the arms race are minuscle compared to the dangers of continuing it. In any case, it is unquestionably a risk worth taking.

The deterrent capability of each of the superpowers is so substantial, each can take unilateral initiatives to break the barriers of distrust between them—without jeopardizing its security. The word "unilateral" terrifies people by conjuring the image of our nation inviting occupation or demolition. But in fact a unilateral initiative can speed multilateral action. When the Russians stopped nuclear testing in 1958 unilaterally—without requiring any American quid pro quo—they in fact accelerated the process of negotiating a test ban. Within months, world opinion caused the United States to follow suit, and after Kennedy came into office the two sides began negotiations on the issue. One-sided initiatives, though limited in what they accomplish, can help achieve a broader purpose—namely, a sense of trust between the parties.

Until now we have had unilateral build-ups, each side doing much as it pleased, and the process of *dis*armament has been subordinate to the process of *re*armament. Most disarmament proposals actually have been predicated on retaining or expanding an advantage. Under the disarmament plan but before the United Nations by Bernard Baruch in 1946, for instance, the United States would have been permitted to continue research, development, and manufacture of nuclear bombs, while the Russians, who did not as yet have the Bomb, would have been required to end their research program and allow inspectors to monitor their land. From the Truman era to the Reagan era, that has been the general rule—"arms control" proposals that either escalate the armament levels or put the United States in a superior position. This approach is understandable – if not accept-able – because Washington presently equates military superiority with national security. But once that mind-set is cleared away and we be-come reconciled to a no-war world, disarmament can proceed with-out too many hitches.

It would be idle to discount other impediments to disarmament. There are physical, psychological, and historical questions that are not fully answered. Many people – including some social scientists – believe that war is endemic to human nature, that nothing can be done to change it. The popular expression is that "there have always *been* wars, there will always *be* wars." But that is a bit too glib, for it means that a thinking, innovative animal capable of reaching the moon and releasing the hidden energy of the atom is incapable of preventing its own suicide. "War has so long been a part of human life," writes Bertrand Russell, "that it is difficult for our feelings and our imaginations to grasp that the present anarchic national free-doms are likely to result in freedom only for corpses."[10] Whatever the psychological reality, however, to allow ourselves to be pessimis-tic about human nature is a luxury we cannot afford.

There are other subtle obstacles that hobble disarmament – such as a vulgar nationalism that insists we must be "number one" or the alleged need of a nation to focus on an "outside enemy." It seems to be a characteristic of human nature that if you give a people some-one or something to hate, they love you for it. Hitler gave the Ger-mans the Jews to hate, our leaders give us the communists. This is a formidable matter to overcome, requiring adjustments in education and behavior. But it certainly cannot be more formidable than split-ting the atom or launching a space vehicle toward the planet Mars. Demilitarization itself will spur the adjustments and other devices, only beginning to be explored, will also reorient human attitudes. It is worth reminding ourselves that a large section of the clergy that once believed there was such a thing as a "just" war no longer be-lieves a just war possible.

If we put aside the long-term behavioral difficulties, the short-term problems of the actual disarmament agreement are manageable. These include: which weapons to dispose of first; what to do with the plutonium–239 and uranium–235 from the dismantled bombs; how large a conventional force to allow for internal, domestic secu-rity; how to verify that the terms are being agreed to; how long the process should take; and how to punish violations. These are not simple questions to grapple with, particularly after so many decades in which militarism has been institutionalized, but there are answers to all of them that Soviet and American negotiators can work out if they stop seeking one-sided advantage. ("No country has permanent friends or permanent enemies, but only permanent interests," the late Secretary-General of the United Nations, U Thant, once said.)[11] The issue of inspection, for instance, is already partly resolved by the space satellites that monitor and photograph Soviet military installations. Which bombs and delivery systems to dismantle first may be more complicated since each side would want the other to give up those it considers the biggest threat at the moment (for the U.S. that might be the Russian SS–18s). But herculean as the task appears, it is not impossible. The reductions can be made based on megatonage, costs, lethality, or a combination of criteria and, as already indicated, would be mitigated by the fact that both sides have such a sizable overkill capability that the reduction process could begin almost anywhere without jeopardizing their security.

* * * * * * *

Disarmament, unfortunately, is not a self-enclosed system whereby you get rid of the weapons and everything else remains the same. Just as the process of rearmament dictated a whole set of institutional changes—collectively called the National Security State—so the process of disarmament will dictate institutional changes. If nations give up their troops and bombs, what will replace them as the final arbiter in international disputes? While the superpowers are disarming, they will confront a corollary set of problems: how to convince the rest of the world to follow suit; how to police and adjudicate international disputes in the interim—and afterwards, how to deal with the social problems that have led to both intranational and international violence so often; how to take up the slack left in economies by arms reductions; how to find a modus vivendi between social systems so different from each other. None of this can be done without thinking in *supra*national terms, that is, without the nations of the world giving up—or being forced to give up—part or all of their sovereignty. That is a problem of a new dimension, alien to our pigeonholed existence as "Americans," "Germans," "Russians," and so on. Still, it is not an altogether new idea; it was not only bruited about by a good part of the postwar intelligentsia in such books as *One World or None*, but alluded to occasionally in government proposals. Tired of having been put to the ordeal of two world wars, postwar leaders in many places recognized that some sort of international police mechanism had to be interposed between rival nations to keep them from fighting. Truman records in his memoirs how impressed he was by the "Grand Design" of King Henry IV of France, which "called for a kind of federation of sovereign states in Europe to act in concert to prevent wars."[12] The United Nations charter provided vaguely for an international police force to enforce peace, and some hoped that such a force might one day take the place of national armies. Supranationalism was an idea being explored in many places.

President Truman's statement that it would be good if the whole world were covered by a single *enforceable* legal structure to resolve international disputes may have been an off-hand remark without further significance, but in his first disarmament proposal—the 1946 Baruch Plan—he at least paid lip service to the idea of curtailing sovereignty for the United States, the Soviet Union, and the other nations. Under its provisions, an International Atomic Development Authority would assume "various forms of ownership, dominion, licenses, operation, inspection, research, and management" of everything associated with nuclear atomic energy throughout the world, including uranium mines and fission bombs.[13] The Baruch Plan was filled with items that made it suspect even to American leaders, including former atomic energy chief David Lilienthal. As with proposals Washington would make for many years thereafter, it was long on inspection but short on disarmament. Be that as it may, it is significant that the Truman Administration, if only for a short period, was willing to accept limitations on American sovereignty. Unfortunately, the idea receded into history's memory box in cadence with the Cold War. But it was an idea to which the intelligentsia returned repeatedly.

In April 1948, the Emergency Committee of Atomic Scientists issued a policy statement that reflected the opinion of many American intellectuals. There are "three possible lines of policy" for the West, it said. One was a "preventative war" while the United States still had a monopoly of the bomb; but, it said, "let us not delude ourselves that victory in such a war would be cheap and easy. At the outset the Russians would occupy all of Europe up to the Atlantic seaboard. . . ." The second possible policy outlined was "maintenance of an armed peace in a two-bloc world, which, historically, has always led to war." The third possibility was "the drive for world government . . . the creation of a supranational authority with powers sufficient to maintain law among nations."[14] Among those with similar notions were Robert Maynard Hutchins, Walter Lippmann, and Bertrand Russell. Even British conservative Harold Macmillan, as minister of defense in March 1955, urged the House of Commons to adopt a disarmament plan that would "provide effective international, if we like supranational, authority invested with real power. Hon. Members may say that this is elevating the United Nations, or whatever may be the authority, into something like world government; be it so, it is none the worse for that. In the long run this is the only way out for mankind."[15]

The tragedy of the postwar period, it is clear in retrospect, is that our government felt so sure it could police the world by itself. Armed with the atom, it shelved consideration of a world authority that unlike the United Nations, would have "real power." Today, having delayed for a third of a century, we are back to our dilemma, for there can be no enduring peace unless military and other power is taken from the hands of individual nation-states and put in the hands of a supranational body. And there can be no effective disarmament unless such supranational institutions are put in place concurrently, for the nations that are in the process of disarming would have justified fears that the nations that have not yet disarmed would use the opportunity to invade neighbors or lay claim to Third World territory. Without supranational law that can be enforced by a supranational military body, disarmament would become a dead letter. "Law is a farce," Bertrand Russell once observed, "unless there is power to enforce it. . . ."[16]

The need for supranationalism arises from yet another source, namely, the internationalization of many problems other than armaments. Nuclear radiation is one such problem, for if the nuclear bomb should ever be used again, its radiation would cross international borders with impunity. An estimate made by a committee of experts headed by Jerome Wiesner in 1974 concluded that in a limited nuclear war in which Soviet missiles struck "ICBM fields alone" with one-megaton bombs per silo, there would be 3.5 million to 22 million dead in the United States, plus 800,000 dead and 400,000 wounded in Canada.[17] Thus, a war in which Canada had no part would take a toll of five percent of its population.

Another internationalized problem arises from the ozone layer, which shelters us from ultraviolet rays and hence, cancer. In the last ten years the layer of ozone has been depleted at the rate of about 0.5 percent per year, as a result, among other things, of the increased propulsion of carbon dioxide into the atmosphere.[18] Obviously that cannot continue indefinitely, but it is not a problem that can or should be resolved by a single nation. Nor can a single nation exploit the many trillions of dollars worth of minerals in the ocean without havoc and perhaps war. Satellites in the stratosphere pose still another international problem, since either of the superpowers can, if it wishes, cause chaos with communications on Earth by detonating a nuclear bomb 125 miles overhead or just emplacing a supply of plutonium in a satellite on high. Disease, pollution, hunger, and other facets of our lives are also steadily becoming internationalized and hence call for supranational bodies to cope with them.

The blueprints suggested for such bodies tend to fall under two classifications: federative and functional. Under the federative approach, the armies of various nations, for instance, would be federated into a single army, under a single international leadership, beholden to no individual nation-state. Some of the theorists on this subject have suggested a tight federation, others a loose one. A few months after the Bomb was dropped on Hiroshima, Albert Einstein proposed that

> the secret of the bomb should be committed to a world government, and the United States should immediately announce its readiness to do so. Such a world government should be established by the United States, the Soviet Union and Great Britain, the only three powers which possess great military strength. . . . The fact that there are only three nations with great military power should make it easier, rather than harder, to establish a world government.[19]

Einstein, though a pacifist, felt that the great powers might have to pressure reluctant nations—even militarily—into international amalgamation. On the other hand, Bertrand Russell in 1961 suggested "a *voluntary* agreement among nations to pool their armed forces and submit to an agreed International Authority." (Emphasis added.) To obviate the possibility that a national contingent might be called on to fight its own people, Russell urged establishment of an orderly legal structure—a world constitution, a world legislature, and a world executive with "irresistable military power. Irresistable military power is the most essential condition and also the most difficult to fulfill."[20] The nations would have to agree in advance, Russell insisted, to forswear the use of nuclear bombs and to reduce their armed forces to a level compatible with internal security, no more. Russell had other ideas for preventing a coagulation of power — organizing mixed armed units of many nationalities and giving higher commands to "men from small countries which would not entertain any hope of world dominion." The world government would have the right to verify that affiliated governments were abiding by their disarmament schedule.

There is obviously a range of possibilities for the formation of world government, some not necessarily as all-encompassing as either the Einstein or Russell plans. For instance, the United States and the Soviet Union might jointly undertake a program of forming customs unions in various areas and eventually, after some experience with each other, "internations": a United States of North Africa, a United States of South America, a United States of Sub-Sahara Africa, a United States of Southeast Asia, and so on. These internations would be a transitional step toward world government.

A functional supranational body, in contrast to a federative body, would operate in a single area, impinging only partially on the sovereignty of individual nations. The Baruch Plan is an example of this approach. The plan, as already noted, had flaws that made it unacceptable, but purged of those flaws, it would have ended the nuclear arms race and established an embryonic form of world government.

In 1969, the late Secretary General of the United Nations, U Thant, proposed four supranational agencies to deal with the proliferation of nuclear weaponry, pollution, population, and poverty — the "four p's." "I do not wish to seem overdramatic," Thant told the U.N., "but I can only conclude . . . that the Members of the United Nations have perhaps ten years left in which to subordinate their ancient quarrels and launch a global partnership to curb the arms race, to improve the human environment, to defuse the population explosion, and to supply the required momentum to development efforts."[21] He feared, he said, that unless this were done "the problems [he] mentioned will have reached such staggering proportions that they will be beyond our capacity to control." U Thant was wrong on his timetable, but there is little doubt that an increasing number of problems demand international solution. And that is true not only insofar as the interests of weak nations are concerned, but even the strong.

According to the U.S. Bureau of Mines, all but one of the eleven most needed minerals will be exhausted a few decades from now. If somehow the resources are quintupled, the supply of bauxite, copper, lead, natural gas, petroleum, and silver will run out in six or seven decades, tin and tungsten a few years later; only the supply of coal will be adequate for the long run.[22] Perhaps the supplies can be increased by a factor of ten or twenty, but that poses derivative questions: How will the ersatz industries be subsidized? What will happen to the developing nations whose resources are depleted? How will the conflict between nations rich in resources and those poor be resolved in a period of shortage? None of this seems amenable to solution without the global partnership U Thant spoke of, and that is equally true of the arms issue. Supranationalism is clearly an urgent item on history's agenda, and though most of us would prefer nationalist solutions to all our problems, we are much in the position of Britain after Dunkirk when it offered France immediate unification as a single state in order to keep it in the war. We are in the same kind of emergency, only this one encompasses the whole planet.

* * * * * * *

It would be misleading to minimize the problems of either joining the revolution of rising expectations or initiating disarmament. There are objections every step of the way. The various supranationalist proposals that have been put forth since 1945 are almost certainly too schematic, too simplistic, and inadequately detailed. They do not come to grips with myriad problems. For example, if you leave weapons in the hands of an army, won't the people who control that army eventually establish a dictatorship? (John M. Swomley, Jr., a well-known pacifist professor, argues that "a world government is feasible *only* in a disarmed world.")[23] Can a capitalist society live in harmony with a communist or socialist society? Can a democratic regime work with a dictatorial one? How would a world legislature be selected or elected? Who would initiate legislation? How would it be passed? Would the international judicial system supersede national ones, or exist side by side, functioning in its own area of jurisdiction? Should those nations that refuse to join be punished, and if so, how? Can poor nations be enticed into world government unless assured of utimately erasing their poverty? To make changes so sweeping requires more than intellectual speculation, for what we are discussing is blending scores of nationalisms and cultures that took centuries to evolve. To expect them to blend easily and harmoniously would be foolhardy. The record for political blueprints in fact is fair at best. Adam Smith's free enterprise system was supposed to be immune to depression; it wasn't. Karl Marx's socialist system was supposed to be immune both to economic problems and social injustice; it hasn't been. Even the best of plans, like the best of machines, need fine tuning and adjustment.

Though the goal may be in accord with historical necessity, there are a host of unknowns in the uncharted plans for world government. Even its strongest advocates concede the point. Bertrand Russell, in his book *Has Man A Future?*, wrote of the "grave psychological obstacle . . . that there would be no outside enemy to fear. Social cohesion, insofar as it is instinctive, is mainly promoted by a common danger or a common enemy."[24] We tend to establish both our individual and national identities in relation to adversaries. No doubt this is a resolvable problem, for we cultivate the cooperative spirit as well, and that can be powerfully reinforced through education. Yet we have never done such educating on a mass scale; it needs the work of thousands of experts and millions of teachers.

Other factors that urge us to proceed cautiously include the method by which we move from nationalism to supranationalism. Will that in itself require a violent revolution? Do we need a new political party to mobilize for such a revolution? Can the transformation take place peacefully and in stages? Will world government come about in one fell swoop, or as part of a long process? What domestic changes will become necessary as we erect the framework for supranationalism? If we save hundreds of billions in our military budget, to what extent will we use that to broaden the welfare state – to introduce, for instance, national health insurance and similar reforms? Supranationalism is not a formula for communism (the communists in fact seldom talk about it anymore), but neither is it a formula for retaining the social status quo. Once the disarmament process gathers momentum, key facets of our present way of life are bound to change.

The same is true of the Soviet Union. The centralized form of communism is not likely to survive disarmament, if only because it will release hundreds of billions of rubles for capital formation and consumer goods in the Soviet orbit and China.

What all this suggests is that, in light of the many unknowns and variables, it would be wise for humankind to proceed cautiously into the new tomorrow. The best procedure probably would be to begin disarmament and create an international agency to dismantle and destroy nuclear weapons and monitor the world against new proliferation. With this, the nations might establish an international police force, an international court whose edicts it would enforce, and an international body to deal with world poverty. Such steps may not be as exhilerating to idealistic hearts as an all-encompassing blueprint. But it has the merit of being workable, and for idealistic persons who long for an end to the war system, that may be the greatest exhileration of all.

Many on the Right very likely would say that such a program turns the world over to communism, but in fact it saves the world from suicide. Many on the Left would charge that none of this is possible until capitalism is first overthrown through world revolution, but in fact the struggle against war is *the* world revolution. The important point is to heed the clarion and move persistently in its direction—no matter how far away it is at the moment.

NOTES

CHAPTER ONE

1. H.G. Wells, *The Outline of History*, New York: Macmillan, 1922, p. 402.
2. Herbert Aptheker, *The American Revolution 1763-1783*, New York: International Publishers, 1960, p. 119.
3. W.N. Weech, ed., *History of the World*, London: Odhams Press Limited, n.d., p. 567.
4. Ibid., p. 568.
5. Winston Churchill, *The Gathering Storm*, vol. 1, *The Second World War*, Boston: Houghton Mifflin, 1948, p. 475.
6. Thomas M. Johnson, "As The War Begins," *Current History*, October 1939, p. 24.
7. Pierre Belperron, *Maginot of the Line*, London: Williams and Morgate Ltd. 1940, p. 111.
8. Robert Stausz-Hupe, "France Goes To War," *Current History*, November 1939, p. 24; Winston Churchill, *Their Finest Hour*, vol. 2, *The Second World War*, Boston: Houghton Mifflin, 1949, pp. 30, 32, 33.
9. Strausz-Hupe, op. cit., p. 24.
10. "Gallicus," "The French Military Problem," *19th Century*, March 1939, p. 314.
11. "Underground Forts," *Literary Digest*, January 29, 1938, pp. 17-18; Belperron, op. cit., p. 108.
12. Dorothy Thompson, *Current History*, June 1940, p. 52.
13. "Underground Forts," op. cit., p. 17.
14. Strausz-Hupe, op. cit., p. 24.

15. Belperron, op. cit., *Maginot of the Line*, p. 112.
16. Ibid., pp. 113, 124.
17. Churchill, *Their Finest Hour*, p. 191.
18. Ibid., pp. 31, 40, 43.
19. *Chicago Sun-Times*, January 29, 1982, p. 4.

CHAPTER TWO

1. Lewis Broad, *Winston Churchill, A Biography*, New York: Hawthorn Books, 1958, p. 186.
2. R. Palme Dutt, *World Politics 1918-1936*, New York: International Publishers, 1936, p. 47.
3. Isaac Deutscher, *The Prophet Armed*, Oxford: Oxford Press, 1954, p. 443; Philip S. Foner, *The Bolshevik Revolution*, New York: International Publishers, 1967, pp. 30-32.
4. William Henry Chamberlin, *The Russian Revolution, 1917-1921*, 2 vols. New York: Macmillan, 1935, vol. 2, p. 156.
5. Walter Lippmann and Charles Merz, "A Test of the News," *New Republic*, August 4, 1920, p. 288.
6. Victor Serge, *From Lenin to Stalin*, New York: Pioneer Publishers, 1937, p. 63; Leon Trotsky, *The Revolution Betrayed*, New York: Pioneer Publishers, 1945, pp. 33, 35; Walter Duranty, *The Story of Soviet Russia*, Philadelphia: Lippincott, 1944, pp. 44 ff; Foner, op. cit., p. 32.
7. Duranty, op. cit., pp. 46, 50.
8. A. Mitchell Palmer, "The Case Against The Reds," *Forum*, February 1920.
9. For more details, see my *Radicalism in America*, New York: Thomas Y. Crowell, 1969, pp. 262-63.
10. Lewis Broad, op. cit., p. 183.
11. "Soviet Russia and the United States," *Current History*, September 1920, p. 931.
12. Brynjolf J. Hovde, "Russian-American Relations 1917-1927," *Current History*, November 1927, p. 235.
13. See Duranty, op. cit., ch. 10, pp. 117 ff. For a general economic picture of the Soviet Union in its early days: Manya Gordon, *Workers Before and After Lenin*, New York: Dutton, 1941. For the U.S. attitude toward the Soviet Union: Frederick L. Schuman, *American Policy Toward Russia Since 1917*, New York: International Publishers, 1928.
14. David Horowitz, *The Free World Colossus*, New York: Hill and Wang, 1965, p. 61 footnote.
15. Hugh Seton-Watson, *From Lenin to Malenkov*, New York: Praeger, 1954, p. 223.
16. D.F. Fleming, *The Cold War and Its Origins, 1917-1950*, 2 vols., New York: Doubleday, 1961, vol. 1, p. 51.

17. Browder's altered attitude toward capitalism is dealt with in some detail in Irving Howe and Lewis Coser, *The American Communist Party*, New York: Praeger, 1962, pp. 424–30.

18. Robert E. Sherwood, *Roosevelt and Hopkins*, New York: Bantam Books, 1950, vol. 1, p. 440.

19. Ibid., vol. 2, p. 475.

20. Milovan Djilas, *Conversations With Stalin*, New York: Harcourt Brace and World, 1962, p. 114.

21. Elliot Roosevelt, *As He Saw It*, New York: Duell, Sloan, and Pearce, 1946, p. 41.

22. The provisions are listed in encyclopedias and almanacs of various kinds. I have copied this section from *Information Please*, 1970, p. 564.

23. James F. Byrnes, *Speaking Frankly*, New York: Harper, 1947, pp. 35–36.

24. Barton J. Bernstein and Allen J. Matusow, *The Truman Administration: A Documentary History*, New York: Harper Colophon Books, 1966, pp. 221–24.

25. James P. Warburg, *The United States in a Changing World*, New York: Putnam, 1954, p. 413.

26. Gar Alperovitz, *Atomic Diplomacy: Hiroshima and Potsdam*, London: Secker and Warburg, 1966; Martin J. Sherwin, *A World Destroyed*, New York: Knopf, 1975.

27. William D. Leahy, *I Was There*, London: Whittlesey House, 1950, pp. 351–52.

28. Lloyd C. Gardner, *Architects of Illusion*, Chicago: Quadrangle, 1970, p. 130.

29. Robert A Divine, ed., *American Foreign Policy*, New York: Meridian Books, 1960, pp. 264–65.

30. Adam Ciolkosz, "Poland," in Dennis Healey, ed., *The Curtain Falls*, London: Praeger, 1951, pp. 38, 41, 44, 46.

31. Walter LaFeber, *American, Russia and the Cold War, 1945–1971*, New York: Wiley, 1972, p. 17.

32. Divine, op. cit., pp. 264–65.

33. Warburg, op. cit., p. 416.

34. Clifford let me read this document in his office in 1976. I was allowed to make notes but not to xerox it. He said it was still classified.

35. George F. Kennan, "The Sources of Soviet Conduct," *Foreign Affairs*, July 1947, pp. 566–82.

36. LaFeber, op. cit., p. 55.

37. George F. Kennan, *Memoirs 1925–1950*, Boston: Little, Brown, 1967, p. 364.

38. Revealed by Senator Henry Jackson, *Time*, January 28, 1980. p. 13.

39. James Burnham, *Containment or Liberation*, New York: John Day, 1953, pp. 158–66.

40. Harry S. Truman, *Memoirs*, vol. 1, *Years of Decision*, New York: Doubleday, 1955, p. 87.
41. *Time*, September 11, 1950, p. 22.
42. *Time*, September 4, 1950, p. 12.
43. Jeane J. Kirkpatrick, at the American Enterprise Institute meeting, December 8, 1981.
44. Norman Podhoretz, *The Present Danger*, New York: Simon and Schuster, 1980, p. 21.
45. Ibid., p. 37.
46. For the full story see William Shawcross, *Sideshow, the Secret War in Cambodia*, New York: Simon and Schuster, 1979.
47. Podhoretz, op. cit., pp. 32-3.
48. James Fallows, *National Defense*, New York: Random House, 1981, pp. 144-45.
49. *New York Times*, January 18, 1982, p. 21.
50. George F. Kennan, "The Sources of Soviet Conduct," *Foreign Affairs*, July 1947.
51. J. Wszelaki, *Communist Economic Strategy: The Role of East Central Europe*, Washington: National Planning Association, 1959, pp. 68-77.
52. Zbigniew K. Brzezinski, *The Soviet Bloc, Unity and Conflict*, New York: Praeger, 1963, pp. 94-7.
53. Samuel Pisar, *Coexistence and Commerce*, New York: McGraw-Hill, 1970, pp. 125-26.
54. *Defense Monitor* (published by the Center for Defense Information in Washington), January 1980, p. 4.
55. *New York Times*, March 10, 1946.
56. *Multinational Monitor*, November 1981, pp. 19-20.

CHAPTER THREE

1. Harry S. Truman, *Memoirs*, 2 vols., *Years of Decision*, vol. 1, New York: Doubleday, 1955, p. 421.
2. Ibid., p. 87.
3. Ibid., p. 343.
4. Barton J. Bernstein and Allen J. Matusow, eds., *The Truman Administration: A Documentary History*, New York: Harper & Row, 1968, pp. 43, 46.
5. John M. Swomley, Jr. disputes my position as to why the Soviet Union withdrew. In his *American Empire* (Macmillan 1970, p. 101) he argues that the Soviets withdrew under "real pressure" from the U.N. Security Council and because they had concluded an agreement to establish "a joint Iranian-Russian oil company which would give the Soviet Union control of the company for the first twenty-five years of a fifty-year con-

cession, and equal control for the next twenty-five years." After the Soviet withdrawal, the Iranian parliament "refused to ratify the oil agreement."

6. *Chicago Sun-Times*, May 20, 1981.

7. *New York Times*, June 26, 1976.

8. P.M.S. Blackett, *Studies of War*, New York: Hill and Wang, 1962, p. 9.

9. Raymond Aron, *The Great Debate*, New York: Doubleday Anchor, 1965, p. 14.

10. Published in *National War College Review*, May–June 1975, pp. 51, 65, 81.

11. Blackett, op. cit., p. 9.

12. Ralph Lapp, *Arms Beyond Doubt*, New York: Cowles Book Co., 1970, p. 175.

13. Blackett, op cit., pp. 11-12.

14. *National War College Review*, op cit., pp. 66, 68, 97.

15. Herman Kahn, "The Nature and Feasibility of War and Deterrance," in Walter F. Hahn and John C. Neff, eds., *American Strategy in a Nuclear Age*, New York: Anchor, 1960, p. 219.

16. *Chicago Sun-Times*, November 6, 1981, p. 45.

17. Stockholm International Peace Research Institute (SIPRI), "Armaments or Disarmament?" Brochure, 1982, p. 12.

18. *Chicago Sun-Times*, January 20, 1981, p. 18.

19. The speed of a missile is computed in D.G. Hoag, "Ballistic Missile Guidance," in *Impact of New Technologies on the Arms Race*, B.T. Feld, T. Greenwood, G.W. Rathjens and S. Weinberg, eds., Cambridge, Mass.: M.I.T. Press, 1971, pp. 19-108.

20. Robert Jungk, *Brighter Than a Hundred Suns*, New York: Harcourt Brace, 1958, pp. 183-84, 349; The Franck Committee report was published in the *Bulletin of The Atomic Scientists*, May 1946, pp. 2-4, 16.

21. The Eisenhower quote is from a speech delivered to the Republican National convention in San Francisco, August 23, 1956. The MacArthur quote is from a speech delivered by him to the Joint Session of Congress of the Philippines, July 5, 1961. Printed in the *Defense Monitor* (published by the Center for Defense Information, Washington, D.C.) vol. 9, no. 6, 1980.

22. For more on this issue see Sidney Lens, "The Case Against Civil Defense," *Progressive*, February 1962.

23. Interview Ren F. Reed of Defense Civil Preparedness Agency, 1976. This strategy is called "Crisis Relocation."

24. *Life*, September 15, 1961.

25. Leslie Brown, director of the State Department's Office of International Security Policy, notes that if Crisis Relocation were put into effect it would "take on a somewhat irreversible character to those observing [on the other side] ... It's a damn drastic thing to do." He points out that

even during the 1962 October missile crisis President Kennedy did not call on the people to leave the cities. "I don't think any President would want to tip his hand to that extent."

26. For a congent discussion of the ABM issue see Abram Chayes and Jerome B. Wiesner, *ABM: An Evaluation Of The Decision To Deploy An Antiballistic Missile System*, New York: Harper & Row, 1969, pp. 3, 15, 16, 17.

27. Ibid., p. 14.

28. Ibid., p. 25.

29. See two articles by Bob Aldridge in the *Nation*, March 25, 1978. p. 333; October 18, 1980, pp. 369-70.

30. *New York Times*, March 29, 1981; *Chicago Tribune*, April 11, 1981, p. 6.

31. *Bulletin of the Atomic Scientists*, May 1981, pp. 52-3.

32. Chayes, Wiesner, op. cit., p. 14.

33. James Fallows, *National Defense*, New York: Random House, 1981, pp. 148 ff.

34. *Science*, May 29, 1981, p. 1009; June 12, 1981, pp. 1248, 1250-51.

35. *Science*, June 12, 1981.

36. Letter by Dr. Michiu Kaku of City College of New York to author.

37. *New York Times*, November 26, 1975, op-ed page.

38. Fallows, op cit., pp. 149 ff.

39. *Washington Post*, January 26, 1969.

40. *Chicago Sun-Times*, February 1, 1981, p. 6.

41. Center for Defense Information, press release, Washington, D.C., August 3, 1981.

42. Stefan Leader, *Philadelphia Inquirer*, July 20, 1975.

43. Fallows, op. cit., pp. 144-45.

44. Quoted in "Quotes: Nuclear War," Center for Defense Information, Washington, D.C. No date, p. 11. From B.H. Lidell Hart, *Why Don't We Learn From History?* London: Allen & Urwin, 1944.

45. Jerome H. Kahn, *Security in the Nuclear Age*, Washington, D.C.: Brookings Institution, 1975, p. 330.

46. Dean Acheson, *Present at the Creation*, New York: Norton, 1960, pp. 478-80.

47. H.R. Haldeman, with Joseph DiMona, *The Ends of Power*, New York: Dell, 1978, pp. 81-85, 97, 98; Richard M. Nixon, *RN: The Memoirs of Richard Nixon*, New York: Grosset and Dunlap, 1978, pp. 393-414.

48. *Chicago Sun-Times*, March 15, 1977, p. 32; Richard J. Barnet, *The Giants: Russia and America*, New York: Simon and Schuster, 1977, pp. 18-20.

49. C. Wright Mills, *The Causes of World War III*, New York: Simon and Schuster, 1958, p. 82.

50. *Congressional Quarterly*, May 23, 1969, p. 760.

51. Leonard Rodberg and Derek Shearer, eds., *The Pentagon Watchers*, New York: Doubleday Anchor, 1970, p. 45.

52. Arms control report, U.S. Arms Control and Disarmament Agency, July 1976, p. 18. Reported in *Washington Post*, July 30, 1976.

53. *Time*, May 22, 1977, p. 15.

54. Center for Defense Information Quotes, op. cit., p. 30.

55. Quoted Bulletin of the Friends Committee on National Legislation, Washington, D.C., February 1981, p. 4.

56. *Boston Globe*, December 8, 1978, p. 2.

57. Vice Admiral Hyman G. Rickover, testimony before the Subcommittee on Appropriations, House of Representatives, June 19, 1973.

CHAPTER FOUR

1. See Gar Alperovitz, *Atomic Diplomacy: Hiroshima and Potsdam*, London: Secker and Warburg, 1966; Martin J. Sherwin, *A World Destroyed*, New York: Knopf, 1975.

2. Harry S. Truman, *Memoirs*, vol. 1, *Years of Decision*, New York: Doubleday, 1955, p. 87.

3. Milovan Djilas, *Conversations With Stalin*, New York: Harcourt, Brace, and World, 1962, pp. 181–82.

4. D.F. Fleming, *The Cold War and its Origins, 1950–1960*, New York: Doubleday, 1961, vol. 2, p. 1060; Isaac Deutscher, *Russia: What Next?* New York: Oxford University Press, 1953, pp. 99–101.

5. John W. Spanier, *American Foreign Policy Since World War II*, New York: Praeger, 1960, p. 37.

6. *New York Herald-Tribune*, July 12, 1946.

7. See Richard J. Barnet, *Intervention and Revolution*, New York: World, 1968, pp. 84–85.

8. Richard Hofstadter, *The American Political Tradition*, New York: Vintage, 1954, p. 349.

9. Ibid., p. 348 footnote.

10. Noam Chomsky, *Towards A New Cold War*, New York: Pantheon, 1982, p. 98.

11. Noam Chomsky, "The Cold War and the Superpowers," *Monthly Review*, November 1981, p. 1.

12. William Appleman Williams, *The Tragedy of American Diplomacy*, Mountain View, Calif.: World, 1959, p. 148.

13. Lloyd C. Gardner, *Economic Aspects of New Deal Diplomacy*, Madison: University of Wisconsin Press, 1964, pp. 282–83.

14. David W. Eakins, "Business Planners and America's Postwar Expansion," in David Horowitz, ed., *Corporations and the Cold War*, New York: Monthly Review Press, 1969, p. 156.

15. Williams, op. cit., p. 166.

16. Gardner, op. cit., pp. 315–18.

17. Truman, op. cit., vol. 1, p. 10.
18. Williams, op. cit., p. 148.
19. Barton J. Bernstein and Allen J. Matusow, eds., *The Truman Administration: A Documentary History*, New York: Harper Colophon Books, 1968, pp. 219–21.
20. Kumar Goshal, *People in the Colonies*, White Plains, N.Y.: Sheridan House, 1958, pp. 266–68.
21. Ibid., p. 268.
22. William J. Pomeroy, *Guerrilla and Counter-Guerrilla Warfare*, New York: International Publishers, 1964, p. 63.
23. Alex Campbell, "The Philippines, Sugar, Rice, and a Great Deal of Ice," *New Republic*, March 12, 1966, p. 23.
24. Robert A. Divine, ed., *American Foreign Policy*, New York: Meridian Books, 1960, pp. 264–65.
25. David Horowitz, *The Free World Colossus*, New York: Hill & Wang, 1965, p. 58.
26. Fleming, op. cit., vol. 1, 1917–1950, p. 183.
27. L.V. Stavrianos, *Greece: American Dilemma and Opportunity*, Chicago: Henry Regnery, 1952, pp. 135–36.
28. Ibid., p. 150.
29. *New York Herald-Tribune*, September 17, 1946.
30. Truman, op. cit., vol. 2, p. 112.
31. Barnet, op. cit., p. 115.
32. Horowitz, op. cit., p. 164.
33. I.F. Stone, *The Truman Era*, New York: Monthly Review Press, 1953, p. 75.
34. Barnet, op. cit., p. 229.
35. Ibid., p. 230.
36. Ibid., pp. 232–33.
37. Dwight D. Eisenhower, *Mandate For A Change*, New York: Doubleday, 1963, pp. 422–23 footnote.
38. *New York Times*, January 28, 1982, p. 23.
39. *Parade* Magazine, January 24, 1982, p. 17.
40. *Parade* Magazine, October 10, 1971.
41. Eisenhower, op. cit., p. 422.
42. Interview with author.
43. Interview with author.
44. Eisenhower, op. cit., p. 160 footnote.
45. Barnet, op. cit., pp. 226–27.
46. Andrew Tully, *CIA, The Inside Story*, New York: William Morrow, 1962, p. 88; Also see Davis Wise and Thomas B. Ross, *Invisible Government*, New York: Random House, 1968.
47. Barnet, op. cit., p. 228.

48. Joseph W. Stilwell, *Stilwell's Papers*, New York: W. Sloane Associates, 1948, p. 320.

49. Fleming, op. cit., vol. 2, p. 549.

50. K.S. Karol, *China: The Other Communism*, New York: Hill and Wang, 1967, p. 66.

51. Kumar Goshal, *People in Colonies*, White Plains, N.Y.: Sheridan House, 1948, pp. 69-71; Karol, op. cit., pp. 65-67; W.J. Hail, *Tseng Kuofan and the T'ai P'ing Rebellion*, 1926.

52. Hans J. Morgenthau, *Defense of the National Interest*, 1951, p. 257.

53. Foster Hailey, *Half of One World*, New York: Macmillan, 1950, p. 51.

CHAPTER FIVE

1. Letter to author, November 9, 1981.

2. Elliot Roosevelt, *As He Saw It*, New York: Duell, Sloan, and Pearce, 1946, p. 41.

3. For a left-wing account of pre- and postwar nationalism in the colonies: Kumar Goshal, *People in the Colonies*, White Plains, N.Y.: Sheridan House, 1948.

4. This story has been told in many places. Additional sources are: A. Roselli, "Guerrilla War as it Really Is," *Harper's*, August 1953; "Dead End in Vietnam," *New Republic*, October 12, 1963; Jean Lacouture, *Vietnam Between Two Truces*, New York: Random House, 1966. For a broader view of events in the continent: Virginia Thompson and Richard Adloff, *The Left Wing in Southeast Asia*, New York: William Sloane, 1950.

5. Nejla Izzeddin, *The Arab World, Past, Present and Future*, Chicago: Regnery, 1953, pp. 105-6, 114, 138. John Gunther, *Inside Africa*, New York: Harper, pp. 201 ff.

6. Thomas Patrick Melady, *Profiles of African Leaders*, New York: Macmillan, 1961. This section is also based on interviews by author in Kenya and Ghana.

7. Much of this material on Latin America is gathered from interviews on the spot during a number of trips to Latin America. Other sources: John Gerassi, *The Great Fear*, New York: Macmillan, 1963; Samuel Shapiro, *Invisible Latin America*, Boston: Beacon, 1963; Albert Weisbord, *Latin American Actuality*, Seacaucus, N.Y.: Citadel, 1964; Richard Gott, *Guerrilla Movements in Latin America*, New York: Anchor, 1964.

8. Jeffrey Stein, "Graduate School for Juntas," *Nation*, May 21, 1977.

9. *Progressive*, January 1967, p. 31.

10. For more details on the Guyana story, see Sidney Lens, "Lovestone Diplomacy," *Nation*, July 5, 1965; Sidney Lens, "Labor Lieutenants of the Cold War," *Progressive*, April 1967.

11. For more details: Warren Hinckle and William Turner, *The Fish Is Red*, New York: Harper, 1981, pp. 102-3; Richard Barnet, *Intervention and Revolution*, New York: World, 1968, p. 156; Tad Szulc, *Dominican Diary*, New York: Dell, 1965, p. 28 ff.
12. *New York Times*, May 3, 1965.
13. Martin J. Sherwin, *A World Destroyed*, New York: Knopf, 1975, pp. 204-5.
14. Barton J. Bernstein and Allen J. Matusow, eds., *The Truman Administration: A Documentary History*, New York: Harper Colophon Books, 1966, pp. 219-21.
15. Clifton Brock, *Americans for Democratic Action*, Washington, D.C.: Public Affairs Press, 1962, p. 46.
16. Robert Borosage, "The Making of the National Security State," in Leonard S. Rodberg and Derek Shearer, eds., *Pentagon Watchers*, New York: Anchor, 1970, p. 47.
17. *New York Times*, April 9, 1969.
18. Senate Select Committee on Intelligence Report, 1976, pp. 42-43.
19. Borosage, op. cit., p. 15.
20. Report prepared by Library of Congress, Senate Foreign Relations Committee, December 1971.
21. Borosage, op. cit., p. 45.
22. Frank Donner, "HUAC: The Dossier Keepers," *Studies on the Left*, I, no. 4 (1961): 12-13.
23. Borosage, op. cit., p. 50.
24. Ibid.
25. Marshall Knappen, *An Introduction to American Foreign Policy*, New York: Harper, 1956, p. 337.
26. Senate Foreign Relations Committee, 1966; The Clark quote appeared in a Pennsylvania union paper. Trade Union Courier, January 1967.
27. Amaury de Riencourt, *The American Empire*, New York: Dial, 1960, p. 96.
28. Senate Committee on Foreign Relations Hearings on Nonproliferation Treaty, February 18, 20, 1969, p. 509.
29. Dr. Herbert J. Schiller, "The Use of American Power in the Post Colonial World," *Massachusetts Review*, 9, no. 4.
30. John Fischer, *Master Plan U.S.A.*, New York: Harper, 1951, p. 84.
31. Hanson W. Baldwin, *New York Times*, February 24, 1954.
32. Herbert L. Matthews, *The Cuban Story*, New York: Braziller, 1961, pp. 54 ff.
33. Leo Huberman and Paul M Sweezey, *Anatomy of a Revolution*, New York: Monthly Review Press, 1960, p. 29.
34. Hinckle and Turner, op. cit., pp. 20, 25-26, 36-37, 75-79, 107, 124, 126, 173-4, 189, 213, 217, 268.

35. Ibid., p. 9.
36. Samuel Shapiro, "Cuba, A Dissenting Report," *New Republic*, September 12, 1960, p. 15.
37. Hinckle and Turner, op. cit., p. 33.
38. Ibid., p. 98.
39. Shapiro, op. cit., p. 15.
40. This information was given to the author in two interviews with Regino Boti, Cuban Minister of Economics.
41. *Wall Street Journal*, January 19, 1982.
42. Shapiro, op. cit., p. 15.
43. Offer given to author and transmitted to Adlai Stevenson, who sent it on to Kennedy, January 1961.
44. *Guardian* (New York), November 14, 1970, p. 11.
45. Beau Grosscup, "Kissinger's Africa Policy: What Else is New?" *Progressive*, October 1976.
46. See Arthur Gavshon, *Crisis in Africa*, New York: Penguin Books, 1981.
47. Ibid., pp. 234, 252.
48. Ibid., p. 243.
49. John Stockwell, *In Search of Enemies*, New York: Norton, 1978, p. 188.
50. See Gerald Clark, *The Coming Explosion in Latin America*, New York: David McKay, 1962, p. 263 ff.
51. Ibid., p. 261.
52. For a description of these events see "Report on the Americas," NACLA (North American Committee on Latin America.) May–June 1980.
53. Noam Chomsky and Edward S. Herman, *The Washington Connection and Third World Fascism*, Boston: South End Press, 1979, p. 284.
54. Penny Lernoux, "Latin America: A Political Guide to Thirty-three Nations," *Nation*, August 22–29, 1981, p. 143.
55. *New York Times*, January 18, 1982, p. 10.
56. Lernoux, op. cit., p. 137.
57. Marvin E. Gettleman, ed., *Vietnam: History, Documents and Opinions of a Major World Crisis*, New York: Fawcett, 1965, p. 89.
58. Roscoe Drummond and Gaston Coblentz, *Duel At the Brink*, New York: Doubleday, 1960, p. 121.
59. Committee of Concerned Asian Scholars, *The Indochina Story*, New York: Bantam, 1970, p. 35.
60. Ibid., p. 34; And in Marvin Gettleman, op. cit., pp. 211 ff.
61. A. Roselli, "Guerrilla Warfare As It Really Is," *Harper's*, August 1953.
62. Mansour Farhang, *U.S. Imperialism; From The Spanish–American War To The Iranian Revolution*, Boston: South End Press, 1981, p. 148.
63. Ibid., p. 147.
64. Ibid., p. 147–48.
65. Ibid., p. 145.

66. Ibid., p. 139.
67. Ibid., p. 146.
68. "Repression's Friend," *New York Times*, October 10, 1974.
69. Thomas A. Bailey, *A Diplomatic History of the American People*, New York: Appleton-Century-Crofts, 1969, p. 661.
70. See Harry Magdoff, "International Economic Distress and the Third World," *Monthly Review*, April 1982.
71. John Buell, "After Reaganomics, What?" *Progressive*, July 1982, p. 22.

CHAPTER SIX

1. *New York Times*, January 18, 1982, p. 21.
2. Michael T. Klare, *Beyond The "Vietnam Syndrome": U.S. Intervention in the 1980s*, Washington, D.C.: Institute for Policy Studies, 1981, p. 6.
3. Robert W. Tucker, "The Purposes of American Power," *Foreign Affairs*, Winter 1980/81.
4. Norman Podhoretz, *The Present Danger*, New York: Simon and Schuster, 1980, p. 49.
5. *Business Week*, March 12, 1979, pp. 3-4.
6. Klare, op. cit., p. 21.
7. Noam Chomsky, *Towards A New Cold War*, New York: Pantheon, 1982, p. 189.
8. *New York Times*, October 4, 1979.
9. Klare, op. cit., p. 36.
10. For the full list, see *New York Times*, November 23, 1981, p. 14.
11. Klare, op. cit., p. 36.
12. *Time*, March 29, 1982, p. 19.
13. *Defense Monitor*, June 1980, p. 1.
14. Caspar Weinberger, *Annual Report to the Congress, Fiscal 1983*, February 8, 1982, p. II-3.
15. Military Budget Manual, *A Report by the National SANE Education Fund*, Washington, D.C.: April 1982, p. 1.
16. *Chicago Sun-Times*, February 18, 1982, p. 20.
17. Military Budget Manual, op. cit., p. 8.
18. Michael T. Klare, "Reagan's Gun Collection," *Mother Jones*, February-March 1981, p. 6.
19. Military Budget Manual, op. cit., p. 8; Bob Aldridge, "The Pentagon On The Warpath," *Nation*, March 27, 1982, p. 361.
20. Edgar Ulsamer, "Realism In The Defense Budget," *Air Force*, April 1982, p. 46.
21. *The Washington Spectator*, June 1, 1982, p. 3.
22. Ibid.

23. Institute for Policy Studies, *The New Generation of Nuclear Weapons*, Washington, D.C., p. 10.

24. Aldridge, op. cit.; Military Budget Manual, op. cit., p. 12.

25. Military Budget Manual, op. cit., p. 12.

26. Institute for Policy Studies, op. cit., p. 12.

27. Ibid.

28. Klare, "Reagan's Gun Collection," op. cit., p. 6.

29. *New York Times*, May 30, 1982.

30. *Time*, March 29, 1982, p. 19.

31. *Chicago Sun-Times*, June 29, 1982, p. 25.

32. Alan Worlfe, "In Search of Autonomy," *Nation*, February 27, 1982, p. 244.

33. In 1961, after President Kennedy revealed his plan for fallout shelters, I had a talk with a deputy to Defense Secretary McNamara. "You know these shelters are useless," I told him, "why do you go ahead with them?" "Maybe so," he said, "But it will force the Russians to spend large sums, reduce the living standards of their people, and increase hostility to the government. What's wrong with that?"

34. Henry Kissinger, "Trading With The Russians," *New Republic*, June 2, 1982, p. 15.

35. *Inquiry* magazine, Editors, July 1982, p. 4.

36. Ground Zero, *Nuclear War: What's In It For You?* New York: Pocket Books, 1982, app. C.

37. *Chicago Sun-Times*, July 19, 1982, p. 51.

38. *Business Week*, July 19, 1982, p. 51.

39. The first act of civil disobedience against the Vietnam War in 1965 attracted 200 people.

40. Norman Podhoretz, "The Neo-Conservative Anguish Over Reagan's Foreign Policy," *New York Times Magazine*, May 2, 1982.

41. John W. Fulbright, "The Fatal Obsession in U.S. Foreign Policy," *Progressive*, September 1958.

42. *Business Week*, October 19, 1981, p. 72.

43. *Boston Globe*, July 18, 1982, pp. 1 and 11.

44. V.M. Chernov, *Great Russian Revolution*, translated and abridged by Philip E. Mosely, New Haven: Yale University Press, 1936, p. 164; William Henry Chamberlin, *The Russian Revolution: 1917–1921*, vol. 1, New York: Macmillan, 1935, pp. 223, 236.

45. Walter Duranty, *USSR: The Story of Soviet Russia*, Philadelphia: Lippincott, 1944, p. 44.

46. George F. Kennan, *Russia and the West Under Lenin and Stalin*, Boston: Atlantic, Little Brown, 1960, p. 79.

47. David Horowitz, *Empire and Revolution*, New York: Random House, 1969, p. 130.

48. For more details on the Burkharin–Trotsky–Stalin dispute, see: Boris Souvarine, *Stalin*, New York: Longmans, Green, 1939, pp. 421–24; Leon Trotsky, *The Revolution Betrayed*, New York: Pioneer Publishers, 1945, pp. 25–33; Sidney Lens, *A World in Revolution*, New York: Praeger, 1956, pp. 117–23.

49. Souvarine, op. cit.

50. Hugh Seton–Watson, *From Lenin to Malenkov: The History of World Communism*, New York: Praeger, 1954, p. 107.

51. Victor Serge, *From Lenin to Stalin*, New York: Pioneer Publishers, 1937, p. 63.

52. Ibid., pp. 58, 61, 77.

53. Most of the material in this section comes from research during a number of visits to Yugoslavia. I have written a brochure on the subject for the *Foreign Policy Association* and articles for the *Progressive*. The last of my articles appeared in the *Progressive*, October 1981.

54. Interview of Praxis leaders in Belgrade, July 1981.

55. Denis Healy, *New Leader*, December 31, 1960, p. 3.

56. Yugoslav government fact sheet.

57. Interview, July 1981.

58. Isaac Deutscher, *The Unfinished Revolution: Russia 1917 to 1967*, Oxford: Oxford University Press, p. 49.

60. Interview with leading Czech economist, August 1968.

CHAPTER SEVEN

1. *Mexico Today*, pamphlet published by First National City Bank, Mexico City.

2. Otto Nathan and Heinz Norden, eds., *Einstein on Peace*, New York: Shocken Books, 1960, p. 4.

3. Barton J. Bernstein and Allen J. Matusow, eds., *The Truman Administration*, New York: Harper Colophon Books, 1968, p. 163.

4. Ibid., p. 222.

5. Ibid., p. 225.

6. *SIPRI Yearbook of World Armaments and Disarmament, 1968/69*, New York: Humanities Press, 1969, pp. 188–89.

7. Committee for Economic Development, brochure, 1976.

8. I.F. Stone, *New York Review of Books*, April 23, 1970, p. 18.

9. Richard J. Barnet, "Challenging the Myths of National Security," *New York Times Magazine*, April 1, 1979.

10. Bertrand Russell, *Has Man A Future?* New York: Penguin Books, 1961, p. 79.

11. Walter Millis, "How To Compete With The Russians," *New York Times Magazine*, February 2, 1958.

12. Harry S. Truman, *Memoirs*, vol. 1, *Years of Decision*, New York: Double-day, 1955, p. 271.
13. Louis Henkin, ed., *Arms Control: Issues for the Public*, New York: Prentice-Hall, 1961, pp. 19–20.
14. Nathan and Norden, op. cit., pp. 470–72.
15. Bertrand Russell, op. cit., pp. 72–73.
16. Ibid., p. 79.
17. Foreign Relations Committee, *Analysis of Effects of Limited Nuclear War*, September 1975, p. 45.
18. Jonathan Schell, *The Fate Of The Earth*, New York: Knopf, 1982, p. 92.
19. Nathan and Norden, op. cit. pp. 347–48.
20. Bertrand Russell, op. cit., pp. 72–74.
21. Donella H. Meadows et al., *The Limits of Growth*, New York: New American Library, 1972, p. 21.
22. Robert L. Heilbroner, "Growth and Survival," *Foreign Affairs*, October 1972, pp. 140 ff.
23. Letter to author.
24. Bertrand Russell, op. cit., p. 82.

INDEX

ABM system, 44
Acheson, Dean, 51, 61, 62, 83–84, 98
Afghanistan, 25, 101; and Soviet Union, 31, 128, 146
Africa, 90–91
Albania, 16
Algeria, 8, 33, 72, 80, 84, 87–88, 105
Allen, Richard, 57
Allende, Salvador, 93
Alperovitz, Gar, 19
Alsop, Joseph, 60, 112
American Civil War, 149–50
American Mission for Aid to Greece, 70
American Relief Administration, 136
American Revolution, 2–3, 80, 86, 149
Amnesty International, 75
Anderson, Orvile A., 23, 40
Angola, 105–108; and South Africa, 25; and Soviet Union, 25, 31, 107–108; and United States, 25, 101, 105, 107, 120
Anticommunism, 54, 98
Antinuclear movement, 126, 130, 131
Anti-satellite capabilities, 45
Antiwar movement, 53, 97, 126, 130
Arbenz Guzman, Jacobo, 72–74, 76
Arevalo, Juan Jose, 72, 91, 93
Argentina, 91–93, 157
Armed peace, 161–62
Arms control negotiations, 126, 130, 158
Aron, Raymond, 39
Aspin, Les, 45
Atlantic Alliance, 130–32

Atlantic Pact, 71
Atom/atom bomb, 18, 26, 41, 86, 94, 154, 155; as indicator of U.S. superiority, 37–38, 95; potency, 41
Atomic energy, 42
Atomic Energy Act, 96
Atomic Energy Committee, 94
Atomic partnership, 18–20, 63, 94, 155
Australia, 99
Austria, 20, 32, 80, 140
Azerbaijan, 38, 53

Bader, George W., 106
Balaguer, Joaquin, 94
Barnet, Richard, 78
Baruch, Bernard, 37, 155, 158
Baruch Plan, 161, 164
Batista, Fulgencio, 101–102
Bavaria, 11
Bay of Pigs, 93, 103
Belgian Congo (Zaire), 34, 91, 108
Belgium, 16, 21, 91; German invasion of, 6; revolutions in, 33, 101
Belperron, Pierre, 6
Bender, Frank, 103
Benes, Eduard, 29, 33
Berlin, 52
Betancourt, Romulo, 92
Biddle, Francis, 97
Bilateral freeze, 130
Bishop, Maurice, 110

Blackett, P.M.S., 39–40
Blacklisting, 97–98
Blast shelters, 43
"Blockbuster" bomb, 86
Bohlen, Charles E., 63
Bolivia, 91–92
Bolles, Blair, 96
Bolsheviks/Bolshevism, 9–11, 35, 135
Borosago, Robert, 98
Bosch, Juan, 93–94
Botha, Pieter, 108
Branco, Humberto Castelo, 93
Bravo bomb, 43
Brazil, 34, 64, 93, 116, 157
Brezhnev, Leonid, 57, 121, 128, 133
Britain, 91, 157; boycott of Iranian oil, 77, 79; and Burma, 153; capitalist revolution in, 80–81; colonial repression policy, 21; colonialism, 61; defeat at Dunkirk, 6; defeat in American Revolution, 2–3; and Ethiopia, 106; and Greece, 68–69, 70; and India, 26, 33, 72, 88–89; and Indonesia, 89; and Kenya, 91; Labour Party, 15; and Madagascar, 87; military strategy in World War II, 16; nuclear arsenal, 55; and Russian Revolution, 11; socialist revolution in, 138; Soviet policy, 12, 21; and Soviet Union, 12, 136, 137; and Suez, 90; and United States, 79–80; victory in Spain, 3; and Vietnam, 112; in World War I, 9–10
Broad, William J., 46
Brock, William E., 131
Browder, Earl, 15
Brown, Harold S., 41–42, 56
Buell, John, 118
Bukharin, Nikolai, 12, 135, 136–37
Bulgaria, 16, 20, 69; and Soviet Union, 28, 68, 143
Bullitt, William C., 10
Bureau of the National European Resistance (CNR), 13
Burgoyne, John, 3
Burma, 67, 90, 112, 153
Burnham, James, 23
Byrnes, James F., 23, 37, 59

Caamano Deno, Francisco, 93
Cabell, C.P., 102
Caetano, Marcelo, 107
Cambodia, 25, 111
Campbell, Alex, 66
Canada, 99, 162
Capitalism, 15, 34; and communism, 21–23, 31, 32, 139, 147; laissez-faire, 150; and slavery, 149–50
Cardenas, Lazaro, 152

Carillo, Justo, 103
Carter, Jimmy: defense spending, 27; 120; and Iran, 114, 121; and Middle East, 121; and Nicaragua, 110; and SALT II, 121; and U.S.–Soviet relations, 132
Castillo Armes, Carlos, 73–74
Castro, Fidel, 26, 101–105, 110
Center for Defense Information, 31, 49
Central America, 85, 109, 132
Chamberlin, William Henry, 10
Chiang Kai-Shek, 14, 15, 25, 52, 79, 83–84, 90
Chile, 64, 92, 93
China: aid from U.S., 25, 83–84; aid to Angola, 107, 108; communism in, 14, 26, 83–84, 90, 134; economic growth, 142; and Korean War, 24, 52; Manchu Dynasty, 81, 82; nuclear arsenal, 55; revolutions in, 15, 23, 33, 81, 82–84; and Soviet Union, 31, 83, 166; Taiping Rebellion, 81–82; and United States, 61, 64, 99, 101
Chomsky, Noam, 61
Chou En-lai, 90
Church, Frank, 96
Churchill, Winston, 15, 87, 88; iron curtain speech, 21; and Stalin, 60, 68; Soviet policy, 21; on United States, 17; and World War II, 3, 6, 7, 9, 11, 16; at Yalta Conference, 18
CIA, 57, 71, 96, 125, 146, 152; in Angola, 107–108; in Chile, 93, 110; in Cuba, 102–105; in Guatemala, 73–75; and Iran, 8, 78–79, 114
Circular error probable (CEP), 48
Civil defense, 43–44
Civil rights protests, 97
Clark, Gerald, 109
Clayton, William L., 64, 71
Clifford, Clark M., 21
Coexistence, 18–20, 63, 85, 103
Colby, Bainbridge, 12
Cold War, 54, 60, 161
Collins, Arthur, 56
Colonialism, 61
Columbia, 92
Committee for Economic Development, 157
Committee on the Present Danger, 121
Common market(s), 153–54
Communism/communists, 12, 100–101, 159; and capitalism, 21–23, 31, 32, 139, 147; in China, 83–84; future of, 139, 144; and justifiable intervention, 72; postwar purges, 29; and revolution, 60; and socialism, 143; in Soviet Union, 82; and supranationalism, 166; and Third World, 76; in United States, 95, 97–98; U.S. view of, 75; war communism, 138–39

Communist Information Bureau
(Cominform), 140
Communist International, 15
Computer false alarm, 128
Concert of Europe, 32
Congo, 31
Containment policy, 22, 85, 101, 116, 122,
129, 133, 157; and antinuclear movement,
129–30; 131; and Atlantic Alliance,
130–32; defined, 1–2; domestic opposi-
tion to, 96; economic containment, 12,
28; economic effects of, 129; failure of,
28, 34–35; goals of, 31, 34–35; in Guate-
mala, 75; liberal view of, 27–28; moderate
containment, 119–20; World War II to
present, 14–18. *See also* U.S. foreign
policy
Contingency agreements, 98
Costa Rica, 66
Council for Mutual Assistance (Comecon),
31
Council on Foreign Relations, 61
Counterinsurgency, 92
Counterrevolution, 154
Cruise missiles, 55, 122, 124, 128, 131
Cuba, 26, 38, 52; Bay of Pigs, 93, 103;
communism in, 102–103; revolutions in,
33, 84, 92, 94, 101–105; and Soviet
Union, 31, 105, 128; and United States,
66, 101–105, 116
Cuban missile crisis, 38, 50, 51, 52, 105
Customs unions, 153, 164
Czechoslovakia, 16, 30, 143; communism
in, 145; decline of industry, 31; economy,
144–45; free trade, 62; socialism in, 134,
144–46; and Soviet Union, 145–46;
trade with West, 145

Davidon, William C., 86
Dawes plan, 117
DefCon (Defense Condition) alerts, 52–53
Defense Department, 126, 128
De Gaulle, Charles, 13, 87
Demilitarization, 151, 157, 159
Democracy, 86
Democratic Alliance (Philippines), 65
Denmark, 80
Detente, 24, 121, 122
Deterrence, 46, 51–57
Deutscher, Isaac, 143
De Villiers, Philippe, 112
Diaz, Porfirio, 82
Diem, Ngo Dinh, 79, 111, 112
Disarmament, 155–62 *passim*, 165, 166
Disarming first strike, 45–46, 125, 127, 150
Divine right of kings, 86
Djilas, Milovan, 59, 142

Dominican Republic, 93–94, 116
Domino theory, 105, 112
Doolittle, Hooker, 88
Drug abuse by military personnel, 49
Dulles, John Foster, 52, 74, 100
Duranty, Walter, 10, 136
Dutch East Indies, 88–89

EAM (National Liberation Front) (Greece),
68–69
Early-warning radar system, 51
East Germany, 30, 31, 134, 146; Berlin
revolt, 144
Eastern Europe: communism in, 14, 26; and
free trade, 62; industrialization after
World War II, 19–20; postwar elections,
20–21; and Soviet Union, 23, 29, 84
Ecuador, 92
Eden, Anthony, 68
EDES (National Republican Greek League),
68
Egypt, 69, 81, 125
Einstein, Albert, 154, 163
Eisenhower, Dwight D., 67; aid to Iran, 77;
and antiballistic missile defense, 44; and
Castro, 102–104; and Guatemala, 74; and
Korea, 24, 26; nuclear policy, 52; on
nuclear war, 42; opposition to nuclear
bomb, 94; and public opinion, 132; and
secrecy, 96; threatened use of atomic
bomb. 38; and Vietnam, 112
El Salvador, 105, 110; civil war in, 75, 92,
110–111; and Soviet Union, 32; and
United States, 110–11, 132–33
Electromagnetic pulse (EMP), 46–47
Electronic systems (on missiles), 48
Ellsberg, Daniel, 52
ELAS (National Popular Liberation Army)
(Greece), 68
Emergency Committee of Atomic Scientists,
161
English Revolution, 32
Ethiopia, 25, 31, 32, 101, 105–107, 120,
128
Europe: antinuclear movement, 131; econ-
omy, 131; reconstruction after World War
II, 60; as target for nuclear war, 131
European common market, 154
Export Control Act, 30

Fallout shelters, 43–44
Fallows, James, 46
Farouk, King, 90
FBI, 96–97
Fear psychology, 123
Ferguson, Homer, 95
Fink, Daniel, 44, 46

Finland, 21, 27
Finlandization, 27, 45, 119, 127
First strike, 45, 54, 123, 125, 128. *See also*
    Disarming first strike; Retaliatory strike
Fischer, John, 100
Fleming, D.F., 15, 60, 80
Foreign Affairs article by George F.
    Kennan, 20, 22–23
Foreign Policy Association (U.S.), 11
Formosa, 67
Forrestal, James, 22
France, 21, 91, 157; and Algeria, 72,
    87–88; communism in, 13; in Indochina,
    16, 26, 61, 72, 89–90; and Madagascar,
    87; Maquis, 60; and Morocco, 87–88;
    nuclear arsenal, 55; Popular Front govern-
    ment, 15; revolutions in, 33, 80, 86; and
    Russian Revolution, 11; socialist move-
    ment in, 16; and Soviet Union, 15, 136;
    and Tunisia, 87–88; and United States,
    79–80; and Vietnam, 88, 112; in World
    War I, 9–11; in World War II, 13, 17
Franck, James, 42
Franco, Francisco, 135
Free-enterprise system, 69, 71
Fulbright, John W., 133

Gairy, Eric, 110
Gaitan, Jorge Eliecer, 92
Garibaldini (Italy), 13, 60
Garwin, Richard L., 45
Geiger, H. Jack, 41
Geneva Accords, 112
Germany, 69, 100, 117, 118; communism
    in, 60; and Maginot Line, 6; nuclear
    arsenal, 55, 157; recovery after World
    War II, 17; revolutions in, 11–12, 80,
    138; and Soviet Union, 15, 28, 136; and
    United States, 117, 146; use of technol-
    ogy in World War II, 7; war of movement
    strategy, 7
Ghana, 91, 153
Giap, Vo Nguyen, 90
Gold Coast, 91
Gomulka, Wladyslaw, 29
Gordon, Charles George, 81
Goulart, Joao, 93
Government of National Reconstruction
    (Nicaragua), 110
Great Depression, 13, 35, 129, 150
Greece, 16, 59–60, 67–71, 100; capitalism
    in, 135; civil war in, 68–69; and Soviet
    Union, 69
Grenada, 110
Griswold, Dwight, 70
Gromyko, Andrei, 38

Guatemala, 67, 72–75, 91, 92, 93, 111
Guyana, 93

Haig, Alexander, 56, 67
Hailey, Foster, 84
Haiti, 66
Handler, Philip, 47
Harsch, Joseph C., 23
Hart, B.H. Lidell, 51
Healey, Denis, 142
Henderson, Loy, 70
Herter, Christian, 103
Hiroshima, 18, 19, 37, 47, 59, 86, 94, 163
Hitler, Adolf, 13, 15, 40, 135, 159
Ho Chi-minh, 89–90
Hofstadter, Richard, 61
Hoi, Dong Minh, 89
Holland, 16, 21, 33, 80, 88–89, 91, 131;
    German invasion of, 6
Honduras, 66
Hoover, J. Edgar, 96–97
Hoover, Herbert, 9
Hopkins, Harry, 16
Hughes, Charles Evans, 12
House Committee on Un-American Activi-
    ties (HUAC), 97
Hsiu-ch'uan, Hung, 81
Hukbalahap (National Anti-Japanese
    Army), 65–66
Hull, Cordell, 61
Hungary, 16, 26, 142; communism in, 134;
    revolution in, 30, 32, 144; socialism in,
    134; Soviet republic in, 11; and Soviet
    Union, 20, 24–25, 28, 68, 143, 146
Hurley, Pat, 79
Hutchins, Robert Maynard, 162
Hydrogen bomb, 41, 86

Ickes, Harold, 95
Ikle, Fred C., 46
Illia, Artura, 93
Imperialism, 88, 89; benign, 60, 63, 65, 67,
    80
India: and Britain, 26, 33, 72, 88; commu-
    nism in, 90; nuclear arsenal, 55; revolu-
    tions in, 81, 84; and Soviet Union, 14
Indochina, 67, 100, 101, 111; communism
    in, 112; French rule in, 16, 26, 61, 72;
    revolution in, 89–90
Indonesia (Dutch East Indies), 64, 67,
    88–89, 105; communism in, 90;
    Dutch rule in, 16, 88
Ingersoll, Bruce, 48
Insurgency situations, 99
International Atomic Development Author-
    ity, 161

International Bank of Reconstruction and Development, 17
International Monetary Fund, 17–18. 19, 34
Iran, 70, 72, 106; hostage crisis, 121; revolution in, 76–79; and Soviet Union, 38, 52, 59; and United States, 26, 67, 77–79, 101, 111, 114–16
Israel, 52–53, 153; nuclear arsenal, 55, 157
Italy, 140; Garibaldini, 13, 60; general strike in, 13; monarchy, 16; nuclear arsenal, 55; revolution in, 32, 80; and Russian Revolution, 11, in World War II, 13

Jackson, Henry, 38
Jagan, Cheddi, 93
Japan, 69, 88–90, 99, 118; atomic attack on, 19, 37–38; defense spending, 146; nuclear arsenal, 55, 157; revolutions in, 80; and United States, 146
Johnson, Lyndon B., 26, 44, 52, 94, 112, 113, 156
Joint U.S. Military Advisory Group (JUSMAG), 66
Justice Department, 103

Kahan, Jerome H., 51
Kahn, Herman, 41
Kaku, Michiu, 47
Kearns, Doris, 26
Kempeitari, 89
Kennan, George F., 20, 22–23, 28, 30, 31, 34, 38
Kennedy, John F.; and Castro, 102, 104–105; civil defense program, 43–44; Cuban missile crisis, 38, 50, 51; and Dominican Republic, 93; and Iran, 114–15; missile gap, 123; nuclear policy, 25, 38, 44, 52; test ban negotiations, 158
Kenney, George C., 40
Keynesian economics, 150
Kenyatta, Jomo, 91
Khomeini, Ayatollah, 26, 115
Khrushchev, Nikita, 144, 147
Killer lasers, 45
Killer satellites, 45, 125
Kinzer, Stephen, 75
Kirkpatrick, Jeane J., 23–24
Kirkpatrick, Lyman, 103
Kissinger, Henry, 27–28, 38, 127; and Angola, 107–108; on the nuclear threat, 49; and Yom Kippur War, 52
Klare, Michael T., 119–20, 132
Kleist, Ewald Von, 6
Korea, 98, 100
Korean War, 24–25, 38, 52, 117

Kostov, Traicho, 29
Kuomintang, 15, 60, 79, 83, 89, 90
Kurdistan, 38

LaFollette, Robert M., Sr., 11
LaRocque, Gene R., 123
Labour Party (Britain), 15
Land reform, 93, 103, 110–11
Lao, Pathet, 25, 38, 52, 53
Laos, 25, 31, 38, 52, 111
Lapp, Ralph, 40
Lasers, 45, 125
Launch on warning, 128
Latin America, 67, 74, 92, 100, 105, 110
Lebanon crisis, 52
League of Communists (Yugoslavia), 141–42
Leahy, William D., 19, 21
Lend-lease, 19, 62
Lenin, V. I., 10–12, 135, 136
Lernoux, Penny, 111
Libya, 14, 31, 101
Lillienthal, David, 161
Limited nuclear war, 49, 56–57, 127, 162
Lippmann, Walter, 10, 22, 162
Lloyd George, David, 10
Lodge, Henry Cabot, 67, 74
Loory, Stuart H., 133
Lovett, Robert A., 52
Loyalty oaths, 96–98
Luce, Henry, 8

MacArthur, Douglas, 24, 42, 56, 65, 75
McCarthy, Joseph/McCarthyism, 156
McNamara, Robert S., 92, 99, 121, 123
Madagascar, 17, 87
Maginot, André, 4
Maginot Line, 2, 3, 4, 95, 154; development and cost, 4–6; defeat of, 6–7
Maginot Line syndrome, 2, 7
Magnuson Act, 97
Makris, Fotis, 69
Malaya, 105
Malaysia, 67
Malenkov, Georgi, 143–44
Manchu dynasty, 81, 82
Mao Tse-tung, 14, 33, 60, 90
Maquis (France), 60
Marshall, George, 79
Marshall Plan, 130, 151
Marx, Karl, 135, 150, 166
Marxism-Leninism, 133
Massive retaliation, 100
Mathias, Charles, 124
Matthews, Francis, 23
Matthews, Herbert L., 102

Maximos, M., 70
Mazzini, Guiseppe, 32
Mau Mau war, 91
Meltdown, 47
Mendlovitz, Saul, 151
Mengistu Haile, Marian, 106
Merz, Charles, 10
Metternich, Klemens von, 32
Mexico, 102, 105, 152; revolutions in,
    82–83
Middle East, 52–53, 70, 85, 120
Military science, 86
Mills, C. Wright, 53
Missile/missile systems, 41, 42; antiballistic
    (ABM), 42, 122; cruise, 55, 122, 124,
    128, 131; electronic systems on, 48;
    fratricide of missiles, 46; issue, 46;
    LoADS, 122; MX, 122, 124–25, 128;
    offensive, 44; oversophistication of, 48;
    Pershing II, 43, 128, 131; Safeguard ABM
    system, 44; Trident, 128; Trident II, 122
Molotov, Vyacheslav M., 19
Mook, Hubertus J. van, 89
Morgenthau, Hans, 116, 118
Morgenthau, Henry, Jr., 95
Morocco, 87–88
Mossadegh, Mohammed, 76–79, 80, 114
Mozambique, 25–26, 31, 101, 107
Mussolini, Benito, 106, 135
Mutual assured destruction (MAD), 51, 53

Nagasaki, 18, 37, 59
Nagy, Imre, 144
Napoleon, 40, 84
Nasser, Gamal Abdel, 90
National Council of Churches, 11
National Front (Iran), 77
National Front for the Liberation of Angola
    (FMLA), 107–108
National Liberation Front (FLN) (Algeria),
    88
National Liberation Front (Greece), 68–69
National Liberation Front of Vietnam, 113
National Planning Association, 62
National Popular Liberation Army (ELAS)
    (Greece), 68
National Republican Greek League (EDES),
    68
National security: and communist con-
    spiracy in Guatemala, 73; and contain-
    ment policy, 1–2, 7, 150–51; National
    Security Agency, 98; and nuclear
    weapons, 7; security agreements, 98–99
National Security Act, 95–96
National Security Agency, 98
National Security Council (NSC), 39, 40,
    95–96

National Security State, 95–101, 103, 118,
    160
National Union for the Total Independence
    of Angola (UNITA), 107–108
NATO, 71, 131
Nazi/Nazism, 13, 15, 87
Nelson, Donald M., 61, 79
Neoconservatives, 119, 132
Netherlands. See Holland
Neto, Agostinho, 107–108
Neutrality laws, 103
New Zealand, 99
Nicaragua, 101. 132; revolution in, 33, 92,
    94, 105–106, 109–111
Nigeria, 8
1962 October missile crisis. See Cuban
    missile crisis
Nixon, Richard M.: antiballistic missile
    defense, 44–45; and antiwar movement,
    113–14; and Castro, 104; and Iran,
    115–16; nuclear policy, 52–53; on
    nuclear war, 43; and public opinion, 132;
    and Vietnam, 26, 52
Nixon Doctrine, 26, 115
Nkrumah, Kwame, 90–91
Nol, Lon, 25
Noninterventionism, 100
North Africa, 17
North Atlantic Treaty, 80, 99
North Atlantic Treaty Organization
    (NATO), 71, 131
North Korea, 31, 38; communism in, 14,
    24, 90; Soviet occupation, 84
North Vietnam, 26, 90, 98, 114
Nossiter, Bernard D., 48
NSC-68, 39, 40
Nuclear arms race, 8, 18, 43, 53, 55, 63, 94,
    128, 157, 164
Nuclear bomb/the Bomb, 2, 18, 19, 35, 38,
    49, 162, 164; American monopoly of,
    38–39; as diplomat instrument, 50; as
    indicator of political superiority, 38–39,
    63; opposition to by scientists, 94; and
    U.S. foreign policy, 59
Nuclear defense, 43–44
Nuclear escalation, 55
Nuclear freeze, 156, 157
Nuclear stalemate, 38
Nuclear submarines, 43, 46, 128; Trident,
    122, 125
Nuclear threat, 49–50
Nuclear war, 8, 45, 127, 150, 157; by acci-
    dent, 51–53; consequences of, 46–51;
    as "double suicide," 42, 56; fatality esti-
    mates, 41–42; human factor in, 49; initia-
    tion of, 52–53; limited, 49, 56–57, 127,
    162; in outer space, 45; physiological

defense against, 49–50; preparation for, 53–54; protracted, 42, 49, 125–26, 127; scenarios. *See* Scenarios for nuclear war. as survivable, 1; uncontrolled, 47; as unwinnable, 49; as winnable, 42–43, 44
Nuclear weapons: effectiveness, 128; over-kill capability, 160; physical defense against, 49–50; strategic, 126; tactical, 56, 126; thermonuclear, 56

oil, 33, 111, 152; and Cuba, 104; in Iran, 8, 77, 114–16; in Middle East, 120, 121; in Venezuela, 92
Oman, 125
Ongania, Juan Carlos, 93
OPEC (Oil and Petroleum Exporting Countries), 8, 111
Opium War, 81
Organization of American States, 104
Outer Mongolia, 31

Pahlavi, Mohammed Reza, 114–15
Pakistan, 55, 85, 116, 157
Panama, 66
Panama Canal, 74
Papandreou, George, 68
Paraguay, 92
Patterson, Richard C., 72
Pax Americana, 17, 62, 66, 70, 88, 110, 116
Paz Estenssoro, Victor, 91
Peralta, Enrique, 93
Perez Jimenez, Marcos, 92
Peron, Juan, 91
Persian Gulf, 8, 26, 115, 121
Petain, Henri Phillipe, 4
Peurifoy, John E., 73, 74, 76
Philippine Trade Act, 64–66
Philippines, 64–66, 67, 72, 99, 105
Physical defense against nuclear weapons, 44–51
Pinochet, Augusto, 93, 110
Plutonium, 156–57, 163
Podhoretz, Norman, 24, 25, 26, 116, 120, 132
Poland, 16, 20, 28, 64, 128, 134, 143; communism in, 144; elections in, 146; martial law in, 131–32, 142–43; revolutions in, 144; and Soviet Union, 20, 147
Popoviv, Milentije, 29
Popular Movement for the Liberation of Angola (MPLA), 107
Porter, Charles O., 104
Porter, Robert, Jr., 67
Portugal, 101, 107
Postwar pacifism, 54
Potsdam Agreement, 28
Proliferation, 55–56, 124, 164

Proxmire, William, 53
Prussia, 32
"Prussians" (U.S. neoconservatives), 119, 132

Quemoy-Matsu crisis, 52, 53

Radar, 51
Radiation, 43, 47
Rajk, Laszlo, 29
Rapid Deployment Force, 120, 122, 125
Reagan, Ronald, 121; and antiwar movement, 131; and arms control, 158; budget cutbacks, 129; defense spending, 129; and El Salvador, 110, 132–33; embargo of grain to Soviet Union, 131–32; embargo of strategic materials to Soviet Union, 130–31; foreign policy, 121–27; and Guatemala, 75, 110; and nuclear freeze, 156; and public opinion, 132–33
Reaganomics, 129–30
Realpolitik, 66
Retaliatory strike, 54, 129
Revolution, 63, 66, 118, 156; bourgeois, 32; and containment policy, 35; and counterinsurgency, 92; cycle of, 80–84; military, 86; permanent, 15; political, 32; popular, 154; of rising expectations, 105, 151–54, 157, 165; social, 32–34, 86, 116; technological, 86; "in the womb of history," 80; world, 167; after World War I, 117; since World War II, 32, 55, 85–94, 101, 117
Rhee, Syngman, 79
Rhodesia, 107
Ribicoff, Abraham, 116
Rickover, Hyman, G., 8, 57
Riencourt, Amaury de, 99
Rio Pact, 99
Roberto, Holden, 107–108
Robeson, Paul, 95
Robins, Raymond, 11
Romero, Carlos Humberto, 110
Roosevelt, Kermit, 78–79
Roosevelt, Franklin D., 15, 109; and capitalism, 150; and coexistence, 19; and communism, 15–16; and imperialism, 88; military strategy, 17; and Pax Americana, 17; postwar projection, 60–61
Roosevelt, Theodore, 67
Roxas, Manuel, 65
Rumania, 16, 28, 68
Rusk, Dean, 38, 67
Russell, Bertrand, 159, 162, 163–64, 166
Russian Revolution, 11, 14, 33, 82
Russo-Japanese War, 33

Sakharov, Andrei, 75
SALT (Strategic Arms Limitations Talks), 156
SALT agreements, 156
SALT II treaty, 121
Sandinista National Liberation Front (FSLN) (Nicaragua), 109–110
Satellites, 45, 125, 163
Saudi Arabia, 8, 61, 116
Savimbi, Jonas, 107–108
Scandinavia, 80
Scenarios for nuclear war: "aggressor for peace," 23; Finlandization, 27, 45, 119, 127; full-scale counterattack, 50; Reagan scenario, 124; standard scenario, 56
Schiller, Herbert I., 100
Schlesinger, Stephen, 75
Schneider, Rene, 93
School of the Americas, 92
Schwarzkopf, H. Norman, 78
SEATO, 99
Second Hundred Years' War, 2
Secrecy, 96, 155
Selassie, Haile, 25, 106
Serge, Victor, 138
Seton-Watson, Hugh, 13
Shah of Iran, 8, 26, 78, 80
Sherwin, Martin J., 19
Sherwood, Robert, 16
Siberian pipeline, 131, 132
Sihanouk, Norodom, 25
Sik, Ota, 144
Slansky, Rudolf, 29
Smith, Adam, 166
Smith, E.T., 102
Socialism/socialist, 11, 14, 82, 87, 90, 106; administrative, 140; and communism, 143; democratic, 34
Socialist Unity Party (E. Germany), 144
Somalia, 106, 125
Somoza, Anastasio, 109–110
Somoza, Anastasio, Jr. ("Tachito"), 109
Somoza, Luis, 109
Sophoulis coalition, 70
South Africa, 25, 55, 107, 157
South Korea, 24, 99, 142
South Vietnam, 90, 114
South Yemen, 31
Soviet blockade of Berlin, 52
Soviet communism, 7, 9–14, 15, 133–39, 147, 166; and capitalism, 32; capitalist reaction against, 21–23; and non-communist elements, 29
Soviet Relief Committee, 136
Soviet Union, 40, 133; alliance with United States, 13; and Angola, 25, 31, 107–108; atomic partnership, 18–20, 63, 94, 155; and Balkan states, 68; and capitalism, 15,

34, 147; and China, 31, 83, 166; civil war in, 135–36; consumer goods production, 144; communism in. *See* Soviet communism. and containment policy, 1–2, 13–14, 28–32; and Cuba, 31, 105, 128; and Cuban missile crisis, 53; and disarmament, 157, 166; economy, 10, 19, 28, 29–32, 57, 62, 127, 135–39; as enemy, 59–60, 122, 123; and Ethiopia, 106–107; and expansionism, 24; foreign credits, 12, 19–20, 62, 136; GNP, 7, 31, 32, 133; and Greece, 69; and Hungary, 11, 20, 24–25, 28, 68, 143, 146; imports from U.S., 121; industrial output, 12; invasion by Germany, 15; invasion of Czechoslovakia, 145; and Iran, 38, 52, 59; and Korean War, 25; lend-lease shipments, 19, 62; military strategy in World War II, 16; military superiority, 27, 28, 39–40; non-revolutionary policy, 15; nuclear arsenal, 28, 54, 55, 86, 123, 158; and Poland, 20, 147; reconstruction after civil war, 136–39; reconstruction after World War II, 28; and revolution, 16, 82–83, 117, 138; Russian Revolution, 11, 14, 33, 82; and socialism, 14; Soviet-Brazilian relations, 93; Soviet empire, 31; threatened use of nuclear weapons, 128–29; trade agreements, 12, 19–20, 28–29, 62; U.S.-Soviet relations, 18–23, 62–64, 66, 127, 132, 147; and world revolution, 14–16, 23; in World War I, 9–10; World War II losses, 19; and Yom Kippur War, 52–53
Spain, 3, 99; revolutions in, 80, 101
Spanier, John W., 60
Spanish-American War, 95
Sputnik I, 43
Stable deterrence, 51–57
Stagflation, 118
Stalin, Joseph, 12, 13–14, 15, 18, 135, 143; and Churchill, 60, 68; and Greek uprising, 59; military strategy, 16; purges in communist party, 29; reconstruction policy, 28, 137–39; secret police, 138, 143; and Tito, 139–40
Standard Oil Corporation, 152–53
State Department, U.S., 61, 75, 102, 103, 126; and Dominican Republic, 93; and Iran, 78
Stavrianos, L.S., 68–69
Steffens, Lincoln, 10
Steinbruner, John D., 47
Stewart, George C., 79
Stillwell, Joseph, 79
Stimson, Henry L., 18, 63, 94, 155
Stockwell, John, 108
Strategic retreat, 27–28

Subversives/subversive organizations, 97–98
Suez Canal, 90
Sun Yat-sen, 33, 82
Sung, Kim Il, 26
Supranationalism, 160–62, 163, 166
Swomley, John M., Jr., 165
Sylvis, William H., 140
Syria, 31
Szilard, Leo, 59
Szulc, Tad, 75

Taft-Hartley law, 97
Taiping Rebellion, 81–82
Taiwan, 64, 142, 151
Technology, 7, 147
Ten Years War (Cuba), 101
Test ban negotiations, 158
Thailand, 67, 112
Thant, U, 160, 164
Thatcher, Margaret, 131, 135
Third World, 80, 162; and communism, 76;
  economy, 33–34, 101, 152–54; revolu-
  tions in, 34, 63; and United States, 120,
  153–54
Thompson, Dorothy, 5
Thorez, Maurice, 60
Tirena, Tomas C., 65
Tito, 14, 60, 139–40
Togliatti, Palmiro, 60
Tonkin Gulf Resolution, 98
Trotsky, Leon, 10–11, 12, 14–15, 92, 135,
  136–37
Trujillo, Rafael, 93
Truman, Harry S., 13, 26, 30, 62, 94, 161;
  and arms control, 158; atomic attack on
  Japan, 37; ban of aircraft sales, 30; China
  policy, 25; and coexistence, 19; and con-
  tainment policy, 34; and Greek crisis,
  70; and Korean War, 24–25, 52, 98;
  loyalty oath requirement, 96; nuclear
  policy, 22–23, 52; and Pax Americana,
  17; and Philippine independence, 64;
  postwar projection, 69–70; and public
  opinion, 132; and secrecy, 96; Soviet
  policy, 20–23, 28, 60, 63; and world
  government, 155
Truman Doctrine, 20, 22–23, 67–68, 95
Tsaldaris, Constantine, 69
Tsipis, Kosta, 45
Tudeh party (Iran), 77, 78
Tully, Andrew, 78
Tunisia, 87–88
Turkey, 34, 67, 70, 100
Turnbull, Walter, 73

Ubico, Jorge, 72, 73, 91
United Fruit Company, 72–75
United Nations, 18, 162

United States: and Angola, 25, 101, 105,
  107, 120; aid to anticommunist China, 25,
  83–84; aid to Holland, 89; aid to Portugal, 26, 107; and Afghanistan, 25; anticommunist sentiment in, 75; atomic capability, 39–40; atomic partnership, 18–20,
  63, 94, 155; benign imperialism, 60, 63,
  65, 67, 80; and Cambodia, 25; and China,
  61, 64, 99, 101; CIA. See separate listing.
  containment policy. See separate listing.
  and Cuba, 66, 101–105, 116; Defense
  Department, 126, 128; defense spending,
  27, 120, 122, 123, 126–27, 129; and disarmament, 157; economic containment
  policy, 12, 28; economy, 60–62, 69–70,
  75, 88, 117–18, 130, 131; and El Salvador, 110–11, 132–33, embargo of military goods, 30; embargo of strategic
  materials to Soviet Union, 130–31; and
  Ethiopia, 26, 106; exports, 121, 127;
  FBI, 96–97; foreign policy. See U.S.
  foreign policy. and Germany, 117, 146;
  GNP, 7–8, 133; and Greek crisis, 68–71;
  and Guatemala, 72–75; imperialism, 98,
  100; import policy, 131; and insurgency,
  99–100; investments abroad, 100; and
  Iran, 26, 67, 77–79, 101, 111, 114–16;
  and Japan, 146; Justice Department, 103;
  lend-lease shipments, 19, 62; loans to
  Britain, 94–95; loans to West Europe,
  117; and Mexican Revolution, 82; and
  Middle East conflict, 53; military options,
  57; military power, 7–8, 24; military
  strategy in World War II, 17; National
  Security State, 95–101, 103, 118, 160;
  and Nicaragua, 109–110; nuclear arsenal,
  54, 55, 86, 119, 122–23, 128, 158;
  nuclear policy, 22–23, 26, 52–53,
  100–101, 129; nuclear superiority, 39,
  127; nuclear weapons to France, 52, 53;
  Pax Americana, 17, 62, 66, 70, 88, 110,
  116; post World War II objectives, 61; and
  revolution, 85, 92–93, 100, 118; security.
  See U.S. security. and South Africa, 107;
  Soviet policy, 20–23; State Department.
  See separate listing. technological innovation, 117–18; and Third World, 120,
  153–54; trade agreements, 130; trade
  markets, 61–62, 69; troop counts, 95;
  U.S.-British relations, 79–80; U.S.-French
  relations, 79–80; U.S.-Soviet relations,
  13, 18–23, 62–64, 66, 127, 132, 147;
  and Vietnam War, 26, 27, 113; in World
  War II, 9–14
U.S. foreign policy, 59, 111, 119; affected
  by antinuclear movement, 131; and blacklisting, 97–98; and military force, 95;
  based on nuclear strength, 59, 154–55;

under Reagan, 121-27; and revolution, 85, 94-95; and secrecy, 96; under Truman, 20-23; and Vietnam, 111-14; and Western Europe, 88; after World War II, 71, 79-80. *See also* Containment policy
Uruguay, 92
Ustinov, Dimitri, 128-29

Vandenberg, Arthur, 54, 96
Vanderbilt, Cornelius, 109
Venezuela, 8, 92
Viet Minh, 52, 89-90, 112
Vietnam, 31, 52, 67, 88, 101, 105-106, 116, 120; communism in, 112; GNP, 8, 113
Vietnam Syndrome, 120
Vietnam War, 24, 26, 27, 98, 112, 118, 132

Wallace, Henry A., 63, 79, 95
Wallop, Malcolm, 45
War/warfare: atomic, 22; biological, 22; containment strategy. *See* Containment policy. defensive, 4; erroneous assessment and preparation for, 2-4; preventive, 23, 40, 161; war of movement strategy, 7; war of position strategy, 4, 6
War-avoidance policy, 53
War communism, 137-39, 145
War Powers Act, 120
Weech, W. N., 3
Weinberger, Caspar W., 42, 122

Welfare state, 150
Wells, H.G., 2
Western Europe, 70, 71, 130
Wheeler, Earle, 52
Wiesner, Jerome, 162
Wilson, Woodrow, 10, 11
Win-the-Peace Conference, 94
Wolfe, Alan, 126
World Bank, 19
World government, 155, 162, 163
World War I, 3, 9-14; death toll, 86; and Maginot Line, 4
World War II, 3, 13, 15-18; Allied defeat at Dunkirk, 6; death toll, 86
World War III, 51, 53
Wszelaki, J., 28

"X" article (in *Foreign Affairs*), 22-23

Yalta Agreement, 28
Yalta Conference, 18
Ydigoras Fuentes, Miguel, 73
Yom Kippur War, 52-53
Young plan, 117
Yugoslavia, 16, 31, 68, 71, 100; communism in, 14, 134, 139-42; revolution in, 84; self-management system, 140-42

Zahedi, Fazollah, 78
Zaire (Belgian Congo), 34, 91, 108
Zapata, Emiliano, 82
Zhdanov, Andrei, 29
Zuckerman, Solly, 45

ABOUT THE AUTHOR

Sidney Lens, a well-known writer and lecturer, is senior editor of *The Progressive*. He has published numerous articles in such magazines as *Harper's, Harvard Business Review, New Republic, Nation*, and innumerable newspapers; and has lectured and taught at many universities. His many books include *The Day Before Doomsday, The Military–Industrial Complex, The Labor Wars*, and *Radicalism in America*.